THE 'CENTURIES' OF JULIA PALMER

Kate Gould

5th February 1977 – 9th October 2017

From a collection of books gathered by Kate Gould for her PhD on the ways in which media coverage of "pink Viagra" represented and constructed female sexuality; in her years at the front line of gender politics as part of the global sisterhood; and as a passionate campaigner for the truth and rights of women.

Critical Sisters posted this on
hearing of Kate's death:

'Love and anger course through the radical feminist community compelling each of us to question, debate and create change. Many of us never met Kate in real life, and yet she spoke our truth often in the face of hostility. Her clear and unwavering voice rang out through her writing - righteous, powerful and insightful. Without ego and free from artifice - Kate's bravery, shining intellect and warmth have inspired many of us. Kate gave to each of us; and her memory and work continue to give us strength. We will miss our sister.'

THE 'CENTURIES' OF JULIA PALMER

Edited, with an introduction and notes, by Victoria Burke and Elizabeth Clarke

TRENT EDITIONS

Published by Trent Editions, 2001

Trent Editions
Department of English and Media Studies
The Nottingham Trent University
Clifton Lane
Nottingham NG11 8NS

Printed in Great Britain by Goaters Limited, Nottingham
ISBN 1 84233 061 6

Contents

Acknowledgements

Victoria Burke would like to thank the William Andrews Clark Memorial Library at UCLA for granting her a visiting fellowship which allowed her to transcribe the manuscript and to check her transcription, and both The Nottingham Trent University and the Arts and Humanities Research Board for providing funding for a return trip to the Clark for a final proofread. She is grateful to the staff at the Clark Library for all of their help, and to Jeanne Ross for her hospitality in Los Angeles.

Elizabeth Clarke would like to thank the staff at the City of Westminster Archives Centre for permission to reproduce the cover illustration, and for their assistance during research visits. March Pons identified many Biblical references.

We would like to thank Jeremy Maule for telling us about the manuscript and for commissioning us to edit it in his series *Renaissance Texts from Manuscript*, where it would have appeared if not for his untimely death in 1998.

The cover illustration is taken from *A Plan of the Cities of London and Westminster, and the Borough of Southwark, with the Contiguous Buildings. From an actual Survey, taken by John Roque, Land Surveyor, and Engraved by John Price. Begun March 1637. Published 1746.* (London Topographical Society, 1919). The editors are grateful to the Westminster Archive for permission to publish it.

Introduction

It is very difficult to trace middle-class women from the seventeenth century, but fortunately Julia Palmer thought so highly of her manuscript that she bequeathed it to men who left their mark in seventeenth-century records.

> I Leave this Book to Mr Joseph
> Bisco senior. if he out Live
> me otherwiss. I Leave itt to
> Mr James pitson Apothicary.[1]

In fact both men mentioned here were wealthy apothecaries: Joseph Biscoe (1637-1718) was an officer in the Society in the early eighteenth century, becoming Master in 1711-1712, and he took James Pitson (born c.1658) as his apprentice on 7 May 1672. Pitson was freed in 1680 and was active in the Society, holding several positions, including Master, in 1723-1724.[2] Biscoe was based in Westminster and owned a great deal of property there. Nothing is known of Julia Palmer's parentage. Based on the evidence of her poem entitled, 'Some few perticular mercy (amongst many) taken notice of throug the whole course of life', it is possible she was an orphan: she thanks God for being 'most kinnd/ unto the fatherlese' (see below, p. 119). The following tentative information is based on the fact that Julia is a very unusual name in this period. Julia Palmer is probably the Julia Hungerford who married Nicholas Palmer on 12th May 1664.[3] She is probably the same Julia, married to Nicholas, whose son Samuel was baptised at St. Margaret's Westminster on June 17th 1667:[4] she must have moved to Westminster soon after her marriage. The inscription on her manuscript suggests she was contemporary with Joseph Biscoe the elder: he was married in 1658 and died in 1718. Samuel Palmer, probably her son, was apprenticed as an apothecary in 1682: he is listed as the son of Nicholas Palmer, deceased.[5] It is possible that the dedication of this manuscript to two prominent apothecaries was an attempt to curry favour for her son, who never in fact completed his apprenticeship.

This evidence seems to suggest a Westminster context for this manuscript, and a connection with the apothecary trade. Joseph Biscoe's father, brother and nephew were all Westminster apothecaries. However, the dedication of the manuscript to Biscoe also suggests an affiliation with Nonconformist religion and politics. Joseph's nephew John married the granddaughter of Vincent Alsop, minister of the Presbyterian church at Westminster from 1677, at the same church in which Julia Palmer was married—a suggestive connection, especially as All Hallow's London Wall is a stone's throw from the famous Dissenting meeting place, Pinners' Hall. Biscoe's will includes a bequest to the minister of his Independent congregation John Nesbitt.[6] He was a preacher at the famous Presbyterian/Independent lecture at Pinners' Hall: Vincent Alsop, of Westminster, was a lecturer there from 1685-1694.[7] Joseph Biscoe was probably moving in a wide and influential Nonconformist circle.

That Julia Palmer was herself a Nonconformist is confirmed by the theology and spirituality of the poems in the manuscript. She is a strong Calvinist, a theology typical of Presbyterianism. The overview of Protestant history in poem 78 of the 'First Century' is characteristic of the Nonconformist community, and there are many echoes of Presbyterian devotional texts noted in this edition. It is most likely, therefore, that while she lived in Westminster Julia Palmer attended the large Presbyterian church 'gathered' by Thomas Cawton after he became chaplain to Lady Armine in 1665.[8] This may well be why there is no trace of her or her family records after 1667 in the register of St. Margaret's, Westminster: Nonconformist churches usually had their own registers. It is also possible that she moved away from Westminster, as we shall see.

The two years during which Julia Palmer composed her poetry, 1671-1673, were crucial to the fortunes of Nonconformists, who had suffered severe persecution since the Restoration of Charles II in 1660. Her carefully-dated poems begin during the buildup to one of the most significant events in the history of Nonconformity: the Declaration of Indulgence, finally enacted in March 1672.[9] The Declaration of Indulgence allowed freedom to preach and to worship for Nonconformists under licence, and came as a relief to ministers and people who had been harassed and imprisoned, during the ten years since the ejection of nonconforming ministers from the Church of England in 1662, in an attempt to stamp out congregations of Presbyterians, Independents, Baptists and Quakers. Measures such as the Five Mile Act, which kept ministers at least five miles away from their place of worship, and the Conventicles Act, allowing no more than five people to congregate together if they were not of the same family, did not succeed in quashing Nonconformity, and protests had reached their height in London in 1670, when thousands of people took to the streets.

The Declaration of Indulgence, therefore, was not a straightforward gesture of goodwill towards Nonconformists. In 1671 state papers show the government desperately trying to get Nonconformist leaders on side in preparation for a Dutch war: the Dissenters' natural sympathy with the Dutch was thought to constitute a real threat to civil peace.[10] Several agents were used by Joseph Williamson, Secretary of State, whose brief was to get the ear of Nonconformist leaders, try to influence them, and report back on their state of mind. An important person in this enterprise was a Westminster Presbyterian, James Inness, who lived in Axe Yard, King Street (located approximately where Downing Street is now), on the very fringes of Whitehall Palace. The location of his house meant that he was able to introduce government officials to Nonconformist ministers: Lord Ashley, powerful member of the Cabal, spent time there in the autumn of 1671 and in November Inness introduced the more radical Presbyterian leaders to the King himself.[11] This group were known as the Ducklings, because of their readiness to 'take to water'—to embrace permanent Dissent and its implications. The opposing group, the Dons, consisting of Edmund Calamy, Richard Baxter, and William Bates, were the Presbyterian 'elder statesmen', still hoping for reconciliation into one national church, and less willing to break the law. The Ducklings—Thomas Watson, Samuel Annesley, and the Vincent brothers—were much more important to the government because of their perceived influence over large numbers of the middling sort, merchants and businessmen and their wives whose acquiescence was crucial to the success of a Dutch war. The younger, more fiery Vincent, Nathaniel, had been further radicalised by a recent stay in a Westminster prison, the Gatehouse.

Thomas Cawton's church, surprisingly considered its closeness to Whitehall, had escaped the more draconian persecution meted out to City churches under the Five Mile Act and the Conventicles Act. Perhaps this was because of the personal esteem in which he was held by Charles II: Thomas Cawton the elder, a distinguished Oxford orientalist, had been one of the conspirators in the unsuccessful Presbyterian Plot of 1651 to put Charles II on the throne, and prior to the King's eventual restoration a royal letter was sent to the Cawtons in exile in Holland asserting their worth and asking for their support.[12] The King did not forget Presbyterian loyalty as quickly as some of his ministers. Figures such as James Inness received both favour at Court and an allowance: he asked for £800 a year, and was designated 'a great rogue' by Secretary of State Joseph Williamson.[13] In return, however, he and his fellow agents were to try and ensure that there was no Presbyterian uprising. State Papers reveal that the aim of the

Declaration of Indulgence, rather than the exercise of Royal grace and favour that it was announced to be, was entirely political: the agents' secret meetings with the Ducklings had made it clear that Nonconformists were not to be appeased in any other way, and the evidence from Julia Palmer's poems is that the misgivings about the Dutch War went very deep. Moreover, the assiduity with which government agents such as Inness helped ministers apply for licences was not surprising: the condition on which a licence was granted was that the full address of the meeting house was given. The surrender of this precious information, which had in some cases eluded government agents on surveillance operations, turned the Declaration of Indulgence into a triumph for Lord Arlington's secret service: they now had a list of every location where preaching was taking place.

Thomas Cawton's licence for preaching at his house in St. Ann's Street was one of the very first to be issued, and one of the first to be picked up: G. Lyon Turner suggests that the co-operation of the most important ministers was a priority for the government and he imagines Cawton's walk to Whitehall on 3rd April 1672. In his mind's eye he sees Thomas Cawton

> leave his house in St. Ann's Lane, pass Dean's Yard, cross the Sanctuary, go along King Street, and through Holbein's arched gateway into Whitehall, pass the Privy Garden and the Banqueting Hall, into the Great Court on the right, and returning to its farther corner on the south-east, turn sharp to his right into Lord Arlington's Office.[14]

His route probably led him very close to where Julia Palmer lived: in 1694 her son was living in Orchard Street, just around the corner from Thomas Cawton's house. If Joseph Biscoe were already living in the Sanctuary and Deanery, where he was living at great expense in 1694, Thomas Cawton would have walked straight past his house too: in the embattled community of Nonconformity, Cawton and Biscoe would certainly have known each other, even if they did not attend the same church.[15] Since all licences had to be picked up in person, many ministers or their representatives from all over England passed through Westminster in the months after the Declaration of Indulgence, probably putting in an appearance at Thomas Cawton's church in the process, although James Inness' son advertised himself as an agent who for a fee would apply for a licence and pick it up on behalf of a customer. Emboldened by the new political situation the Presbyterian community built themselves a meeting house in New Way, off Orchard Street and close to Tothill Street, which was licensed for preaching in November.[16]

How much did Julia Palmer know of all this? She probably knew nothing of the secret meetings and intrigues at the highest level of Presbyterian leadership. However, poem 5 of the 'Second Century', in the middle of an anxious sequence for June 1972, refers to 'this sad news', perhaps the news of the Dutch war: there had been murderous fighting, and hundreds of Dutch refugees had been fleeing from the French, England's allies. If the Declaration of Indulgence had been conceived to keep Nonconformists happy, it was not working for this woman. This is the more significant, as her husband Nicholas had benefited directly: on 12th June 1672 he received a licence to preach at the Presbyterian congregation at Windsor, meeting 'at Mrs Jane Price's new house, Frogmore'.[17] He had visited this church at least once before, in 1669, and this move may have been part of a Presbyterian church-planting programme, made possible by the Declaration of Indulgence.[18] Nicholas Palmer does not appear in Calamy's famous memorial to Nonconformist ministers. It is possible that he is the Nicholas Palmer, 'pleb.', who matriculated at Magdalen Hall, Oxford, in 1659.[19] If so, the Restoration probably intervened before he could be ordained.

Nicholas died in Windsor in February 1681.[20] The records are silent about whether Julia moved there with him, but presumably she was back in London at the time that she dedicated her manuscript to Joseph Biscoe, which was probably after 1690: her inscription suggests that Joseph Biscoe the younger, who was born in 1676, had reached adult status at the time that she wrote it.

No explicit political opinion is expressed in the poetry, which is not surprising: Nonconformist women's devotional writing in this period was valued entirely for its spirituality, which was seen in direct opposition not only to politics but to all secular circumstance. It is worth remembering, however, that contemporaries who read the poetry would have known exactly to which events Palmer was referring, however obliquely. Palmer's carefully dated poetry bears a close resemblance to the spiritual journal, which women were encouraged to keep as valued records of their spiritual experience: as Ollive Cooper, Nottingham Presbyterian, announced in her journal, the 'Temporall favours' of one's life, by which she means external circumstance, are 'but the dark side of gods goodness': 'Spirituall favours' only should be recorded.[21]

This belief, obliterating as it does so many details of pious women's lives, is deeply frustrating to students of women's history. However, the very timbre of Palmer's spirituality has a political resonance in the 1670s. Her constant theme is her love for Jesus, which is so extreme that she wishes only to die and to be with him. Poems such as 26 and 64 of the

'Second Century', 'The soull courting death', and 'The souls, longings to be gone', may seem excessively morbid to a modern reader, but in fact such sentiments are the logical conclusion of Nonconformist teaching in this period. The 'mystical marriage' trope in which the believer becomes the Bride of Christ, to achieve consummation at death, is characteristic of periods of persecution for the Reformed church: it permeates Protestant martyrology and its generic successor, exemplary biography. Moreover, there is evidence that in the Restoration period this teaching was particularly aimed at women: in *Christ the Best Husband, or an invitation of Young Women unto Christ* (London, 1672) Thomas Vincent advocated the mystical marriage as eminently superior for women to physical marriage. He preaches this commitment in exactly the absolute terms used by Julia Palmer:

> If you be espoused unto Christ, then you do embrace him in the arms of your dearest love; then you love the Lord Jesus in sincerity, and you love him with the supremacy of your love; if you love father or mother, houses or lands, riches or honours, delights or pleasures, or any thing in the world, more than Christ, you have no true love to Christ, and be sure are not espoused to him. (p.13)

It is no wonder that when her fanaticism is questioned by Mr. H., who ventures to suggest that it might be acceptable to wish for a long life on earth rather than an early union with Jesus in death, Palmer reacts with indignation (see poem 56 of the 'Second Century').

The trope of the mystical marriage had political implications, however, which became explicit after the repeal of the Declaration of Indulgence in March 1673. In 1674 William Sherlock expressed his anxiety about an intimate relationship with God that transcended all worldly authority, in *A Discourse Concerning the Knowledge of Jesus Christ, and our Union and Communion with him.*[22] His targets were Thomas Vincent, Presbyterian minister Thomas Watson, and the Independent minister John Owen. Both had written spiritual treatises in 1657 asserting the intimacy of a marriage relationship between Christ and the believer. Sherlock redefines the 'person' of Christ as a kind of Scriptural metaphor. Thus the relationship suggested by an allegorical interpretation of the Song of Songs is entirely inappropriate: the trope of the Bride should be enlisted only to describe the Church. It was the immediate access to Christ implied by idea of a marriage relationship that so disturbed Tory Anglicans, who wanted to preserve the authority of hierarchies, both Church and State. Nonconformist reaction was immediate and vocal: for them, this was an attack on the central experience of Reformed Christianity. John Owen's assistant Robert Ferguson, in one of the most effective responses to Sherlock, identified this political intent in the reluctance of Church of England theologians to recognise the metaphorically encoded union of believers with Christ: 'by our *Fellowship with Christ* which the Sacred Writers so Emphatically speak of, we are told there is only meet such a Political Union, as is betwixt a Prince and his Subjects, between Superiours, and Inferiours'.[23] Another famous Nonconformist contribution to this controversy was Vincent Alsop's *Antisozzo*, written as an attack on William Sherlock. Although he did not know this Northampton preacher personally, Thomas Cawton asked on his deathbed in 1677 that whoever wrote *Antisozzo* should be his successor.[24] Thus Vincent Alsop became leader of the Westminster church, and the political leader of the Nonconformists in London.[25] But Sherlock may have been right about the revolutionary implications of the mystical marriage trope: both Robert Ferguson and Alsop's son Benjamin, the father-in-law of Joseph Biscoe's nephew, fought with Monmouth in the 1685 rebellion against Charles II's brother, James II.

Julia Palmer's poetry

The word 'century' is not Julia Palmer's own, but it would have resonated with any seventeenth-century English Presbyterian. William Barton had made an attempt to get his psalm paraphrases substituted for the Sternhold and Hopkins Psalter in 1645: whilst the Lords had backed the volume, the radical and therefore anti-rhetorical Commons had rejected it. This did not stop Barton publishing various volumes of 'Centuries', groups of one hundred hymns, in the Restoration. In 1670 Barton had published *Two Centuries of Select Hymns Collected Out of the Psalter*, and it is possible that this volume was a stimulus to Julia Palmer's poetic composition. The arrangement of her poems into two series of 100 each was obviously important to her: her numbering system breaks up a close chronological sequence of thirteen poems dated from June 13th to June 28th 1672, leaving half in one 'Century' and half in another. However, Palmer's subject matter is not the rather impersonal, Old Testament paraphrase of Barton's hymns. Palmer is entirely concerned with her own spiritual experience, and the intimate, emotional timbre of the poetry is more like the eighteenth-century nonconformist hymn than anything published in the seventeenth century. Isaac Watts, who wrote his first hymn in an effort to improve on Barton, complained about the often violent Old Testament rhetoric of the psalm paraphrases, which did not for him convey the spirituality of the Gospel. His description of his own work could be applied to Julia Palmer's, although she was writing thirty years before him: 'the most frequent Tempers and Changes of our Spirit, and Conditions of our Life are here copied, and the Breathings of our Piety expresst according to the Variety of our Passions ... as they are refined into Devotion, and act under the Influence and Conduct of the Blessed Spirit; all conversing with God the Father by the new and living Way'.[26] Perhaps it is not too fanciful to suggest that this stanza from the 'Second Century' could even have been written by Watts himself:

> A burning beacon, of pure love
> Still strongly, flaming up to thee
> I'de be, untill thou doe remove
> Mee up, where love. shall perfect be. (II, 67, ll.1-4)

In fact, if the poems were being sung or read at Pinners' Hall in the early eighteenth century, as is quite possible, Watts might have encountered them: he led a congregation that met there, from 1704-1708.[27]

To a modern reader, the first impression of Palmer's poetry is often made by the eccentric spelling. In fact, her spelling is not bad by manuscript standards. Spelling was not standardised in the seventeenth century, and most authors expected their printers to correct their manuscripts during the publication process. If Palmer had been able to afford a scribe, the same revision would have happened during copying. More significant is the form of the poetry in the manuscript. Most of the poems in the 'First Century' are in four-line simple stanzas with alternate rhyming. This is not surprising for a woman beginning to write poetry in 1671: a form for women's religious poetry had become established since the beginning of the seventeenth century. Printed works by pious women, such as Dorothy Leigh's *A Mother's Legacie* had invariably been written in prose, yet often there was an example of the author's poetry attached at the beginning or the end of the volume. Several of these poems—Elizabeth Richardson's 'My owne Prayer in Meeter' attached to *A Ladies Legacie to her Daughters* (1645) and Frances Cooke's psalm of thanksgiving, attached to an account of a shipwreck in the Irish Sea in 1650—are very similar in form to the poems in Julia Palmer's 'First Century'.[28] An analysis of such poetry perhaps gives the twenty-first century reader a sense of what the spiritual ideal of female-authored poetry was thought to be. All these poems are in a very simple metre, usually ballad metre, which was reminiscent of the Psalms sung in church: the connection with 'holy' poetry may have added to the sense that this was legitimate rhetorical endeavour. Many of the happiest rhythms in the poems are actually Biblical ones, for example the first two lines of number 13 of the 'Second Century': 'thy ways, ar ways of pleasentnese/And all thy paithes, ar peace', taken directly from Proverbs 3.17. That there was an illegitimate poetics for the religious author is seen in, for example, the struggles of George Herbert to produce a poetry uncontaminated by rhetorical display and self-seeking. It is safe to assume that this kind of restraint operated even more strongly for women: Palmer expresses her sense of being silenced by conventions of 'modesty', which she describes as 'sinfull' (the 'Second Century', no. 72, l. 15). Even Isaac Watts felt that he should not only restrict the metre and tone down the metaphor of his religious lyrics, but deliberately ignore aesthetic considerations: he said of his immensely popular hymnbook, 'Some of the Beauties of Poesy are neglected, and some wilfully defac'd'.[29]

Theology and spirituality

It is possible to trace a distinctive Nonconformist theology in the poetry. Julia Palmer is constantly celebrating free grace, the strongest aspect of the Gospel for Nonconformists: this is the name for the completely undeserved mercy of God in saving people in the first place and then sustaining them with blessings. ('Free love' is another common term for the same phenomenon: Frances Cooke called her daughter 'Freelove', a rather startling appellation to the modern ear.) Palmer believes in a particularly strong version of God's sovereignty, double predestination: not only did God choose those who were to be saved, the 'elect', from the beginning of time, but he also chose those who were to be damned. Every event in Palmer's life is appointed by God, a belief that causes her some problems in interpreting difficult or negative occurrences. Her spiritual autobiography, which she gives us in poem 70 of the 'First Century', is a typically Nonconformist one: the highlight is the 'covenant' with God. This is a profound transaction whereby Palmer surrenders all right to self-determination but in exchange receives God's strength for a holy life.

> I gave my self to thee, by vow
> and resignation
> And am my own, noe longer now
> but thine, and thine alone. (ll.65-68)

Such benefits are defined with the preceding adjective, 'covenant', as in 'cov'nant streams' (the 'First Century', no. 19, l. 52), 'cov'nant priviledges' (the 'First Century, no. 75, l. 45) and even 'gods new cov nant court/From whence he doth receive, a safe pasport' (the 'Second Century', no. 48, ll. 59-60). Palmer is dependent upon God in everything. Her values are self-consciously different from those of the world around her and many of the poems define the distinctiveness of the Christian life and chart her struggle to maintain holiness. This involved the mortification ('putting to death') of many 'carnal' desires and lusts ('carnal' means 'of the flesh', the opposite of 'spiritual'). Her vocabulary is distinctive: she uses the verb 'give in' rather than the straightforward 'give' to describe God's direct blessings. This jargon is used by other Nonconformist women.[30] Palmer is very convinced of the necessity of 'ordinances' and 'duties'—set services such as Holy Communion—which means she is more likely to be Presbyterian than a member of a more radical sect. The spirituality of the poetry, with its echoes of Presbyterian publications by writers such as Thomas Watson, helps to establish her as Presbyterian.

An unusual feature of the manuscript is the dating of so many of the poems, which were apparently written within a two-year period, and are arranged in chronological order.[31] Given the almost exclusive concern with the progress of her relationship with God, this turns Julia Palmer's manuscript into a document very similar to the seventeenth-century spiritual journal, a common form of woman's writing in this period.[32] Three of the poems of the 'First Century' are entitled 'Experience', the technical term for the subject matter of the spiritual journal.[33] The closeness to Biblical discourse in this 'feminine' poetry seems to have represented a further guarantee of its spirituality. The notes at the end of this edition reveal how great is Julia Palmer's dependence on Biblical tropes and near-quotation. It is sometimes possible to deduce which Biblical passages she was reading at a certain time: poems 58 and 60 of the 'Second Century' seem to indicate that she was reading Matthew 25 in early May 1673. Like most religious poets of the seventeenth century, Palmer asks for God's aid in her opening poem, therefore suggesting that the following poetry is divinely inspired: 'Blessed spirit, doe thou endite'. The mode of Biblical interpretation represented here is distinctively Nonconformist. She employs jargon to describe her spiritual experiences, of the kind Simon Patrick had criticised in *A Friendly Debate Between a Conformist and a Nonconformist* (1669), such as the 'quickening' and 'enlarging' of 'affections': he would particularly have objected to her often-used rhyme of 'soul' and 'roll', as the rolling of the soul onto Christ was a Nonconformist expression of surrender and dependency.[34] In poem 85 of the 'Second Century', she talks about 'that sweet art, of contentation' in an echo of the title of a 1653 book by Thomas Watson, *The Art of Contentment*, which was reprinted numerous times in the seventeenth century. On the whole, however, 'contented' is not what Julia Palmer is. Her poems are full of longings and desires, and for her the worst sin is to 'sit down' rather than continually strive after Christ. In poem 99 of the 'First Century' she admits that she is not even sure what she is longing for: poem 71 of the 'Second Century' is a response to fellow believers who were probably frustrated with her: 'Why ask you me, what tis that I would have?' She becomes completely confused when her holiness is questioned, on May 6th 1673:

> Love unto Christ, is cal'd self love
> And that which came not, from above. (II, 58, ll.5-6)

When she can express what she desires it is usually in physical terms—she wants a 'taste' or a 'sight' of Christ. However, in the Reformed tradition she has been taught that only with death comes the full consummation of union with Christ, which is why she wishes for death, and the tropes of the mystical marriage pervade this manuscript. Although to a modern reader this preoccupation seems excessively morbid, Palmer is only responding to what she has been taught: the idea of Christ as husband, affianced in this life and to be married only in death, seems to have been preached by Nonconformists to women in particular. Thus, she is distinctly irritated by Mr H., who suggests to her that it is legitimate to wish for long life:

> Then worthy sir, why do you say
> Tis good to live, here many a day
>
> Ar ther soe many, in the throng
> Of this world, that, doe truly long
>
> In their redeemers arms to lye
> That you should thus, att them let fly. (II, 56, ll.53-8)

Nevertheless, some of the manoeuvres here show a struggle with profound inner contradiction. Her reaction to the loss of 'a deer freind brother Gilbert' is to renounce dependence on human companionship: yet this renunciation is clearly in the interests of self-protection.

We joy a litle in a freind
But oh how soon, this joy doth end

They do;nt so much refresh the hart
As gaule when we from them do part. (II, 34, ll.9-12)

However, she goes beyond much rather shallow contemporary teaching. She is aware of her own changes of mood (see the 'First Century, no. 84) and learns about her own state by observing the behaviour of children (see the 'First Century', no. 79). She realises that human understanding comes far short of God's dealing with believers (the 'Second Century', no. 25). Unlike most of her contemporaries she recognises that contentment is not always a sign of God's favour, and on June 22nd 1673 she plumps for holiness rather than immediate happiness, in a use of what must have been a rather novel trope in the seventeenth century:

I'de trust thee, with my hapynese
to store itt up, in bank. (II, 69, ll.27-8)

Form

In the 'Second Century', Julia Palmer moved away to some extent from Biblical tropes, and from stanzaic simplicity. Whilst her 'First Century' had contained 11 poems with complex stanzaic forms, several of which are duplicated, the 'Second Century' contains more than twice that number, with only two repeated patterns. This metrical variety is very unusual, and, it must be said, represents an unfortunate change of direction: on the whole, Palmer is much better at simple stanza forms. In fact, some of the most interesting poems in the 'Second Century' are in rhyming couplets with no stanzaic breaks. These often concern personal incident, such as Mr H's challenge to her spirituality (II, 56), or the meditation on the life and death of Christ that ends in a kind of swoon (II, 16). Heartfelt meditation seems to slip easily into iambic pentameter. This raises the question of whether the lyric forms are intended for public singing in the congregation. Some of the lyric forms would fit the tunes suggested in Barton's hymnal: most of them are combinations of eight syllable, six syllable and four syllable lines, the standard components of the hymnbook. Isaac Watts' early hymns were written in manuscript and 'lined out' to the congregation: perhaps Palmer's were too. There is certainly a sense that the manuscript was intended for the benefit of other Christians, as the very first poem indicates:

> Blessed spirit, doe thou endite
> Help me to speak thy praise
> That soe I may others envite
> To love thee, all there days.

Several of the poems suggest that other Christians were jealous of her reputation for spirituality, a reputation that may have been enhanced by the circulation of her poems, or the use of them as hymns.[35] It may be significant that Palmer sometimes uses the vertical lines characteristic of psalmbooks to show line divisions: this practice, which we have only seen elsewhere in manuscripts of Mary Sidney's psalm paraphrases, may indicate that Palmer is perceiving her writing as hymns rather than poetry—a distinction which would have been very important to her.

However, it may just be that the lyrics of the 'Second Century' show Palmer gaining more confidence as a poet. Although the rhetoric is hardly more sophisticated, remaining simple and conversational, the tropes are no longer exclusively biblical. A suggestive cluster of imagery concerns merchant shipping:

> The Christians trade, is always heavenly
> His marchandise, is for eternity
> He drives an hiden, cecreet, unknown trade
> With heaven, and comes home, still richly lade. (II, 48, ll.26-30)

Poem 24 of the 'Second Century' is entitled 'The best trade', and poem 39 of the 'Second Century' describes a spiritual disaster in terms of a shipwreck at sea. This reference to the boom in overseas trading in the later seventeenth century is typical of the wider reference shown by the poems of the 'Second Century' when compared with the first. There is also more than a suspicion of the influence of another poet, George Herbert. Much as his volume, *The Temple*, can be described as a record of spiritual conflict (Herbert's own description), so Julia Palmer's 'Centuries' chart the vagaries of the spiritual life: there is the same pattern of joy followed by despair, and an overwhelming Calvinist sense that the true Christian is never allowed to sense his or her own progress. In some places there is an echo of Herbert's own phraseology; poem 45 of the

'First Century' begins 'How sweet ar thy returning rays' in an echo of Herbert's 'The Flower': 'how sweet and clean/Are thy returns!' Poem 55 of the 'Second Century' has more than a ring of the refrain of Herbert's poem 'Home':

> Oh manefest thy self to me
> Or fecth me up in hast. to thee. (ll.17-18)

The rather close echoes suggest that Palmer had read *The Temple* for herself, rather than picking up the allusions in Nonconformist sermons, for example. Herbert's poems were the one kind of poetry that would have been considered appropriate reading matter for a Nonconformist woman.

Until more can be unearthed about Julia Palmer's background and material circumstances, we can only speculate about the amount of education she received. Relatively wealthy Nonconformist families did send their daughters to school, as the diary of Elizabeth Turner reveals.[36] Julia Palmer's poetry offers little evidence of a formal education beyond the ability to read and write, and an obvious immersion in the Biblical text and other works of religious devotion. Clearly Palmer did not see herself in a contemporary elite poetic tradition. During the years in which she wrote her 'Centuries', Milton was still alive, Cowley's works were selling well, and Dryden was establishing his career. Her work was not intended to be read alongside this kind of poetry, but she clearly considered it to have value of its own. Much of that perceived value is hard to recover outside of the context of religious persecution in which it was composed. However, someone considered this manuscript worth preserving well after the death of its author and the people to whom she bequeathed it: the manuscript found its way into a London bookshop, and then into the library of Sir Thomas Phillips, when he was amassing his huge manuscript collection in the early nineteenth century. This manuscript marks a moment in the development of authorship for non-elite women. It also represents an early effort in the kind of poetic that was to produce the simple sublimity of the eighteenth-century nonconformist hymn. However, to assign the poetry an importance outside of its literary historical significance will require the deployment of rather different literary critical paradigms than are usually in use in seventeenth-century research.

Elizabeth Clarke

Notes

1. William Andrewes Clark Memorial Library, UCLA, MS P1745 M1 P744 1671-3 Bound, f.i.

2. John Challenor Covington Smith, *Pedigree of the Family of Biscoe* (London: Mitchell and Hughes, 1887), 4-7; Arthur Meredyth Burke, ed., *Memorials of St. Margaret's Church Westminster Comprising the Parish Registers, 1539-1660 and the Churchwardens Accounts, 1460-1603* (London: Eyre and Spottiswode, 1914), 134; Court Minutes of the Society of Apothecaries 1651-80, MS 8200/2, Guildhall Library, f. 160; Court Minutes 1680-94, MS 8200/3, f. 6; Penelope Hunting, *A History of the Society of Apothecaries* (London: The Society of Apothecaries, 1998), 302; C.R.B. Barrett, *The History of the Society of Apothecaries of London* (London: Elliott Stone, 1905), 122-131. See Court Minutes 1694-1716, MS 8200/4; Court Minutes 1716-26, MS 8200/5; and Court Minutes 1726-1745, MS 8200/6 for Biscoe's and Pitson's activities as officers of the Society. Since apprentices were usually bound to a master when they were 14 (Hunting 45), Pitson was probably born in 1658. The last mention of Pitson in the Court Minutes is 16 March 1732/3 so he may have died shortly afterwards.

3. E.G. Withycombe, *The Oxford Dictionary of English Christian Names*, 3rd edition (Oxford: Clarendon, 1977), 183. Withycombe says that the name was not current until the eighteenth century, but points out that the name Julia was used by Shakespeare, in *Two Gentlemen of Verona*, and by Herrick. Guildhall Library MS 5085, f.55v.

4. Parish Records of St. Margaret's, Westminster: Harl. Soc. Parish Registers, LXIV, 64.

5. Guildhall Library MS 8200/3, p. 64.

6. Will of Joseph Biscoe. City of Westminster Archives Centre, Will Accession 120/1853, f. 128. Will proved 11 December 1723.

7. See Walter Wilson, *The History and Antiquities of Dissenting Churches and Meeting Houses in London, Westminster and Southwark*, 4 vols.(1808-14), II, 252-4, III, 282-287.

8. Wilson, *History and Antiquities*, IV, 61.

9. For further reading on this phase of religious history, see Richard Greaves, *Enemies Under His Feet: Radicals and Nonconformists in Britain* (Stanford University Press, 1990).

10. Calendar of State Papers Domestic, 1671, 554, 563.

11. Ibid., 497, 562.

12. See *The Life and Death of that Holy and Reverend Man of God Thomas Cawton* (1662). Its author was anonymous but the preface 'to the

Reader' was signed by prominent Presbyterians such as Edmund Calamy, Thomas Watson, and Simeon Ashe, most of whom had been involved in the Presbyterian Plot.

13. Calendar of State Papers Domestic, 1671, 497: 1671-2, 29.

14. G. Lyon Turner, *Original Records of Early Nonconformity*, 3 vols.(1911-14), I, 206.

15. See *A Plan of the Cities of London and Westminster, and the Borough of Southwark, with the Contiguous Buildings. From an actual Survey, taken by John Roque, Land Surveyor, and Engraved by John Price. Begun March 1637. Published 1746* (London Topographical Society, 1919) for the plan of these streets. The Presbyterian meeting-house is marked in New Way. Corporation of London Record Office MS tax rating for the inhabitants of St. Margaret's Westminster, 'For war v. France', 1st quarter 1694, p.54, shows Samuel Palmer living in Orchard Street North, assessed at £6. Joseph Biscoe is shown living in The Sanctuary and Deanery (p.46) and assessed at £30. He owns many properties in the parish including several in New Way near the meeting-house (p.51).

16. Lyon Turner, I, 576.

17. Calendar of State Papers Domestic, 1672, 55, 196.

18. *Calamy Revised*, ed. A. G. Matthews (Oxford 1834), 380. This visit is here ascribed to Anthony Palmer, but the Christian name is not specified in the reference, and it is much more likely to be Nicholas, in view of the fact that he became preacher to the Windsor congregation in 1672.

19. Nicholas Palmer does not appear in *Calamy Revised*. He may be the Nicholas Palmer in *Alumni Oxoniensis 1500-1714*, ed. Joseph Foster (1891), III, 1109.

20. Berkshire R.O., MS D/P/49/1/1, February 28th 1680/81.

21. Dr. Williams Library MS 24.49, f.19v.

22. Sherlock explicitly criticises Thomas Watson's *Christs Lovelines* (London, 1657) and John Owen's *Of communion with God: the Father, Sonne and Holy Ghost, each person distinctly; or, The Saints' fellowship with the Father, Sonne and Holy Ghost, unfolded* (Oxford, 1657).

23. Robert Ferguson, *The Interest of Reason in Religion* (London, 1675), 187.

24. Wilson, *History and Antiquities II*, 61. The text in question is Vincent Alsop, *Antisozzo sive Sherlocimuss Enervatus. In Vindication of Some Great Truths Opposed and Opposition to Some Great Errors Maintained by Mr. William Sherlock* (London, 1675).

25. It was Alsop who published William Waller's *Divine Meditations upon several occasions* (London, 1680), a classic text of piety in vindication of the Presbyterian Civil War general.

26. Isaac Watts, *Hymns and Spiritual Songs in Three Books*, 10th ed. (1728), vii.
27. *Dictionary of National Biography:* 'Isaac Watts'.
28. Frances Cooke, *M^ris*. *Cookes meditations, Being an humble thanksgiving to her Heavenly Father, for granting her a new life, having conclnded* [sic] *her selfe dead, and her grave made in the bottome of the Sea, in that great storme,* Jan *the 5th. 1649* (London, 1650).
29. Isaac Watts, *Hymns and Spiritual Songs in Three Books,* 10th ed., 1728, ix.
30. See Katherine Sutton, *A Christian Womans Experiences of the Glorious Workings of Gods Free Grace* (Rotterdam, 1663), 44 where she says of her poems 'I assure you Courteous Reader these are not studed [sic] things, but are given in immediately'.
31. There is one exception to this: in the 'Second Century', poem 48 is dated 26th Sept. 1672, poem 51 is dated 22nd Sept. 1672, and poem 52 is dated 25th Sept. 1672.
32. See Elizabeth Clarke, 'Diaries and Journals', in *A Companion to English Renaissance Literature and Culture,* ed. Michael Hattaway (London, 2000), 609-614.
33. See the headings in the ideal spiritual diary laid out in Isaac Ambrose, *Media* (London, 1657), 87-88, 163-68.
34. Simon Patrick, *A Friendly Debate Between a Conformist and a Non-conformist* (1669), 33-48: Samuel Parker, *A Discourse of Ecclesiastical Polity,* (London, 1667), 158.
35. Note the 'complaint' of poem 58 of the 'Second Century': 'What Jealousies, doth me surround … Love unto Christ, is cal'd self love / And that which came not, from above'.
36. Kent Archives Office, MS F. 27, [f.53v].

A Note on the Text

Julia Palmer's devotional poems, now in the William Andrews Clark Memorial Library at UCLA (MS P1745 M1 P744 1671-3 Bound), exist in an autograph fair copy. Though they are arranged into two groups of 100 poems, only 199 poems are in fact present in Palmer's manuscript: there is no poem 62 in the 'First Century'. In the 'Second Century' she has skipped number 88, but has two poems numbered 96, making the total for the second part of the manuscript 100. On the first flyleaf Palmer has written her name, the date 1671, some shorthand, and the note 'I Leave this Book to Mr Joseph Bisco senior. if he out Live me otherwiss. I Leave itt to Mr James pitson Apothicary'. This note and signature are in the same hand as the rest of the manuscript, strongly suggesting that the manuscript is autograph. The manuscript contains authorial revisions and deletions but it is for the most part neatly produced. Horizontal lines that run the width of the page separate each poem. Page numbers are enclosed in parentheses and appear centred at the top of the page. At several points Palmer skips ahead in her transcription, needing to delete a word or an entire line, indicating that she was copying from another source of her poetry. The 265-page octavo volume is prefaced by three flyleaves and followed by three blank leaves, plus a stub. Its cover measures 174 by 118 mm and its pages are 169 by 112 mm, with the exception of pp. 92-95 which are conjugate deckle edge leaves, measuring approximately 162 by 112 mm. It is bound in contemporary brown calf with only ruling in blind for ornamentation, though a zigzag gilt roll has been used on the edges of the boards and the pages are edged in dark green. The horn watermark is similar to Heawood 2715 (1668) and 2722 (1665), but it is difficult to make out any distinguishing marks due to the tightness of the binding. The Clark Library acquired the manuscript in 1951, and it was rebacked by them in June 1999 with the original spine laid down.

We have chosen to follow the editorial principles set out by Michael Hunter in his 1995 article, 'How to Edit a Seventeenth-Century Manuscript: Principles and Practice' published in *The Seventeenth Century*, volume 10, pages 277-310. Hunter has called for consistency in editing, making a strong case for following the practices of a seventeenth-century printer: silently expanding abbreviations (such as 'y^e' and 'w^{ch}' to 'the' and 'which'), normalizing u's and v's, i's and j's, but retaining original spelling and punctuation, with some latitude. We have silently emended Palmer's use of commas instead of apostrophes (e.g. we have changed 'cov,nant' to 'cov'nant'). We chose to follow the 'clear text' presentation of the text, noting insertions and deletions in the textual notes. We have termed something 'inserted' when it has been added by Palmer in different ink; if a word is superscripted but in the same ink, we have not termed that an insertion, but have silently lowered it (e.g. as in the case of 'To,th', which we have changed to 'To'th' in order to preserve the line metrically). A word has been noted as 'deleted' when Palmer has either crossed out or erased it. We have not noted line breaks in titles of poems, nor the few places in which titles have been cropped. Palmer uses tildes frequently to represent missing letters, most of which we have silently expanded when the missing letter was obvious (these letters are the five vowels, n, m, p, b, c, d, and t, and on two occasions the syllable 'ber' in the name of a month). Examples of the following are: 'aproch' to 'aproach', 'surly' to 'surely', 'proclame' to 'proclaime', 'droping' to 'drooping', 'shold' to 'should', 'triumphat' to 'triumphant', 'imortalyty' to 'immortalyty', 'suply' to 'supply', 'climed' to 'climbed', 'thiker' to 'thicker', 'adition' to 'addition', 'inshuting' to 'inshutting', 'octo' to 'october'. We have not expanded several tildes when it was not clear how to do so; these appeared above letters in 'cant', 'canst', 'amaze', 'mirth', 'saint', 'those', 'hindrance', and 'thine'.

Palmer uses shorthand at several points in her manuscript. On the first flyleaf, beneath her signature and date, she has written 'not I' followed by 13 shorthand symbols. Shorthand is used in five titles: 'The struclings of faith october, 7 71' is followed by 7 symbols ('First Century', 14); 'The soull veiwing Christ in his humiliation' is surmounted by 7 symbols ('First Century', 86); 'mr H' is followed by 16 symbols ('Second Century', 56); 'An occationall addition June 16 73' is followed by 7 symbols ('Second Century', 68); 'July 11 73' is followed by 6 symbols ('Second Century', 96). A single symbol (a dash whose edges curve upwards) is used in three titles in the 'Second Century': poems 14, 79, and 99. It may have the meaning 'the'. We have not been able to match Palmer's system with any of the three most popular forms of shorthand by Thomas Shelton (used by Samuel Pepys), Theophilus Metcalfe, and Jeremiah Rich. We also tried unsuccessfully to match Palmer's shorthand with Thomas Bright's much earlier *Characterie*. Palmer's shorthand may be her own invention, and it seems to have been used to obscure personal details, such as the identity of Mr. H.

Victoria Burke

The First Century

Blessed spirit, doe thou endite
Help me to speak thy praise
That soe I may others envite
To love thee, all there days

A blessed sun, oh Lord thou art   5
Let still thy beames of glory dart
To warm, and quiken, my dull hart

2.   Longings to goe hence.   p. 1

From earths dark den, fain would I fly
That in thy bosome, I might lye

Oh dearest Jesus, come away
My sweetest Lord, make no delay

My soull longs to be Lodg'd above   5
In'th armes, & bosome, of thy Love

From sin, & sorow, then shall I
For ever be, sett up on high

No intervening, cloud shall be
To hide thy lovly face, from me   10

Long absence Lord, I cannot bear
The thoughts of itt, doth wast, & wear

Oh fill me with, thy grace, and love
& fitt me for the Joys above,

help me dear Lord, to mend my pace   15
That I may quikly, see thy face

In thine arms, I can freely venture
Oh Christ, my only hope, and centor

By faith, and love, oh lett me, soare
Till I enjoy thee, evermore   20

Then shall I in length of days
Sitt under thine eternall rays

My dearest Jesus come away
To succour me, make no delay

My soull is wracked with desire   25
And yet I cannot get up higher

3   The Love of Christ

Oh what unparaleld love was this
Christ left his fathers throne
And all the glory, that was his
What streames of love here ran

Now mortalls stand, & maze   5
Whilst angells pry, and Gaze

When sin for Justise cry'd aloud   p. 2
Christ came on wings of love
He came with garments dipt in bloud
Love made him swiftly move,   10

Behold what Love is this I see
For Christ to come and dye for me

On fiery, flames of love he rode
This love made no delay
The wine-prese of, gods wrath hee trode   15
Love would not, could not, stay

Whilst wee would of this wonder speak
Our crakt, & narow vessels Leak

What meanst thou thus to darken glory
Its far beyound the pen   20
Of angels for to write this story
Much more of mortall men

They that would in, this work engage
Must wait for an eternall age.

4   Of aproach to god, in ordinances.

I come to ly down att thy feet
Fain I would see thy face
Oh Lord, deny me not, the sweet
Influences, of grace

To pray, to hear, to meditate   5
Is thy declared will.
But Lord att what a wofull rate
To wee thy will, fulfill

A litle length, wee cannot bear
Our harts soon, run astray   10
Here, & there; and ev'ry where
Soon, they ar gone away

And if through chafing, heat we get
Wee quickly cooll again,
And inconsideratly, wee let   15
Our harts grow vile, & vain

Oh oft doe we our selfs content   p.3
With a bare duty done
When many times our harts ar lent,
After the world to run.   20

When wee might hold, converse with god
And get into his hart
We're wandring far, to get a rod
Wh'erby att last wee smart

Duty its self's an empty thing   25
But it is gods command
And he will in it, comfort bring
If wee, by faith attend,

Duty dear god, thou dost apoynt
Whilst wee ar in our way   30
Oh let thy spirit me anoynt
With fresh suplys each day

To thee my god I can apeall
Dutys will not content
If thou thy self, doe not reveill   35
I sorow, and Lament

Yett seeing Lord, thou dost command me
Thy will shall bee my law
And if I never, should enjoy thee
My hart would stand in awe   40

By these sweet streams, let me be Led
With fresh, incomes of strength
Till I injoy the fountain head
And dwell with thee att length

5   The world.

This world's a vain, an empty thing
Her Joys doe reall sorows bring

All things, that ar below the sun
With hast; and speed, away they run

The world our comforts steall, & rifle   5
Whilst wee like Children. play, & trifle

Arise my soull, its not thy rest
The comforts in it ar at best

But briers, that do prick, & smart
And cannot ease, a wounded hart   10

It is a heap of vanity   p. 4
Afording only misery

When wee would of her pleasures tast
Our precyous time doth speand, & wast

When wee doe of its sent pertake   15
It doth but stop, & suffocate

When we would mount above the sky
It pulls us down, & here we lye

Yet wait A while, & thou shalt see
A conquered enemy, it shall bee   20
Through Christ, who gave himself for thee

6   The Complaint of a burdened soull.

Some pity take
Oh god of grace
& speedyly
Shew me thy face

My hart doth ake,   5
I find no rest
To be with thee
Lord, it is best

I cannot mourn,
But like a stone   10
My hart is dead
And sencelese, grown

I want a hart
Enflam'd with love
that I may   15
may faster to thee move,

My unbeleiving
heart makes me,
to start, and run
away from thee.   20

Afections they,
bend to the eearth
And rob my soull
of all true mirth

If I for comfort   25
look within
ther is the guilt
& filth of sin.

Thyne arows they,
Stick in me fast   30
My sorows they,
ar keen, and last

All peace, and Joy,
is from me fled.
In paiths of darknese,   35
I am Led

I am beset
With hels black shade
Through seas of
darknese, I doe wade   40

Life is a burden
unto mee,
Because from sin
I cant be free.

Prefering death,   45
Before a life
That is so full
of wofull, strife

When sin dos stare
me in the face   50
And I seem
destidute, of grace

Tis that I know
not how to bear
My days in greif,   55
doe wast, & wear

But still I shall, & ever must   p. 5
Say thou art righteous, good, & Just.

7   Mixt desires

Thou sitst between the Cherubims
Surounded with the Seraphims
Ther angels see thy face
Oh that I had the wings of love
Then would I flee, to god above   5
Be'ing filled with thy grace

Oh help my weary, restlese soull,
By steady faith, on thee to rowll
This is the work of heaven
Such soulls may surely come to thee   10
As poor, & blind, & empty bee
Self righteousnese, would leaven

A sacrifice Lord, I would offer
But I have none, that's worth the profer
Thou calest for my hart   15
My hart dear Lord, take it to thee
Oh that it were from sin made free
Sorow to Joy, this would convert

Arise, be gone, mount up my soull
Scorning in earths black durt to roull   20
Soe Lord thou knowest I would
A hart burning in flames of love
Send quikly to, thy god above
Oh that in truth, I could

Stand off then from the world, & cretures   25
Be blind to all their lovly features
They will but doe thee harm
Att best the world's a pousen'd bait
Take warning e're, it be to late
Let not its beauty Charm   30

Oh teach me Lord, the holy art
To set this world far from my hart
Then may I, to it say
My hart's reserved for another   p. 6
Dearer to mee, then any brother   35
You may, then goe your way

8   Desires to Love Christ

Though I can nothing for thee doe
Yet grant me my desire
Let Love be strong, & still break through
To'th object I admire,

Dread Soveraign, of all the earth   5
What thing is this I crave
My Love is but poluted breath
Which thou mayst scorn to have

A circumsised hart to love thee
It is thy promise, Lord.   10
Oh let it be, made good to mee
Acording to thy word

Oh might I burn in love, to thee
Though in the hart of hell
T'would be a glorious heaven to me   15
Whilst others, doe rebell

Let, Love increase, still more, & more
Untill the perfect day
And in the croud, of earths afairs
Let love feell no alay   20

When that grace faith, shall wholy cease
And hope, be done away
Love then, shall still, sweetly encrease
And suffer no decay

This is the grace reciprocall   25
Tis lasting, firm, and sure
This is the grace, that's all in all
And ever shall endure

9   Longings after a sence of Christs love.

Dear Lord, away fain would I fly   p. 7
One smile from thee I crave
That in thy bosome I might lye
This is the thing I'de have

The sun doth shine, as well on dung   5
As on the chousest flower
Then shine upon my soull bright sun
By thine almighty power

Ten worlds to me, cant comfort give
When thou dost hide thy face   10
A smile from thee, would make me live
And sweetly run my race

In this worlds sweets, I tast no savour
My soull, drives slowly on
It is thy blessed love, & favour   15
That I would feed upon

Enlighten me soe in my way
That by thy rays devine
I may be able, once to say
Dear Jesus, thou art mine   20

If I must never see thy face
Whilst on this side of glory
Oh lett me move apace, in grace
Towards, the uper story

But if thou'lt say, I cannot take   25
Any delight in thee
Then here am I, Lord, of me make
What seemeth good, to thee

If dye I must, Lord. this I crave
And doe not me deny   30
Under thy feet I'le make my grave
And by thy hand I'le dye

Thy soverainty I will adore
Both now, henceforth, & ever more.

10   Admirings of Christ & longings to be with him,   p. 8

Oh my redeemer dear
How excelent thou art
Oh that thou wouldest, now draw neer
To iradiate every part

Oh sinner why so loth   5
To come, and take a part
His name's an oynment poured forth
It Chears, and glads the hart

Oh heavens, blush before
The brightnese of this sun   10
Which still shall shine, for ever more
When sun, & moon be gone.

Oh when, shall I goe see
The glory of this sight
The world thou knowst, is durt to me   15
Compared, with thy light

Thou art a mase, of love
Oh sweet, and sacred, dove
Oh when shall I, with joy, remove
To him, that dwels above   20

Then shall I sitt, and sing
With hapy, sinlese spirits
Thou art oh Lord, my god, and king
Oh sweet fruit, of thy merits

I wait, for that sweet day   25
When I shall sin no more
When sorow shall be done away
And I shall still adore

Those whom thou lovest best
Thou calst for soon away   30
To take their everlasting rest
Where joys, doe ne're decay

Ther's but a litle space
And thou shalt follow after
Thosse blessed soulls, that have through grace   35
Exchang'd their sighs, for laughter

Then Chear up, drooping soull   p. 9
The time is very short
Upon his word, & promise roull
I doe thee now exhort   40

Let Christ, have his due praise
Whilst thou hast any breath
Both now, & ever, all thy days
Till thou art Laid in earth

Then shalt thou blese his name   45
To all, eternity
With saints, spreading his gloryous fame
With pleasing, harmony.

11   prid, and humilyty.

T'was prid that hurl'd the angells down
From their high glorious station
How doe for ever, now lye bound
In cords, of desparation

The blessed angels, that stand fast   5
Ar said to vaill there faces
If thou wouldst have thy station last
Hold fast, this queen of graces

Wouldst thou be ranked in the row
Of those that humble are   10
A sight of god will lay thee low
To stir, prid will not dare

The soull that doth it self debase
Shall be set up on high
Whilst that the self exallting race   15
Shall on the dung hill lye

The humble soull, the Lord will make
His cecreets for to know
And such, shall of his grace pertake
Wher by apace, they grow   20

But those that love, & live in prid
He knows them afar off
And such with scorn, ar laid aside
god from From them stands aloof

Humilyty, will bring renown   25   p. 10
When thou hast run thy race
It is the blessed angels crown
Who dayly see gods face

be willing then, to let thy name
Ly buried, in the dust   30
Thy god, will surely clear the same
And wipe off all the rust

Unto the praise of man, be deaf
Esteem it not att all,
It is a sure presage of wrath   35
And thou art neer, a fall.

The devill, he is stil'd the king
Of the, Children of pride
This sin it will, all mischeif bring
If it in thee, abide   40

Take heed my soull, of cecreet pride
From man, thou mayst conceall't
But by thy god, t'will be espy'd
And he'l att last reveill it

Mans aprobation, will not steed thee   45
When thou must naked stand
Before the dreadfull god, to bee
Aquited, or condemn'd

The humble, contrite, broken, soull
Is gods own dwelling place   50
And he will give in, many a dole
To such seekers of grace

The kingdome of heaven is theirs
That poor in spirit bee
They ar the right, & lawfull heirs   55
Of that heritage free.

Such soulls ar calm under gods hand
They dare not once, rebell
Its mercy Lord, I'me not consum'd
I might have been in hell.   60

Now wouldst thou truly, humble bee
Then cast thine eyes within
And thou wilt quikly come to scc   p. 11
How black thou art by sin

With holy law, compare thy hart   65
Vew thy self, in that glase
When thou dost see, how vile thou art
T'will make thee sore abash

Then thou wilt think, there's none like thee
In all the world abroad   70
And truly willing, thou wilt bee
Under foot, to be tro.d

Look to thy body, that's but clay
And thou must, shortly dye
Thy name, & fame, will soon decay   75
When thou in dust, shalt lye

Then pluck up pride Lord by the root
Which way thou seest fitt
Although thou tread me, under foot
I will not gainsay it   80

Humility's, a cov'nant grace
Thy promises, ar free
Tis that for which, I seek thy face
Lord, give itt, unto mee.

12   Of faith, and Love.

faith, and love, are a comly pair
These two goe both togather
Nothing will part, thesse graces rare
Till death thesse two, doe sever

Then love, like Ruth, shall to us cleave   5
And, to heaven with us soare
When faith shall of us, take her leave
'Cause, we need her no more

Is he not said, in god to dwell
That hath made love his nest   10
Oh hapy, blessed, citadell
Oh sweet, & pleasing, rest

13   desertion.

The full asurance of thy love
I never yet atain'd
Yet could I goe, to god above
My suit, was not disdain'd

My sins, & sorows, I could tell   5   p. 12
Easing my mind oprest
Unto the god, of Israell
Alas, these days, ar past

Against me bitter things, he lays
Making me to possese   10
The inniquitys, of former days
My soul's a wildernese

Afections they, were quik, and flowing
But now, alase, they flag
My love on wing, to heaven soaring   15
But now, I feell it lag

Its sad to be deny'd thy face
And comforts, of thy spirit
Its worse, to be depriv'd of grace
Which once, wee did inherit   20

I dare not ask, what is the cause
My sins doe Loudly tell
It might have been, far worse with thee
Thou mights have been, in hell

Once I could say, Lord, I doe love thee   25
But now I question all
When I would in, thy presence bc
My spirits sink, & fall.

Thou seemst to bid me, goe away
Oh whether should I goe   30
My trouble, that finds no alay
but dayly high'r grow

Soe hartlese, many times I am
I know not how to speak
It is not fears, that thou wilt damne   35
That makes my comforts leak

But tis a cursed frame of hart
That I doe see, & feell,
Which makes me, dayly for to smart
Till thou be pleasd, to heall   40

The cutting sence of thy displesure
From th hiding of thy face
Is that which in soe great a measure
Imbiters, my short race

When I look into my own hart   45   p. 13
I know not what to make on't
All things ar there, soe black & dark
I am, even, afraid on't

I'me brought to this dilemma sad
To cry, what shall I doe   50
Through paiths, of darknese, I am led
My soull is full of woe

I cant find out, this enemy
That has this mischeif done
And fils me, with perplexety   55
Enlighten me, bright sun

But this I know, thers cause enough
It should be thus with me
And that I should be handled rough
Seeing noe smile from thee   60

My way, is hedged up with stone
I cannot find my paith
My soull doth grope, in dark alone
No true suport it hath

Look thou, on mine afliction   65
My sore, & pained, hart
And take away coruption
Which makes me for to smart

What I have left, is only thus
Some secreet it may be 70
The Lord will yet, be gracious
And pitifull, to mee

With, a cloud, thy self, thou coverest
My prayer cannot pase
I have rebeled, & transgrest 75
My soull, noe pardon has

In darknese, I am made to dwell
As those that long ar dead
Being neer a kin, to those in hell
Whose hope is perished 80

To make my moane, to man, its vain p. 14
To thee Lord, I will come
And if thou dost, my suit distaine
I can but, be undone

The best that man; can doe for mee 85
Is to extend, their pity
The grace to help, must come from thee
or else, I shall be needy

Thou art the potter, I thy clay
And thou mayst doe with me 90
What thou seest good, all I would say
Is, to, Justifie thee

Though I should never, with thee dwell
But be thrown to, the lowest hell

Might my requests, be given in 95
I never would, against thee sin

Whilst thou art powring wrath on me
I'de burn, in flames of love to thee

And alwais I, would Justifie
Thy spotlese, Just, severity   100

But heres my grief, this cannot bee
Thou'lt not turn hell, into heav'n for me.

14   The struclings of faith october, 7 71

Why lookest thou, soe sternly att me
As if thou wer't my foe
Through grace, I'le cleave, & cling, to thee
I'le not be put of soe

When sin, and saten, greatly rages   5
to Thee Lord, I will fly
Thou art that blessed, rock of ages
On whom, I will rely

I know, it is not meet, to give
To dogs, the Childrens bread   10
Yet blessed Lord. the dogs to live
With crums, from the boards head

Into thine arms, I'le throw my soull   p. 15
On this, I doe resovle
Come life, come death, on thee I'le roull   15
Then Lord, thou must absovle

A covenant with me, thou hast made
Its lasting, firm, and sure
It is a strong, foundation laid
Which ever, shall endure   20

Sin cannot break, the knot that's knitt
By compact, long agoe
Into thy hands, I will commit,
Both soull, & body, too

The bond, my god, is seal'd with bloud   25
The bloud of thine own son
See thou to itt, to make it good
For me, Christs bloud, did run

The mountains may, depart away
The hills, they may remove   30
Thy Loving kinndnese, cant decay
To one, whom thou dost love

Thou hast, oh Lord, commanded me
To lay hold, on thy strength
And I shall make, my peace with thee   35
To an eternall length

My faith, though weak, takes hold on thee
And on thy strength oh Lord
Then I shall make my peace with thee
According to thy word   40

In thee it is, the fatherlese
Doth tender mercy, find
To the fatherlese, & frindlese
Thou'lt shew thy self, most kinnd

What though a mother, may forget   45
Her tender sucking Child
My god, is more compationet
More mercyfull, & mild

Thy truth, & oath, my soull rests on   p. 16
Within the vaill it enters   50
Christ is the food faith feeds apon
On him, it sweetly centors

Thou hast bid me, come take my fill
Of waters, that run free
Without money, or prise, I will,   55
Lord, I will come, to thee

Once more, I throw my soull, oh Lord
Down att thy blessed feet
Depending, firmly, on thy word
That thou wilt safly keep't   60

Then why art thou soe sad, my soull
And why soe much cast down
I doe thee now, on Jesus roll
Truth cant, reverse whats done

Thy truth, & honour, lys att stake   65
If into hell, I fall
And in this, I will comfort take
Though Saten, rage, & baule

15   faiths triumph

Then now my soull, rejoyce, & sing
Sing praises to, thy god, and king

For now the love of Christ, stands sure
and shall eternaly endure

Hee'l be thy god, & guide for ever   5
Nothing from thee, his love can sever

Not life, nor death, nor nakednese
Nor any other, such distrese

In fire, & water, he'l be with thee
In death, and danger he'l releive thee   10

It is a cov'nant promise, free
All things shall work for good, to thee

Ar afflictions, for thee, best
They shall be added, to the rest

Aflictions, triels, and the rod   15
Ar the love tokens of thy god

Wereby he fits, & carveth thee   p. 17
An holy temple, for to bee

Thy name is written on his hart
And in his love, thou hast a part   20

By his spirit, he will guid
Till thou in glory do reside

When in dust, thou buri'd art
He will take care, of ev'ry part

A dust of thee, shall not be lost   25
In'th book of life, thy name's endorst

When time, & days, ar done away
Thy body shall, no longer stay

A glorious body, he'l give to thee
From sin, itt shall be wholy free   30

A crown of glory, he will give
For ever, with him thou shalt live

With blessed saincts, thou then shalt sing
The praise, & honour, of thy king

Eternity, is not enough   35
To praise him, to, his macthlese worth

But stay, my soull what dost thou meane
Thy praises, they, ar thin, & leane

My conscience, gives to me, the lye
Whilst I would fain, to heaven fly   40

I cannot say this, with my hart
But fear, I act, anothers part

Till thou doe full asurance, give
And from my fears, & doupts, repreive

Then I will in, thy praises, soare   45
And still admire, thee more, & more

16   thankgiving or an acknowledgment of mercy

When I on faith, my thoughts pitch'd last
Thou gav'st thy self to me
Oh that I may always, hold fast
Thy grace extended free

To me thou threw'st, a bond of love   5   p. 18
Sealling, it in my breast
Which made me sweetly, for to move
Towards, eternall rest

Thou put'st a joyfull song of praise
Into my sinfull lips   10
Oh that it may, my hart soe raise
I ne're, forgett these sips

My soull, return unto thy rest
God hath done well for thee
Hee has, 'g'in Christ which is the best   15
Thing, he could give to thee

When I was overwhelm'd with greif
And ready, quit to sink
He speedily, sent me releife
Saving me, from pitts brink   20

Oh whence is this, that thou shouldst look
On me poor sinfull dust
Who hadst not thou, compasion took
Perish'd, for ever must

I cannot now, with patience stay   25
Why what, my soull, dost ayl
Love is impatient of delay
Till't get within the vaill

I thurst, I thurst, I am of fire
And yet my spirits sink   30
I cannot live, upon desire
I must get up, & drink

Drink my fill, att fountain head
Were I shall thurst, no more
Being drench'd in love, I shall be led   35
To Learn, how to adore

Oh lift me up, in holy praise
And thankfullnese, that I
The short remainder of my days
Thy name, may glorifie   40

17   The soull clouded after a clear sight of Christ.   p. 19

Thou hast my hart, my god, my Lord
What is it, thou wouldst have
My comforts ar like Jonays gourd
Tell me the cause I crave

What Lothsome smoke, has turn'd thee out   5
Of thine own dwelling place
In mercy Lord, now turn about
Least I faint in my race

Ther is somthing, has g'ven ofence
And made thee goe away   10
To ev'ry sin I am propense
In me, thou canst not stay

I wander whilst I musing lye
Att thy great condesension
That ever thou, shouldst cast an eye   15
Towards, so black a dungeon

When as the sun, forsakes the earth
The flowers fade, & dye
So on my soull, there is a dearth
When thou remanst on high   20

Yet somthing Lord thou leavst behind
As pledg of thy return
An akeing hart, & troubled mind
Whilst after thee, I mourn

Thou hidst thy face from me, yet on   25
On thee, I will rely
Oh God, of my salvation
Thou'lt surely hear my cry

18   God demand, & the souls reply

My son give me thy hart, thou sayst
My hart Lord, I will give
An obligation, sweet thou layst
I'le make thy hart to live

My god, my Lord, thou madst my hart   5   p. 20
Tis therfore then by right
With flaming love, fill ev'ry part
Let it in thee, delight

For it thou hast, ernestly sought
Its given thee by vow   10
Thou hast it by dear purchace bought
tis mine, no longer now

It was to thee, a deer bought piece
A told down price, of bloud
That was the precious golden fleece   15
Here love, ran like a floud

Its thine Lord, also on my part
By reall designation
Let it apear, to be thy hart
By true, sanctification   20

That which belongs, to princes great
Doth bear some mark of honour
My hart oh Lord, itt is thy seat
Oh stamp thy image there

now let it by thy spirits dints   25
Be charecteris'd for thine
And let it not, bear satens prints
Henceforth, att any time

Thou'lt have the whole, of ev'ry hart
Or else thou wilt have none   30
Let nothing else, then seace on part
To thee itt doth belong

Pull down, what's old, & make it new   p. 21
oh Build itt up, apace
That thou maist love, thy work to veiw   35
Then Satens name out raze

And writ thine own name Lord, on itt
Acording to thy word,
Oh lett itt still, be made more meet
To be fil'd with the Lord   40

My hart is cold, enflam't with love
To love thee is an honour
Thy smiles, will make, itt to thee move
Let thy love, be its baner

My hart is alsoe, proud, and high   45
And that thou wilt not brook
Let it a sight of thee espy
And that will make it stoop

My hart by nature, is a stone
Let it in thy bloud melt   50
Thers nothing else, but that alone
Can make sin, truly felt

My hart is black, Lord make it white
Thy bloud has that efect
My hart is dark, be thou itts light   55
Thy glory, their erect

Then be thou to it, all in all
And all, in eve'ry part
A sacrifice, now ofer'd whole
Let be, to thee, my hart   60

19   Rich suplys of grace, in Christ

In Christ ther is, a full supply
For ev'ry one, both great, & small
That can by livly faith aply
They'l.find him, to be all, in all

Dost thou feell sin, to smart, & prick   5   p. 22
Then come to him, & thou'lt find ease
Set faith on work, his wounds to lick
And thou wilt find, thy pain to cease

If thou shalt say, sin is to strong
I cannot get it subdued   10
To Christ, as king, doth this belong
To lay thy sin, att thy feet dead

Dost thou desire, to grow in grace
Aply his bloud, to graces root
Then thou wilt surely, mount apace   15
From hence, thou mayst still fecth recruit

Dost thou desire, still more to know
that thou mayst learn, & do his will
Goe thou to his abundant store.
true saving knowledg he'l instill.   20

If thou wouldst have, thy praers ascend
And come up to the mercy seat
Then look to Christ att gods right hand
Thy great high preist, hee'l intercede

Bee sure to put, thy prayers into   25
Thy only mediators hand
And they shall find, aceptance through
His merits, when by them perfum'd

Dos, th greatnese, of thy sins affright
Know Christ, was god, as well as man   30
His godhead t'was that satisfi'd
When united, to the humane,

Wouldst thou have gospell sence of sin,
Look up to Christ, dying for thee
A sight, & sence, of this will bring   35
Repentance to run, kinnd, and free

Wouldst thou have thy afections pack'd   p. 23
And upon heaven, to be set
Tis Christ who by devine atract
must thither thy affections get   40

Dost thou desire, to learn this art
To part with all, & self deny
And willingly, to Loose thy part
Of this worlds vain felicity

Then look to Christ, that rare example   45
Who knew best this earths meane extract
Upon this world, how did he trample
Hee'l teach thee, to tread in his track

Wouldst thou have mercys unto thee
From speciall grace, & love, to grow   50
To Christ beholding thou must be
Cov'nant streams, from him do flow

Wouldst thou from fears, & doupts, be free
And have thy comforts firm, and sure
Anchor'd on Christ, then thou must bee   55
That rock, that doth, and shall endure.

If yet thy pardon be not seal'd
Goe plead the promise of the spirit
Hee, & he only, can reveal't
This's a friut of blessed meritt   60

Dost feell thy self, dead, dull, & low
Christ's the root of spirituall life
Union with him, makes grace to grow
Life in abundance, thou'lt derive

Art thou anoy'd by fresh onset   65
From saten strong, malious rage
Tis Christ, that succours the tempted
His pow'r for thee, he will engage

Doth thoughts of death, thy soull amaze.   p. 24
Christ came to free from fears such as   70
In bondage, ar still all their days
He on this enemy trambled has,

His bloud's the true Catholicon
A universall remidy
Great things, shall still for them, be done   75
That can by faith, unto it fly

Wilt thou now say, whats this to me
I still am poor, and cant atain't
Grace is communicated free
Christ did receive itt, for that end   80

Now if thou wilt, lye down, and dye
When for thy cure, here, is such store
The fault must att thine own door lye,
Christ shall be glorious evermore.

20   The weary pilgrim

This worlds, a prison unto me
A dungeon dark, & black
Lord, I would in, thy presence be
This is the thing, I lack

Like to a banisht prince am I   5
Far from his fathers court
In uncouth places, he dos ly
Forc'd with them to resort

Whilst up, & down, hee's forc'd to range
He meets with usage, bad   10
This cant but be to him so strange
As makes him very sad

He knows, that he is born unto
A kingdome, and a crown
He cannot stoop to actions low   15
To darken his renown

I am a pilgrim, that's my case   p. 25
Whilst in the world I stay
Having no ceirtain, dwelling plase
But in a tent of clay   20

Whilst I am in the world, I grone
I take no true content
I'le never take it for my home
But look upon't as lent

I am a stranger, in this world   25
The world, seems strang to me
Lord, hast to take a stranger home
Who is well known, to thee

This world to me's a borow'd Inne
I Lodg here, for a night   30
And in the morning, I am gone
Fain. I would take my flight

Tis night with me, whilst I am here
I long, for break of day
That when the light, 'gins to appear   35
I may be gone away

No pris'nor bound hands, and feet
With Iron fetters strong
Longs more, with liberty to meet
Then I doe, to be gone   40

I am somtimes amais'd, & tir'd
With this worlds noyse, and bustle
Its guilded glory's not desir d
I care not for its rustle

Dear Lord, what is this world to me   45
(I think) I love it not
For if I could, but be with thee
I would foregoe my lott

Then dearest Jesus, come away   p. 26
Oh make no stay, but come   50
Love is impatient of delay
Oh come, and fecth me home

And though thou seest me unfitt
As yet, to veiw, thy face
I humbly beg, thou'lt make me meet   55
By speedy, growth in grace

What meane I thus to talk of fittnese
I know of no such thing
Tis Christs imputed righteousnese
That I must wrap me in   60

21   A dark glance att the priveledges of a glorified state.

At thy right hand, there's lasting joy
And pleasures evermore
No cecreet sin, shall us anoy
when we shall thither soare

No sorrow there, shall bear a part   5
Nor any vexing care
Nothing ther is, to eat the hart
Of our true plesure there

The sins of wicked men shall not
Att all our souls, anoy   10
The sinfull failings of gods lot
Shall not disturb, our joy

No plots of saten, shall be lay'd
To catch our souls withall
We shall not be of him, afraid   15
When thither, get we shall

Noe wicked sinfull hart shall there
Bee to our souls a greif.
Noe self distracting sinfull care
Shall in, us, longer live   20

No open foe, or flatering freind   p. 27
Shall be within That gate
Ther malice then, & there shall end
With all their cruell hate

Wee shall be far, out of the reach   25
Of ev'ry enemy
No devill there, shall us impeach
He cannot thither fly

In the celestiall orb of glory
Thy soull shall sweetly move   30
Ther shall be known, no other story
But Christs transcendant love

When thou shalt lie att fountain head
Where watters, ar unmixt
To the god of glory, thou'lt be led   35
No sin shall come betwixt

All sighs, & sorrows, there shall cease
Christ wiping off all tears
Ther is nothing, but joy, and peace
Whilst ther's no room for fears   40

Thy pleasures there, run paralell
To an eternity
Striving each other to excell
With sweet variety

(But stay my soull, what dost thou ayle   45
Thou canst not hea'en reach
Thou dost but o're it draw a veill
Till sight, & tasting teach)

Wee shall not then, need meat, & drink
That which we toyle for here   50
Be'ng filled up unto the brink
With nobler, better, Chear

Our food shall be, to love, & praise
Our Jesus lifted high
Our tuned harts, his praise shall raise   55
Whilst on loves wings we fly

Wee not shall there, again need sleep   p. 28
Christ bosome, is our rest
We shall no longer sow, but reap
Of that which is the best   60

Thy garments shall, be always white
No spot shall them polute
Christs righteousnese, both pure, and bright
Shall be thy constant suit

Thou shalt be plunged head, & ears   65
In that bottomlese sea
Of Christs love (not of thine own tears)
Love there bears all the sway

We shall not ther sin, but sing
The praises of our god   70
The praises of our Crowned king
With an harmonious note

There shall bee no devided hart
Among the saints, in glory
But all agree, to act their part   75
In setting forth Christs beauty

Our work shall their, be to admire
And constantly adore
Whilst we shall only, still aspire
To praise him evermore   80

When we shall see him face, to face
Wee shall be transformed
Into the liknese, of his grace
And image of our head

Besids all this thou shalt be free   85
From sin, sicknese, & pain
From greif, & ev'ry malidy
From hatred, & distaine

Thy hapynese, consists in this
Freedome from all that's sin   90
And spotlese, perfect holynese
Thy Joy, shall lye herein

That city hath no need of sun   p. 29
Or moon, to shine in itt
Th glory of god, in itt shall run   95
'The lamb irradiats itt

Alsoe there, is no temple theire
Nor yet no pra'r but praise
The blessed Lamb's the temple where,
Our praises, we shall raise   100

The tree of life that groweth their
Fast by the river side
Twelve sorts of fruit, it still doth bear
Whose friut doth still abide

In the Herusalem above   105
There shall be no more night
Their light. flows, from the god of love
They need no candle light.

The city is transparant gold
On pearl, is eve'ry gate   110
The spirit hath to us foretold,
the glory of the state

Yet here the spirit doth but stoop
To our capacytyes,
The sight of, itt we cannot bear   115
T'would put out our weak eyes,

Tis come, & see, that must reveill
The glory of that place,
When over death, thou shalt prevaill
Then thou shalt see gods face.   120

22   A soull, moving towards its centor:

This world I cannot live upon
Thy self in duty's far beyound
What tounge of angels can say on't

Then blessed Lord, shew me thy self   p. 30
Into thy love, let my soull delve   5
And I'le dispise, this worldly pelf

I cannot love, this painted world
Though it be bravly, deck'd & curl'd
Oh that out of it I were hurl'd

Provided, by thy Lovly hand   10
I were led to emanuells land
Ever before him for to stand

Thou'rt yet on earth, whether dost run
What is itt that thou wouldst have done
I would see, the light of the sun   15

Oh sun, thy beames of glory dart
In duty, still apon my hart
To warm, & quiken, ev'ry part

Thy sweetnese, I doe somtimes tast
But sin, my comforts soon has chas'd   20
Thou wilt not lett them run to wast

It is thy face, Lord, I would see
Extend thy grace, & favour free
Oh call me hence, to live with thee

Thy lovly beauty, I admire   25
This fils, my soull, still with desire
Whilst towards perfection I aspire

Litle small measure's of thy grace
Shall ne're content me, in my race
Oh help me, to grow up apace   30

When stormy winds, my soull doe blow
Let graces root more deeply grow
And att thy feet, lett mee ly low

This world's to me, a meer noyse   p. 31
no true delight, is in her Joys   35
All things below thee, ar but toys

Dear Jesus thou art heavens wonder
Let always, my soull, on thee ponder
Why should time, keep us asunder

Break through the clouds & come away   40
Hasten the blessed marage day
Fecth home thy spouse, without delay

I am thine, by bles'd endenture
Since on thee, I made a venture
Chousing thee, to be my centor   45

Oh pity Lord, a lovsick soull
Doe thou my state, sweetly condole
Whilst fainting, on thee I doe roll

This world I have, & do, disclaim
With all its glory, and its fame   50
Still glor'ing in thy holy name

To thee my god, I can apeall
Since first, thou didst thy self reveill
Have I chouse this world, as my weall

Fain I would bee, safe in thine arms   55
From present sin, and future harmes
And from the worlds, aluring Charms

Hapy am I, who am embark'd
With Christ, though somtimes in the dark
My soull, what needst thou then to cark   60

Though wilt shortly wipe of my tears
Deliv'ring me from all my fears
When that voice shall sound in my ears

Thy sins, & sorrows, have an end
Upon me thou shalt still atend   65
Thy comforts from thee, none shall rend

Lord Jesus, thou hast said I come   p. 32
I hear, and therfore cant be dumb
But must cry out, come fecth me home

Oh lett great grace compensurate   70
My present, distant, absent, state
Untill my time, were out of date

Thou knowst, that I want patience
Because to thee, I cant advance
The thoughts of which doth my soull Launce   75

Whilst I am here, I sigh, I grone
I call, I cry, I make a moane
Like as a widow, left alone

Oh thou that dwelst, in heaven high
Help me to wings, that I may fly   80
To thee, above, the stary sky

Thy holy will, I must abide
Yet I will lye, att watter side
Waiting, for thy blest wind, and tide

To cary me o're to the port   85
Of glory, where thou dost resort
Their I thy praises, shall record

23   The vanity of the world, and instabylyty of creture comforts.

This world is an enchantrese, which
Doth with its suptle Charm
Our poor, & silly soulls, bewicth
And doth us no small harm

Tis vanity, of vanitys   5
vexation, of spirit
An heap of solid misirys
Is all wee, doe inheritt.

If in a freind, we take delight   p. 33
He is soon gone away   10
His businese makes him, take his flight
With us, he cannot stay.

If on relations, wee, begin
To sett too high a rate
Death comes, & cuts the twined string   15
And soon they'r out of date

Their love, and frindship's soon for got
When they ar laid in dust
Only we know, this our lot
That folow them we must   20

If wee enjoy them yet a while
Our comforts ar unfixt
We have with them much greif, & toyle
Our plesure in them's mixt

Somtimes our sweetest deerest friend   25
Dos prove our greatest snare
Whilst love, and anger, our harts rend
Wee know this is not rare

A Child (the staff of parents age)
after our many cares,   30
May soe in ways, of sin engage
As will draw forth our tears

The world it dos devide our hart
Except we keep it under
And slyly steall. away gods part   35
Soe putting, us asunder

Fame, honour, state, traine; bloud, and birth
With all the pomp of kings
Ar fading blosomes of the earth
Poor, empty, sorry, things   40

Honour that makes the man look big
About the world hee'l huff
He can out, on't no plesure dig
Tis but a windy puff

Riches do fly away with wings   45   p. 34
Like to the soaring eagle
Yet How doe these, poor, guilded things
Our silly harts enveagle

Wouldst thou a while, look into pleasure
they ar but vanitis   50
when thou hast had the greatest measure.
they ne're can satisfie.

When with the old, thou'rt tired out
Thou must goe seek for new
And when in them thou'st whirl'd about   55
They'l sting att the reveiw

Thou wer't eternall from thy self
Blessed oh Lord thou art
Away from me, yea worldly pelf
My god has gain'd my hart.   60

24   Experience of the same.

What has this world, been unto thee?
A most unkinnd step dame
This is all it, has been to mee
Then Lord to thee I came

And thou dist sweetly take me up   5
Of me thou hadst a care
Thou fed'st, & also filst, my cup
Thy meat, and drink, is rare

How sweet was this voice once to me
Yea ar not of this world   10
But out of it, I have chousen thee
Therfore it hats, by itt thou'rt hurlt

Bee of good chear, its overcome
Its overcome, for thee
Christ has prepar'd a glorious room   15
With him, thou'lt shortly bee

Hee'th struck thy fingers of from cretures
Oh blessed be his name,!
That thou mayst veiw Christs lovly features   p. 35
To woo thy love, he came   20

Farwell world, I care not for thee
Thou art but durt, to me
Farewell earth, with all thy glory
Lord, call me, home to thee

Thou art the first, & alsoe last.   25
All cretures, they doe faill
Thou art the only, only, best
To thee Lord, I would sayl

On earth, thou never foundst content
In any thing but god   30
When to a creture, love was lent
It surely prov'd thy rod

Of all outward aflictions
This I cannot well bear
Thine own peoples, reflections   35
'Cause they'r to me, soe dear

I know they cannot of me speak
Worse then indeed I am
Why should itt then, my hart thus break
Whi'st I, muse on the same   40

Oh let me not, dishonour thee
Whilst in the world I dwell
If, me hart, doe not deceive me
Tis worse to me, then hell

If that my hart aprov,d may be   45
To thine alseeing eye
Then what though man condemne me
Thou'rt neer to Justifie

How sweet hast thou been unto me
When bitter was my cup   50
pure fountain love, did then run free
When creture streams dry'd up

25   Christ a perfect pattern, & compleat saviour.   p. 36

Without defect, a patern rare
Is Christ, with him none may compare
In him's noe guile
On him's no soyle

Wouldst thou after this coppy write   5
of innocence so pure & white.
turn not aside
from this sweet guide

Christ was lowly, humble, and meek,
His own glory, he did not seek   10
Oh learn of me
Saith he to thee

He was revil'd but revil'd not
But did committ his cause to god
To thee this art   15
He will impart

Wouldst thou learn true self deniell
Christ did himself, to Justise sell
He left his throne
For men forlorn   20

Hee that posesed, heaven wide
Laid his own glory, quite aside
For to impart
To thee his hart

Hee came down here, & dy'd of love   25
To sett poor sinners, up above
In his own throne
Free from all moane

Hee did despise this durty world   p. 37
By it, out of it, he was hurl'd   30
Life he did stake
Down for our sake

Hee went about, still doing good
For our poor soulls, he sought, he wood
He stood not still   35
But shew'd good will

Hee turn'd all that he touch'd to gold
Whilest he did spiritually unfold
Hid misterys
Unto our eyes   40

It was his meat, and drink to doe
His fathers will, which was to woo
Sinners from pelf
Unto himself

The Just sufer'd for the unjust   45
The ofended, sought the offender first
Twas enimies
For whom he dys

Whilst in the dark, his faith was strong
Calling god, father, along 50
When he drank up
The bitter cup

T'was he, that hung upon the tree
From sin, & hell, to sett us free
Apon the Crosse 55
He purg'd our drose

Hee did let out, his precyous bloud
That we might be wash'd in that floud
Here love did flow
On sinners low 60

Hee rose then up, out of the grave
That we firm comfort, still might have
By Justise hee
Was set out free

Hee rode in triumph, up on high 65 p. 38
Whilst that his foes, under feet lye
Att gods right hand
Hee doth still stand

For thee he stands, to intercede
Thy cause, in heavens court, to plead 70
Where hee prevails
And never fails

Oh let me burn, in love to thee
For that which I behold, and see
thy Love will melt, 75
when seen, & felt.

26   Temptation.

Saten has still his sug'red bait
And subtle strategem
Suted to every place, & state
Hes skil'd to play his game

To pictht battell, he comes not out   5
But seeks to circumvent
And cuningly, he wheels about
As if no harm he meant

Hee never, a devise doth want
our silly souls, to cacth   10
He will be sure, us still to haunt
Till we'r out of his reach

But first, and formost, he will tempt
Unto security,
Therby, he doth all fears exempt   15
Whilst he sings lullaby

If this he cannot make, to take
To duty hee'l spur on
That soe a saviour wee may make
Vainly to rest upon   20

If in our selfs, no grace we see   p. 39
Hee then will put us by
That unto Christ, we may not flee
With'ut grace to qualifie

To come to Christ, thou art unfitt   25
It is presumption
Thou hast no grace, thou art not meet
Such, Christ will never own

This we may call, an humble prid
From Saten, it dos flow   30
That we from Christ, may turn aside
Such seed he use to sow

If off from Christ, he canot keep
Thy soull, but their t'will rest
To bring thee, into sorrows deep   35
Hee'l surely, doe his best

Somtimes the praise of men he'l use
To lift thee up on high
And in thy thoughts, he will defuse
That thou art some-body   40

Into the precyous soule, of grace
He'l cast the seed of pride
He knows t'will make god hide his face
'Cause pride, he cant abide

If humbled be, thy soull for sin   45
He'l keep thee, in the dust
Raising such fogs, & mists, within
That dye, thou'lt think thou must

Nay he will yet, goe one step highr
He will not leave thee soe   50
But makes thee to stike, fast in mire
Of unbeleife, and woe

Then with hard thoughts, of god he'l fill   p. 40
Thy soull that thou mayst fly
From him (on whom thou shouldst roll still)   55
As from an enemy.

Somtimes he'l cast in such a thought
Surely their is no god
Because I find, not such things wrought
As scripture, doth report   60

As if we should conclude, & say
There is no Sun to shine
Because I see not now, its ray
Upon this feild of mine

If god on thee, doth lay his rod   65
Then's Sattens busy time
To throw in Jealouse thoughts of god
And of his love design

To tempt somtimes, hee seems to cease
That wee may be cecure   70
That soe he may, with greater ease
Our soulls, to sin, allure

Somtimes he seems, to shrink away
That he may leave us proud
As if we had now got the day   75
And then he'l rage more loud

On while, he stirs up diligence
In our worldly affair
Guilding it o're with this pretence
Of a prudencyall care   80

But if apace in grace thou grow
And long to be in heaven
Thy work he'l tempt away to throw
If thou spy not his leaven

One while he makes us, look on grace   85
As grown to some degree
That soe, we may not mend our pace
But rest contentedly

Anon he'l make thee for to see   p. 41
Thy grace soe weak, thy self soe dull   90
As if their we're, none like to thee
To make thee, unthankfull

Somtimes he'l make thy tounge to walk
That thou mayst surely sin
And to thy soull, by Idle talk   95
Hee will much trouble bring

Another time, thy tounge he'l tye
Soe that thou shalt not know
Which way to speak of the most high
Thy spirits ar soe low   100

Somtims he'l set thee to compare
Thy state, with emenent
Saincts, that seeing their graces rare
Thou mayst despond, and faint

Again he'l place, before thine eyes   105
On that has litle grace
That whilst, thou dost, their grace despise
Thou mayst extoll thy case

If thou has such an enemy
what need hast thou to bee   110
upon thy gaurds continualy
least he break in on thee.

He stirs up all his hellish rout
He knows this is his hour
continually he goes about.   115
And seeks, for to devour.

This enemy, he wants no rage
No malice, nor yett skill
For he hath still in ev'ry age
Drawn souls, unto his will   120

Because he knows, his time is short
His rage doth now encrease
For then he can no longer hurt
With time, his rage shall cease

By neer six thousand yeers practise   125   p. 42
His skill is still encreast
And he is grown exceeding wise
To work his cursed feats

Tis by thy grace, oh Lord, I stand
Doe thou my soull still keep   130
Till on the other side, I land
Wher Saten shall not creep

27   An experience Concerning afliction october 26 71

This day I met, with triels sharp
Which made my soull to bleed
(but god did come, and chear my hart)
Of it their was great need

That sin might be mortified   5
And grace be made alive
That I doe cretures might be dead
And in thy love; might dive

Aflictions give, what thou seest good
So love may mix my cup   10
Thou wilt theirby my sins up root
And shortly take me up

Thou hast made me, this day to see
My foolish Childishnese
In that I would a carver bee   15
Of mine own hapynese

My will was sweetly swalowed
Up in the will of god
Whilst by affliction I was led
To stoop, and kise thy rod   20

It was a triell sweet to me
Which did thy love reveill
By it, thou dist in some degree
Thy favour to me seall,

I could spell nothing out, but love   25   p. 43
In eve'ry peice therof
(And though t'was smart) to god above
It made me sweetly move

I now, doe once again, resovle
That thou shalt chouse for me   30
All my concerns, I doe revovle
On thee, & thy love free

I doe to thee, my self resign
With all that e're I have
Oh cary on thy love design   35
That is the thing, I crave

Oh false, vain world, oh world unkind
I care not for thy love
I'le now with scorn, cast thee behind
My back, & live above   40

Great things, I never did seek after
For, thy sake, I threw them by
Much of thy grace, thy love, & favour
Can only satisfie

If thou wilt but to me give food   45
And raiment to put on
I will acknowledg thee, as good
Whilst in my race, I run

But if thou shouldst deny me this
Ile make up all in thee   50
In thy love, lyes my reall blisc
Thou'rt all, in all, to me

What though my triels, may be smart
They shall be very short
Thou hast love, for me, in thine hart   55
This I beleive, oh Lord

Tis but a litle, litle while   p. 44
And he that shall come, will
Before thou hast, gone many a mile
Hee'l follow att thy heel   60

Eternity, will make amends
For all my sorrows here
Christs bosome, shall, be my defence
securing me from fear

28   Of praer

By prayer, we doe hold
Converse with god, and soe
By frequent use, we grow more bold
And to him, freely goe.

Pray'r is an arrow shot   5
To heaven in a trice
Its foes, hinder itt, they can not
Unto the throne itt flys

Pray'r is a key were by
Wee doe unlock the door   10
Of sacred, holy, tresury
And great, abundant, store

Let mee alone saith god
To Moses, when he prays
Why, who dos hold, that thou canst not   15
Against him, make esays

Tis sweet, to make our moane
To man, much more to god
pray'r finds acese, unto the throne
Wher's help, when man cannot   20

Is it soe good to have,   p. 45
The ear, of some great king
Gods ears atend, to what thou'lt crave
And he will send it in

Through Christs interces'on   25
Great things, ar by itt wrought
Tis by the spirit, still alone
That we, to pray, ar taught

By faith, & pray'r, we thrive
And doe from heav'n draw down   30
That which will make us, soon arive
Unto our glorious Crown

By pray'r it is wee come
To live in heaven here
And frequently, wee visit home   35
A purchase bought full deer

Whilst att gods feet we ly
By pray'r we gain apace
An holy familiarity
To plead, with him for grace   40

Give me, this holy art
By faith, to strive with thee
That I may wind into thine hart
And always thriving bee

29   of death.

Though this be true death is acurst
And still a dreadfull thing
To one, that is not yet in Christ
It doth much horour bring

Yet thou'lt not be att death agast   5   p. 46
Not scar'd at itts pale face
If springled with the bloud of Christ
It will seem full of grace

Death, is the Gate of hapy nese
To let thee, into glory   10
From pain, it gives a writ of ease
And from, the worlds, vain hurry

Whilst on the banks of time, I bide
Comes death the ferry boat
To cary me o're to the other side   15
Where Christ, has paid the shot

Death to my body is a sleep
When in the grave I'me lain
And thou it may be long, & deep
I shall awake again   20

Death is a hapy mesenger
Sent from my fathers court
To fecth, to'th presence Chamber
Where angells, doe resort

Christ rode in triumph over death   25
Att his ascension
Though for a while, tis left on earth
Yet his, shall tread it down

The grave is now become thy bed
Of queit ease, & rest   30
Christ has perfum'd it with his head
Three days it was his nest

And ever since, it smels as sweet
As it of spice t'were made
Thou needst not fear, to put thy feet   35
Into this fragrent bed

Tis their, the weary att ar rest
Nothing doth them disturb
The wicked their, cease to molest
Or by their pow'r curb   40

Oh death, I must, and will stile thee   p. 47
Next to Christ, my best freind
Him thou shalt let, me in to see
puting to sin an end

Death now can neither bite, nor sting   45
Thou mayst look round about
The sting of death, is only sin
And that Christ has took out

Death, is a raging enemy
But to thee, tis the last   50
itts pous'nous malignity
throu Christ is gone, & past

Thou mayst now look death in the face
And bid him, do his worst
Hee can now, only thorow grace   55
Thy bonds, asunder burst

Come then, my soull, sit down, & sing
Upon the grave, thy bed
Oh death, where is thy cursed sting
I shall arise when dead   60

30   The excelency, & sweetnese of the life of faith.

Oh noble life, oh life cecure
What shall I of thee say
t'will make thee, chearfully endure
All hardships, in thy way

Faith is the evedence of things   5
Not seen with mortall eye
Faith, to the soull, the substance brings
Of things exceeding high

Faith will (may I with reverance say)
Soe loud in gods ears ring   10
That he cannot to it say nay
it will the blessing bring

If thou canst, but truly beleive   p. 48
It is but ask, & have
And god will surely, to thee give   15
Whatever thou dost crave

Faith, is a bold advent'rous grace
T'will not let god alone
But tels him to his very face
T'will have, the best or none   20

Faith cannot live on this worlds trash
It feeds on Christ alone
T'will not be daunted or abash
But gets up, to the throne

Faith is a grace, that doth opose   25
And sett Christ opposite
To all itts cruell, hatefull foes
Trampling, upon their spight

Faith is a busie, active, grace
It bears a great command   30
In all, & ev'ry single case.
It will still have a hand

Faith rides in triumph over sin
Saten, the world, & death
Whilst these doe rage, twill sit, & sing   35
As if t'were now grown deaf

This durty world, faith laughs, to scorn
Trampling itt under foot
It is to high, & nobly born
To rake in dung, & durt   40

Faith is a strong, couragious, grace
It will not be out'-dar'd
But can look dangers, in the face
And not be greatly scar'd

Faith is a grace, that's quik of sight   45
And ready to lay hold
It can spy out, a glance of light
And grow theirby more bold   p. 49

Faith can work by great contrarys
It picks life, out of death   50
Joy, out of great extremitys
Sap, out of barren heath

It can from that grave evill sin
Draw out sweet arguments
To plead with god, & to pay in   55
His own free graces rents

Faith, wisely makes its nest on high
Upon the rock of ages
And there, it doth securly Ly
Whilst sin, and saten, rages   60

Faith, is a grace, that take no rest
But ransacks hiden tresures
And picks, & chouses, of the best
Full runing over measures

Faith follows god, close in the dark   65
And lyes down att his feet
If god doth speak, then faith will hark
On what he saith, t'will feed

Faith digs into the golden mine
Of the rich promises   70
And then crys out, all this is thine
Holding fast, what it has

Faith from the precyous promises
Doth feacth both strength, & art
To break through satens falascs   75
And beat back ev'ry dart

This life of faith, doth free the soull
From all distracting care
All its concerns, on god, t'will roll
It feeds on hiden fare   80

Faith knows it shall, have what is best   p. 50
The promise cannot faile
In this, itt finds most queit rest
When trouble doth asayle

When their is no herd, in the stall   85
Nor flock within the fold
Faith can make god, itts all, in all
And its only, strong hold

Faith knows how to rejoyce, & sing
When creatures, ar all gone   90
And to joy in, its crowned king
Liveing on him alone

Faith is thy gift, as well as Christ
Lord to me, give itt down
And then I shall, with sayls up hoyst   95
Hast, to the glorious crown

31   Beauty of holynese

Holynes is thine image bright
Who art, the god, of love, & light
Lord give it unto me
Thou art glorious, in holynese
Thy nature is pure, and spotlese   5
Oh make me like to thee

My dear redeemer, was harmlese
His constant badg, was holynese
Whilst that he lived here
He was spotlese, & undefild   10
With sin, he never was once soy'ld
To him it came, not neer

The angels blise, here in dos lye
That they ar full, of sanctyty
And always see gods face   15
It has a sweet, pleasing aspect   p. 51
Greatly adorning the elect
Whilst they doe run their race

Holynese doth atract the eye
Of thosse that ar, but standers by   20
Gods ways they'l reverance
The more holy, the more comfort
Whilst in the world, thou dost consort
The wicked t'will silence

Holynese is, the only way   25
To plesures that doe ne're decay
To all eternity
The holy, they shall see gods face
When they, have run their weary race
In Christs arms, they shall, lye   30

In holynese, oh ripen me
That I apace, to thee, may flee
Let no sin, me anoy
Purg out my drose, by holy fire
That I may dayly, mount up higher   35
Till I thy self enjoy

32   The soull in an extasy of admiration, at the beauty of Christ,
and the sweetnese, of communion with him,

Oh come and see, oh come, and see,
The beauty of the Lord
And you will find itt for to bee
Far, beyound all report

Behold him in the beauty of   5
His person, cov'nant, grace
And this will make thee burn in love
And long to see his face

Oh come, & tast, oh come, and tast   p. 52
How good and sweet he is   10
And thou wilt find, a blessed feast
Neer kin, to heavens blise

Oh come, and hear, oh come, & hear
And then your soull shall live
To this deer Jesus, draw thou neer   15
He will, thy sins forgive

Oh come and smell, oh come and smell
The sweet perfumes of love
And thou wilt wish to wade through hell
To bee with god above   20

Oh come and walk, oh come and walk
In this delightfull feild
Thou wilt find it no Idle talk
The pleasure that t'will yeeld

His wayes, ar waies of plesentnese   25
And all his paithes, ar peace
Come try, & then thou wilt confese
Here grows, the true harts ease

If some by drops, be so sweet here
What is the fountain head   30
What is that sweet, & better Chear
I shall have when hence fled

Oh what a blessed life is this
In the borders to dwell
Of Canaans land, the land of blise   35
And drink fresh, from the well

Communion with god for one day
Is better then rich treasures
To love, to serve, & to obey
Doth yeeld the sweetest pleasures   40

I challeng men, devils, and hell   p. 53
With the infernall rout
To tell me where, such pleasures dwell
And let them, search, them out

Oh who will help me for to praise   45
This Jesus lifted high
Oh that I could his praises raise
Above the earth, and sky

I cant but wondring, stand, and maize
At that which I now see   50
Oh men, & angels, stand and gaze
At Christs love, which runs free

If one small bunch, of Canaans Graps
Bee soe sweet to thy tast
What will it bee to presse full heaps   55
At the Lambs, mariage feast

Oh that thou wouldst enlarg, and fill
My soull still more, and more
Till I shall climb up Zion hill
To praise, & to adore,   60

Oh that thou woudst throw down apace
This earthly house, for mee
For till thou doe it quite down raze
I cant, come live with thee

33   Reflection.

My soull, my soull, what didst thou get
By wandring from thy god
By running, from thy dearest head
Dost long, to feell the rod

Come tell me now dost like the smart   5   p. 54
Is his displeasure sweet,
Wilt thou on cretures set thine hart
Hee'l spurn thee with his feet

Has god a baren wildernese
Been unto thee my soull?   10
Or yet a land of darknese
That thou from him, didst prole

Oh what! a sottish fooll am I!
To leave the fountain head
And chouse out cirterns, crakt, & dry   15
Which cannot help att, need

Oh when shall I, learn to be wise
By what I still doe feell
And henceforth, take better advise
Then to this world, to kneell   20

Whatever is to me most deer
If't steall my hart from thee
Though to me itt, lye ne're soe neer
Lord tear't away from mee,

My god is Jealouse of my love   25
Hee'l not have cretures share
Oh let me not, from thee once move
Henceforth, for any fare.

If I begin att any time
To stray away from thee   30
Oh pull me back, by that sweet line
Wherwith I'me ty'd to three

Lord bring me home, though in a storm
Suffer me not to stray,
Out of thy pastures wide, and warm   35
Least I, become a prey.

34   the soull under a sence of suspending the answer of prayer. p. 55

How long, oh Lord holy, and true
Shall I to thee, for mercy sue
Shall sin ly, as twere dead
And then get greater head
Ar not my foes, under foot trod   5
By him, that has in triumph rode

Thou seemst to cast my pray'rs behind
Thy back, as if thou hadst no mind
To have any regard
To one, that would be heard   10
My humble suit is yet deni'd
For the which on, thee I rely'd

I cannot, will not, hold my peace
Whilst lasts, this weary short lifes lease
I cannot be said nay   15
oh give, without delay
The thing which I ernestly crave
It is that Lord, which I must have,

With reverance. oh let speak
Thy promises, thou will not break,   20
Thou art god, & not man
Christs bloud has freely ran
And deerly bought the thing I seek
A spirit, truly, humbly, meek

Thou hast all power in thine hands   25
To intercede for me. Christ stands
At thy right hand alway
Thou'lt not to him say nay
Thy spirit now can mortifie
My sin, and make it dead to lye   30

I cannot, will not, let thee goe   p. 56
Untill thou throughly, slay this foe
Oh lett thy spirits dart
Strick it unto the hart
What though thou makest me, to bleed   35
Thou wilt therby, my graces feed

On this I doe resovle through grace
Whilst I have breath, I'le seek thy face
I'le not let thee alone
Till for me, this be done   40
My present stat, I will bewayll
Till through thy grace, I shall prevaill,

Although thou canst not look on me
Remember still, thy promise free
On which I will lay hold   45
And grow theirby, more bold
Oh let me never be asham d
Of that hope, in me, thou hast fram d

Former experience shall bee
A sweet encouragment to mee   50
To wait, & not to tire
Till thou grant my desire
This earnest Lord, let me improve
Untill thou doe, my soull remove

35   of Idlenese

If thou wilt not cutt thy self work
Be sure, the devill will,
About the Idle, he dos lurk
As fitt greist, for his mill

Idlenese is the ready way   5
To fall into all sin
The devill he can soon betray
Our souls, when found therin.

Davids first sin, was idlenese   p. 57
When slothfull on his bed   10
And then he acts, as mercylese
being by saten led

Thy work is great, thy time is short
god will not for thee stay
Bee active then, I thee exhort   15
('my soull') without delay.

The Idle soull, will never thrive
and grow apace, in grace
to thee Oh let me, be alive
and active, in my place   20

The slothfull man, may gape to have
but those desires doe kill
Be diligent, and always crave
if thou wouldst have thy fill

Redeem thy time, be circumspect   25
it is an evill day
Seek thou gods glory to erect,
whilst thou art in thy way,

Ther is no working in the grave
when thou shalt their ly down   30
Bee active, then if thou wilt have
a weighty, heavie, crown.

Oh let thy love, my soull soe fill
that I may active bee
Delighting still, to doe thy will   35
as strongly led by thee.

36   None but Christ

thers none but Christ, thers none but Christ
can fill my empty soull
Oh that I could, with speed, and hast
run to this blessed goal,

I count all things, but lose, & dung   5   p. 58
for thee my saviour deer
Who for me, on the crose, was hung
there did thy love apear.

Ten thousand-worlds cant satisfie,
my soull that's on thee bent   10
Except with love, thou cast an eye
I cannot be content.

Thou art the sweet, shade of a rock,
in this hard, weary, land.
Tis thou must save me from the strock   15
of devine Justise's hand,

Tis thou oh Christ, must be my skreen
(whose love runs full, and free.)
Tis thou alone, must stand between
thy fathers, wrath & me,   20

Let all created glorys blush
before this spleanded sun
Let earthly potentats be hush
Hee'l shine, when you ar gone

Christ is the fairest sweetest rose   25
That grows in paradise
His sweetnese I will still apose
to earthly fragrancys

Thou art my rock, and my strong hold
my refuge, nigh att hand   30
Thy arms, my soull, shall still enfold
thy love, shall comprehand

My soull reaches out after thee
and cannot, be content
Untill with thee, it come to be   35
it swells, & finds noe vent.

It is a sweeter communion   p. 59
and neerer intercourse
Between my soull, & Christ alone
that I would fain, enforce   40

I could (I think) now part with all
Leaving what I have here
To follow thee home, att thy call
thou art to me, most dear

None but thy self. none but thy self   45
Shall give content to me
I'le not be put off, with earths pelf
I must have more from thee.

Then from thy great abundant store
and overflowing grace   50
Let me be fil'd still more, & more
till I shall see thy face

Thine absence is a hell to me
whilst I doe soujourn here
Thy presence, grace, and favour free   55
Brings heavens joy, & chear

This is my motto, none but Christ
whether I live, or dye
Hoping I shall with sayls up hoyst
hast in thine armes to lye   60

Shouldst thou say, here:s heaven for thee
that fair, & spacyous land
Take it to thee, in steed of me
I'de turn it on thine hand

I find desires boundlese to grow   65
Wilt thou not satisfie
Thou knowest I cant sit down below
enjoyment queitly

I cannot live upon desire   p. 60
and breathings after more   70
Whilst att perfection I aspirc
To thee fain would I soare

Thy love I cannot comprehand
let it comprehand me
And let mee come, to understand   75
the depthes that in it bee

37   home, Home

Thou art the only, only, best
Whilst I'me from thee I take no rest

I feell a strangers aking heart
Whilst Christ, and my soull live apart

What ever company, I'me in   5
My joys, they ar but poor, and thin

What ever Lord, I am about
I long for to be called out

Of this dark cell, of misery
Into a blest eternity   10

Where no sin, shall my soull once reach
Her joys, and comforts to impeach

In thy love, itt shall lye, and bleat
Feelling itts warm eternall heat

Oh god thou art my all, in all   15
I will stand att the door, & call.

Crying to thee, oh come away
Hasten my much desired, day

My weary state, doe thou condole
And break the fetters from my soull   20

Dost time, and days, out of the way   p. 61
That I may not long, from thee stay

My soull longs, to be on the wing
To its beloved, it would spring

Whilst I am here, I sink in mire   25
Ready, almost somtimes to tire

Thou lifts me up, & casts me down
Between thy favour, & thy frown

I am still tossed to, and fro
Somtimes hope, somtimes my foe   30

Doth get of me, the uper hand
Soe that my faith, can hardly stand

I never shall, be free from moane
Till I climb up, unto thy throne

This world's a willdernese, att best   35
How can I here, take up my rest

When shall thy weary, absent, bride
With her dear bridgroom still reside

38   Love,

If thou, thy goods givst to the poor
and wantst this grace of love
Thou'lt never get within the door
where dwells, the god above

True love is boundlese in desires   5
untill it terminate
Upon the object, itt admires
breaking through ev'ry lett

True love is conjugall, and chast   p. 62
Its lasting, firm, & sure   10
Unto its object, it doth hast
none from itt, can alure

It takes no rest, but seekes about
and will not be content
Untill itt find the object out   15
upon which it is bent

True love is never weary of
the object whom itt loves
And when it seems to stand aloof
after itt the hart moves   20

It studys always how to please
and fears to gives offence
If angry it seeks to apease
with ernest diligence

Love always, thinks well of itts god   25
when he seems, as unkinnd
It will not keep up one hard thought
or bear a Jealouse mind.

True love to Christ, itt doth constraine
to goe through thick, and thin,   30
Through fire, & water, life, and death
Untill wee come to him,

It will admitt no other Lover,
To bear from him a part,
But preses on with strong endevour   35
To get neerer his hart

The soull, that's touch'd, with this loadstone
Still turns, and restlese is,
Untill it come, to fix upon,
the centor, of its blise.   40

Love runs unto its sweetest freind   p. 63
in all its needs, and straigts
Gods glory, is its only end
for this, it seeks, and waits

It takes delight to speak, or think   45
Of that it most, doth love
Love doth fastly, and strongly link
unto the god above,

It seeks no higher, joy, or crown
then to enjoy its god   50
And in his arms, for to lye down
taking him, for its lot

True love can willingly, lay down
its glory, & its fame
In durt, soe it may bring renown   55
unto his holy name

T'will chearfully it self abase
to lift Christ, up on high
T'would have his glory fly apace
above the earth, and sky   60

Love is a sweet, and holy fire,
mounting upwards apace
Scorching the soull, with strong desire
to see, his blessed face

Oh hasten Lord that blessed day   65
for here, I find no rest
Come fecth my Longing soull away
to be with thee its best

Oh make me one, pure mase of love,
flaming up towards thee,   70
Untill I come, to dwell above
where love, shall perfect bee

39   Perseverance   p. 64

The crown is set, upon the head
of perseviring grace
Such, and such, only, shall be led
to see, his blessed face

Except thou hold out, to the end   5
thy labour will be lost
But if on god, thou still attend
the gain, will quit thy cost

Tis this will bring thee, true renown
when thou hast run thy race   10
Then thou shalt surely, be set down
in gods, prepared place

This blessed grace, it will not tire
with hardships in its way
Although it goe through, durt & mire   15
t'will hold out, all the day

Those that on god, to wait, and cling
ther strength, renew, they shall
Mounting up, as on eagles wing
from him, they shall not fall   20

Such they shall run, & not be weary
they shall walk, and not faint
In their march, to eternity
where saincts, and angells, haunt

Tis by thy mighty power alone   25
through faith, that I am keept
To glory, and salvation
and comforts, fully heap't

Hold out my soull unto the end
with renew'd patience   30
Looking to Jesus, thy best freind
with steady confidence

Behold he saith, I come quickly
hold that fast, which thou hast
That no man take thy victory   35   p. 65
and Crown away at last

40   desires

The neerer I, aproach to thee
The swifter let my motion bee

As I draw neer, unto my end
Lett grace more mightily descend

As I draw neer eternity   5
A clearer light, lett, me espy

When I come, within glorys veiw
Oh let thy grace, my strength renew

When on a death bed I shall ly
Give strength, and suport, from on high   10

Let beames of glory, on me dart
For to refresh, and chear my hart

Throw in devine manefestations
Of love, and glory, and salvation

Let me by faith, behold, and see   15
The arms of love strectht out to me

That I with joy may welcome death
Smelling its Christ perfumed breath

Oh let me render, death lovely
Unto the eyes, of standers by   20

That whilst, I, in thy praises soare
Others may sweetly thee adore

Let me such sweetnese leave behind
That they, thy love, may bear in mind

And may have cause from what they see   25
To blcsc thee to eternity

Oh let me soe thy praises sing
That I may heavens work begin

Thy lovly face, doe thou unveill   p. 66
That I to thee, with joy, may sayl   30

Let an abundant entrance be
Administred then unto me

That soe my soull, may sweetly spring
To its redeemer, and its king

Whilst angels doe my soull convay   35
With joy, and triumph, in its way

Untill they bring it, safe to thee
Whom it desires, and longs, to see

41   The soull admiring Christ longs to be with him.

Come now my soull, let Loose on Christ
thou needst not fear excese
When thy afections ar att high'st
his love deserves no lese

Oh that, I still could gaze upon   5
His transendant beauty
For like unto him, ther is none
That can soe take, the eye

Hee doth all others far excell
cheif of ten thousand hee   10
Oh take me, up with thee to dwell
that I may veiw, and see

Tis he is altogather sweet
sweetnese in the abstract
All creture, beauty, that shall fleet   15
but his shall still. atract

His mouth's like the best wine, causing
even, the lips of those
That ar asleep, to speak, and sing
he's Sharons, sweetest, Rose   20

A glance from Christ soe takes the hart   p. 67
that fain, it would be gone
It cant endure, to live apart
t'would break through to the throne

Thy love is better, then chouce wine   25
it doth procure our growth
I cant but love, thy name devine
an oyntment, poured forth

What the lovesick soull somtimes feels
makes it cry out again   30
Why tarieth, his Char'ot wheels
why run they not amain

It counts the days, and alsoe hours
with sweet impatience
Longing to win, the holy towers   35
where dwells omnipotence

Thy time is best, though it be long
yet give me leave to moane
I will not say, thy ways ar wrong
thou yet, I get not home   40

Oh give me, leave to long, & wait
and joy to see time run
And speedyly wear, out of date
that I may see the sun

Oh pity Lord a lovesick soull   45
that cannot be content
Untill it have a fuller dole
from god, omnipotent

Oh my beloved, now make hast
be like to the young hart   50
Or Roe, upon the mountains wast
let time, no Longer part

The wintor shall be shortly past
the rain, over and gone
Our Jesus cometh, runing fast   55
he is, my only one

My Lovesick fits thou'lt overlook   p. 68
love makes me, long to dye
Love errours, thou wilt not down book
Thy love will pase them by   60

Thou wilt take pity on a worm
when scorched, with thy fire
And give me leave, to sigh, & mourn
till I have my desire

Which is to be engulph'd in love   65
intwisted in thine armes
Safe lodged with thy self above
free from all sinfull harms

Let Christ, & my poor, longing soull
Be handfasted togather   70
For after him, it still doth prole
it can live on no-other

Meane time let beames of glory dart
upon me, day by day
Th' outflowings of thy love impart   75
Whilst I am in my way

42   Concerning the Lords day

Oh blessed, sacred, queen of days
all others stoop to thee
Whilst thou dost sweetly our harts raise
from servile work, wee'r free

Thou hast the stamp of god imprest   5
to make thee, more sacred
In thee we'r called unto rest
on thee, we'r sweetly fed

Thou art a dark, resemblance
of heavens Joy, and blise   10
Whilst thou bringst, to remembrance
what Christ, has done for his

The work of our redemption
was this day brought to light
Which whilst we ruminate upon
we'r brought to clearer sight

It is a blessed, market day
of great, abundant, store
In which we may, fresh food up lay
untill we need no more

This day, rich tresurys of grace
to us ar open laid
That we may take, and grow apace
till fitt for heaven made

On this day, he, to us gives new
outflowings, of his love,
That whilst of itt we, take a veiw
our harts to him, may move

By plesent stremes (we'r this day led)
runing calmly, and still,
Dutys wherin god has been met
and giv, the soull itts fill

God gives this day, variety
least weary, we should bee
Dutys have a sweet harmony
and each of them, agree

pray'r fits for hearing, that for praise
Whilst att his feet we ly
Duty dos sweetly, our harts raise
up to our god, on high

On this day is a blessed feast
The holy comunion
In which we sweetly see, & tast
what Christ hath for us done

p. 69

15

20

25

30

35

40

Upon this day, our Lord arose   45   p. 70
up from out of his grave
Triumphing o're all his foes
and we the comfort have

This day a plentifull infusion
of'th spirit from on high   50
Was poured out, t'was no delusion
But seen, to many an eye

To us this day's a joyfull pledg
of our eternall rest
And of our blessed priveledg   55
when heaven is possest

For in it we ar call'd aside
with god, to hold converse
And whilst we do by him abide
we have gainfull commerce   60

An ernest that he shortly will
us as from cretures call
To come, and take, our joyfull fill
Of him, who's all in all

Those that do strictly, this day keep   65
shall surely thrive, & grow
And of that well of life drink deep
which from above doth flow

Such on ther soulls, shall feel no dearth
hee'l cause them for to ride   70
On the high places, of the earth
His love, he will not hide

They shall have fresh, incomes of strength
whilst they ar in there way
Till they be swalow'd up at length   75
in an eternall day

Thy holy day improve soe let
me, that I grow apace
Speeding to an immediate p. 71
fruition of thy face 80

43   The soull reaching out after what it most desires.

Fain I would dye
That I might lye

Safe in Christs arms
From sinfull, harms

Fain would I fly 5
To heaven high

There being led
To fountain head

Drench'd in the love
Of god above 10

Set free from sin
Then shall I sing

And still adore
Thee evermore

Take pity Lord 15
Of one in ward

In prison I
While here, doe lye

Break ope the door
That I may soare 20

To thee my god
And pleasent lot

Oh come away
Without delay

My only one,   25
Regard my moane

My weary soull
Doth always prole

After its rest   p. 72
And pleasent nest.   30

Thou hast my hart
Why should time part.

Come take me up
With thee to sup

And have my fill   35
On Zion hill

Of that blest Chear,
I cant have here

But by the by,
Which makes me dry   40

And long for more,
Abundant store.

Come riding post,
Over times coast

To fecth thine own   45
unto thy throne

Where I shall see,
And enjoy thee

Eternally,
Without any   50

Thing to anoy,
My canstant joy

Or steall away,
From me one ray

44   The soull greatly clouded novem 20 71

What meanes, this dismall cloudinese
Which doth possese my soull
Filling me full of heavinese
My God, my state condole

Tis that I know not how to bear   5   p. 73
Except suport thou give
My spirits, they doe wast, & wear
I know not how to live

Nothing oh Lord, will satisfie
but a sight of thy face   10
If that to me, thou dost deny
I sink in greif, apace

I turn, and tose, & find noe rest
Because I mise my god
Thy comforts, ar my only feast   15
thy smiles, my pleasent lot

Heaven will not give me content
thou art to me, most dear
Why then dost thou, thy selfe absent
And wilt not now draw near   20

Oh tell me now, the reason why
thou lookst soe strang att me
Thou seemst away, from me to fly
thy smiles I cannot see

I'me plunged, in anxiety   25
unquiet is my mind
All things to me, ar vanity
Except thy self I find

I will not say, thy ways ar wrong
I know that cannot be   30
Supose thou never smilst upon
me, thy actings ar free

Ile call to mind, my former days
what thou to me, hast been
I will reflect, on former rays   35
and wait, for thee again

Doscover now thy pleasent face   p. 74
Let me thy favour see
And give influences of grace
That I may run to thee   40

Lift up, thy lightsome countenance
On my soull in distrese
The price of it thou dost enhance
whilst I walk, in darknese

45   upon Christs return november 22

How sweet ar thy returning rays
now I can say my god,
What warmth, & life thy love displays
thou art my pleasent lot

Welcome deer Lord to thine own home   5
reception thou shalt find
When ever thou'lt be pleas'd to come
thou art to me most kinnd

Thou tookst pity, on me Lord
when I in sorrow lay   10
Oh let me still thy love record
and praise thee all the day

Dear god it was but yester day
that I in sorow sunk
Because thou turnst thy face away   15
and now thy love I've drunk

Thou camest in to me this night
in sweet enlarg'd desire
And gavest mee a tast, and sight
of that, to which I aspire   20

This world I find vain, & unkinnd
but thou to me art sweet
Oh let me always, keep in mind
thy mercy as tis meet

Oh that thou wouldst, be pleasd to draw   25   p. 75
my soull, still by thy love
I care not for this world, a straw
could I be Lodg'd above

Thou canst give meat, the world knows not
thy food, is dayntys rare   30
May I but feed, upon my god
I'le ne're seek other fare

Whilest others trudg, many a mile
to get a litle trash
From thee, my god, I'le seek a smile   35
earths joys, ar but a flash

Oh whence is this, oh what am I
Poor creeping, crawling, worm
That thou shouldst set me up on high
in thy love, let me burn   40

Not unto me, not unto mee
but to thy holy name
Let all the praise, & glory be
to thee belongs the same

But still from satisfaction I   45
am very far as yet
Thy fullnese, that will satisfie
when I to heaven get

Whilst I am here, oh give in more
fill mee up to the brim   50
Till to thy bosome, I shall soare
and in thy love shall swim

46   High expectations, cals for an high, and sutable conversation

What maner of persons ought wee
In thought, in word, in deed, to be   p. 76
who do expect
A bright, uncoruptable crown
Shinning with glory, and renown   5
with the elect

Wee who doe look with Christ to reign
And be still of his blessed traine
when we goe hence
Should we not henceforth always scorn   10
With durt, for to defile our horn
and live by sence

Wee who expect, to live with god
Our glorious eternall lot
on Zion hill,   15
Should surely scorn whilst, we ar here
To live upon earth's, empty chear
which cannot fill

Each sainct expects to be a king
The praises of his god, to sing   20
with joy, and mirth
Shall we not then, take holy state
Living att a more noble rate
then men of earth

Belong not saincts, to, a higher court   25
Then earthly princes, do resort
which here bear sway
Shall such great spirits, stoop so low
As to submit, unto there foe
or once obey   30

Wee do expect eternity
In Christs imbraces for to lye
in sweet solace
Then for to let this world imbrace
Whilst we gaze on its painted face   35
tis sordednese

We that can call heaven our own.   p. 77
And look to sitt, upon Christs throne
Should with distaine
Look down, upon this lower earth   40
As sorry, baren, fruitlese heath
Which yeelds no gain

Wee look for everlasting rest
And to be filed with the best
att fountain head,   45
And shall we soe, love our clay inne
As here our requiem to sing
and home forget.

We who look for a sinlese state
Like to the angells, who doe wait   50
on god alway
Doth it become us to love sin,
Or subject be to itt, as king.
While we obey.

How holy, strict, and circumspect,   55
If posible, without defect.
ought such to be.
Who have whilst here, a ceirtain pledg
Of their grand future priveledg
when hence they flee.   60

47   Experience.

How sweetly dost thou melt my hart
Sometimes, when I can say
My father, and my god thou art
leading mee, in my way

This comfort, I would not exchange   5
for earthly diadems
here I could sweetly all day range
among these pleasent stems

Biding defience to the world   p. 78
scorning itt as my lot   10
Longing out of itt, to be hurl'd
To be with thee, my god

How gladly, could I take my leave
of earthly vanity
And to the crys, of freinds, be deaf   15
leaving them, chearfully

To goe to him, who has my hart,
And my affections,
Thou hast gain'd them, by holy art,
to thee, my all belongs   20

To be endeed, espous'd to Christ
is true nobilyty
Makeing the soull, with sayls up hoyst
hast, to eternity.

To be an heir adopt: of glory   25
and joynt heir, with thy son,
Makes us to love, thy memory
and after thee, to run

Of sin, and absence, I am weary
to be with thee is best   30
Out of this vain worlds, noyse, and hury
my soull would be att rest

My afections they'r ar gone before
what have I then left here
My best goods, ar laid up in store   35
with thee, my god, most dear

Those that aspire, unto a crown
and for a kingdome, wait
Cannot contentedly, stoop down
unto a servile state   40

How easily, could I then wink.   p. 79
This world, of vanity,
to nothing when my faih. doth linke
my soull to god most high

48   The more holy, the more hapy

The grace of god which to us brings
Sallvation, and all good things,
itt doth us sweetly teach.
For to deny, ungodlynese,
Pressing on still to be sinlese,   5
till itt, we fully reach

The pure in hart, they shall see god
Ther pleasent soull, delighting lott
neer to him, they shall creep
Whilst others ar att distence keep't   10
They shall have comforts fully heapt
and of his love, drink deep,

Such do in heaven, still commerce
And with Jehovah, hold converse
that clossly walk with him.   15
His love from them, he will not hide
What they request, sha'nt be deni'd
ther light, shall not shine dim,

Such they doe get many a dole
For to refresh, and chear ther soull   20
in this ther weary race
Whilst they doe neer, to Christs hart ly
They gain much grace, and strength wherby
they come to grow apace

God gives unto such the new name   25
Making them clearly, read the same
tis they have the white stone
The stone, of absolution
Which only they, can feast upon
and only they, alone   30

Such have ther fathers seall imprest   p. 80
And deeply stampt, upon theire breast
his image they do bear
Which god delighteth for to veiw
And more, & more, still to renew   35
till fixt in heavens sphere

They have whilst here, a free acese
Into his presence, for to prese
and wind into his hart
They know the cecreets of his love   40
Which makes them strongly, to him move
himself, he will impart

They that in holynese, excell
Doe of their deer redeemer smell
he doth them always ken   45
And he'l encrease ther stock still more
Into his bosome, they shall soare
Soonner, then other men

Such they, have many a sweet love feast
With Christ wherby there joy's encreast   50
Whilst he doth them imbrace
Of high enjoyments such pertake
And he will never them forsake
in one step of ther race

Such get into Christs house of wine   55
Sitting under his rays devine
which makes ther harts to burn
They dwell always, under his wing
And ar fil'd from the blessed spring
which still, to them, doth run   60

Some few whilst here, have had such high
Manefestations of glory,
that this, has been their song
Lord hold thine hand, or else I break
The vessell whilst here, is to weak   65
to bear, this liquor strong

What an encouragment is this   p. 81
To live this life that leads to blise
and the quik enjoyment
Of our redeemer, and our head   70
Our Jesus, and our advocate
on whom our harts ar bent

49   The soull greatly clouded

What shall I say, what shall I doe
when thou dost hide thy face
It is an embleme, of hels woe.
where is no room, for grace

Thou dost therby, old sins to me,   5
bring fresh unto my mind,
And whilst from thee, no smile I see
what comfort can I find

I am brought to begin anew
what long agoe was done   10
Being forst as t'were to bid adeiw
to what e're was begun

Apon a tendred Christ again
I do afresh lay hold
Hoping his love, will not distaine   15
me, in his arms to fold

I must condemne, my self, & will
still Justifie my god
Though thou with bitternese, dost fill
I have deserv'd this lot   20

Ile bear the indignation
of the Lord, and will say
Thou'rt Just in what afliction
thou shalt upon me lay

Wherin I have done folishly   25   p. 82
Let me doe soe no more
And deall not in severity
and in displesure, sore

Give influences of thy grace
again, unto my soull   30
And let me see, thy smiling face
on thee I will still roll

For time to come, make me afraid
to venture upon sin
Which hath an heavie presure laid   35
and cloudinese, brought in

Which way soever I doe look
no comfort I can take
Till thou blot sin, out of thy book
for thine own mercy sake   40

My soull is as t'were on the rack
tormented ev'ry Joynt
Thy gracyous presence, I doe lack
but this I cannot find

To run from thee, (through grace alone)   45
I neither can, nor will,
Thy faithfulnese I'le roll upon
and rest, although thou kill

50   Concerning Sin

Sin is a contrariety,
unto gods holy natture
It makes us lothsome in his eye
who is himself soe pure

Tis contradictory to his will   5   p. 83
his law itt doth opose
It is the quintesence of ill
from saten, first it rose

It bringeth on us, misery
of eve'ry sort, and kinnd,   10
It subjects unto vanity
and blindnese of the mind

From god, itt doth us separate
itt makes him hide his face,
Tis a continuall makbate,   15
hindring, the rays of grace

Sin in it self, is worse then hell.
for that was made by god,
For pure, & unmixt wrath to dwell,
and be the sinners lott.   20

Sin like a gangreen, doth begin
first on a single part,
And will not leave, untill itt win
the strong hold, of the hart.

Sin is a cursed leprosie,   25
which spreadeth all about.
untill each stone, be quite thrown by
it will not, be got out

Sin is a tirant, and a king
subjecting to its will   30
Our thoughts, our words, & ev'ry thing
till it with horour fill

Sin is a filthy runing sore
a plauge that stricks the hart
'Cept grace step in twill make thee roar   35
when thou shalt feell the smart

Sin is a pousen in the soull
which worketh all about
Defusing it self, through the whole
till death to work it out   40

Sin to the elect is grivious   p. 84
a burden full, of weight
Making them still suspitious
of ther eternall state

As roten wood, doth naturally   45
breed in worms which eat in holes
So sin breeds fears, which multiply
for to distract ther souls

Tis to them, a cruell tirant
acting against their will   50
Contrary, to their graces bent
it domineereth still

Sin dos imbiter, their short race
Causing them for to groan
Its hots persuits, and eager chase   55
Still makes them for to moane

Each sin in us, it dos make way
for a greater to come in
thus itt prevaills and get the day
and footing still doth win   60

It greatly dos, harden the hart
searing the conscience
By custome weaking ev'ry part
from making resistence

It is a, troublesome inmate   65
Which allways goes about
With us, till time wear out of date
When it shall be thurst out

Christ doth subdue this ennimy
in part, for his, whilst here   70
And he'l compleat the victory
When fixt in heavens sphere

51   A desirable day

My god, I long for that sweet day
When Saten shall, noe more esay

Still by temptations for to kill   p. 85
My soull, and it with sorrow fill

No deviating, thought shall bee   5
Once to estrang, my hart from thee

No buding forth, of cecreet pride
Shall cause my god, his face to hide

No remains of hipocrisie
Shall disturb to eternity   10

No pasion bousterous, & strong
Shall any more upon me throng

I shall not moane, for want of love
When fixed, on the god above

From discontent, & freatfullnese   15
I shall for ever be guiltlese

Distractions shall me, no more vex
Or once again my soull perplex

When I am fully, free from sin
All joy shall to me, sweetly spring   20

I shall no more thurst again
When thrown into the ocean main

I shall not then pine for a sight
Of him who is my harts delight

When fixt on him, shall be my eye   25
To'th ages of eternity

A hart untuned for thy praise
Shall in me, no disturbance raise

Under the shadow of thy wing
I shall securly sitt, and sing   30

When I with the triumphant Chore
Joyne, I shall sweetly thee adore

Oh dearest Jesus, come away
Hasten, this blessed, happy day

52   experience.   p. 86

Thou dost oh Lord, prepare our hart
somtimes before we goe
To hear thy word, and take a part
of the seed, though dost sow

Somtimes in duty, before hand   5
thou dost our harts soe fit
That when wee hear, we understand
what thou didst meane by it

Somtimes thou dost imbitter sin
to us, whilst we doe pray   10
And in thy word comfort doth spring
whilst grace, thou dost display

Somtimes thou setest love on fire
drawing us after thee
Then thy word, carieth on desire   15
that we may filled bee

Somtimes we'r filled full of fear
that we ar none of thine
Then in thy word, thou dost us chear
with thy love, as with wine   20

Somtimes thou dost the hart prepare
by laying in the dust
When thou intendest somthing rare
that prid, may not forth burst

53   Contempt of the world and foly of worldlyngs

Alase poor, empty, sory world
where dos thy glory lye
Out of thee, we shall all be hurld
and ev'ry man must dye.

What will thy glit'ring glory then   5   p. 87
Apear to us now here
A thing of nought, empty, & vain
thou shalt at last apear

Att best thou art, a heap of rubish
fit fewell for the flame   10
In which thou speedyly shalt perish
and where is then, thy fame

Oh poor, blind, mortalls what d'e meane
after this world to lag
When passed over is the scene   15
you'l see, t'was but a hag

The world will shortly turn you out
with all your pompe, & state
When in it, you have whirl'd about
you'l see, t'was but a bait   20

Her plesures ar but short, & swift
not worth the taking up
And when shee seems thee up to lift
ther's pousen in her cup

Learn therfore, to be wise in time   25
before it be to late
And broken be your weak lifes line
when time's worn out of date

Come then vain man, take one prospect
of that glory beyound   30
Time, thou'lt not then, thy rest erect
in this earths durty, land

Learn to cast of the world before
the time it casts of you
Your time, will shortly be no more   35
your days, att most are few

The closser you the world to hug   p. 88
the more t'will prick, and smart
The harder att its breasts you tug
the worse t'will be to part   40

This world when hug'd's a heap of thornes
that pricks us, to the hart
Could wee learn wisdome when it warns
we might avoid the smart

54   lets hindring the soull in its speedy progrese, to its desired home.

Fain I would break throug ev'ry lett
That I doe thee, with speed may get

Oh shew the lets, that hinder me
In this my care, I run to, thee

Sin doth out of thy presence lock   5
And in my way lye as a block

Oh let me still take heed of sin
Which will so crop, & clip my wing

As that I shall not fly apace
To the fruition, of thy face   10

Take heed my soull, of secreet prid
For that will surely from thee hide

That sweet, & lovly countenance
Which on thy soull should influence

Each sin will raise, a fog, and mist   15
So that to goe, thou'lt have no list

Vain company will so benum
Thee, thou wilt not know how to run

A lukwarm, dull, indiferency
Thou must be carefull, to espye   20

Much love to any thing, but Christ   p. 89
Will keep thee, that with sayls up hoyst

Thou shalt not move, unto thy port
Nor march with speed, to heavens court

The great block, that will throw thee down   25
In thy swift motion, to the Crown

Is unbeleife, therfore beware
And carfully, avoid that snare

Do thou by grace, each sin out weed
That I to thee, may run with speed   30

Throw ev'ry block out of my way
That would me, in my Joyrney stay

Enlarg my hart; that I may run
And never stop, till time be done

55   Apon the sight of a hasty travelor

When somtimes I do stand, & veiw
earth's busy pasengers
I see some one, to bid adeiw
to's fellow travelors

Giving to them, a quik goe-by   5
as if he were in hast
Whilst others they behind do ly
he'l not let his time wast

And this afresh brings to my mind
What a sweet thing it is   10
With speed, to leave our freinds behind
And hast unto our blise

Then in my thoughts up I doe get   p. 90
and fain, I would be gone
Wishing to break through ev'ry let   15
that I might, be att home

Fain I would be upon the march
never once sitting down
Untill I come, within the reach
of the prepared Crown   20

With David, I wish for the wing
of the poor, harmlese, dove
That I with hast, and speed, may spring
to'th object, of my love

I cannot bear it thus to creep   25
whilst others walk apace
As if I were in slumber deep
or in a stupid. maize

In my race to eternity
let me not walk but run   30
Nay rather, I would chouce to fly
Untill my day be done

Though crowds doe stand thick in my way
I'de break through them to thee
And never stand, or once delay   35
till I thy glory see

Let none out run me, in my race
appounted unto me
But let me walk, and run apace
untill I gett to thee   40

Deer Lord, I need not fear excese
whilst I doe thee aspire
I will sue for a fivefold mese
that I may thee admire

I'me willing to run on the score   45   p. 91
as deptor to free grace
Of holynese, I would have more
then others, in my race

It is not to be seen of men
that I do this, desire   50
I care not one straw, for ther ken
'to thy favour, I aspire,

The reason why, I can apeall.
is to be more like thee,
And that I may, with swift, full, sayl   55
hast with thee, for to bee

56   A lasting name

If thou wouldst eternise thy fame
when thou art dead, and gone
How sweet, and pleasing, is the name
of the Just holy one

some litle time has worn away   5
remembrance of great things,
and mighty monarcks bearing sway
over inferiour kings.

But if thy name, be writen down
in the book of the lamb   10
Thou shalt have true, lasting, renown
and never-dying fame

What if thy name, be light sett by
and troden under feett
God will advance it up on high   15
and wipe all durt from itt

Doth gods dishonour thy soull launce
is his name dear, to thee
In everlasting remembrance
thy name shall surely bee   20

With holynese, thy soull adorn   p. 92
and with humility
Thy god shall then, exhalt thy   horn
'Spight, of the enemy

The name of wicked men shall rott   25
and be, by all abhor'd
But thine, shall never be forgot
but still be on record.

57   Longing desires, & restlese breathings. of the soull, after the full
enjoyment of Christ

Oh when shall Christ, and my soull meet
In each others imbraces sweet
I shall from sorrow, then be quit

Oh that thou couldst, not chouse but come
To perfect, and compleat, the sum   5
And fecth thy bride, unto her home

I shall bee filled, to the brim
When in loves ocean, I shall swim
Which is fed from Christ, that sweet spring

It shall no more, with me be night   10
When I shall always, dwell in light
And have of thee, a constant sight

How can I here, take true content
Who am soe streightly, pinch'd, and pent
Desires do swell, and find no vent   15

Whilst I am here, my joys ar mixt
but when on thee, mine eye is fixt
No cloud of sin, shall come betwixt

Fain would I rest, my weary head   p. 93
In Christs sweet arms, my blessed bed   20
Then with his love, I should be fed

My scorched soull, I would repose
Under the shad, of Sharons Rose
Secure, from the heat, of its foes

My soull like Noahs, weary dove   25
Cant rest its foot; till thou remove
It up unto its ark, above

Then with, the saincts, I shall converse
Who still in heaven, doe commerce
And wonders of, thy love, rehearse   30

When I'me with thee, I need not fear
To find lese, in that blessed Chear
Then I expect, whilst I am here

When I come once, to be entwin'd
In thy sweet arms, then I shall find   35
More, then could here enter my mind

The daintys on which I shall feed
Shall far their name, and fame, exceed
Therfore my soull, make out with speed

And sitt not down, contentedly   40
Till unto heaven. thou shalt fly
And on sweet Jesus, fix thine eye

58   The freenese of grace in its actings

The freenese of thy grace is strange
When we consider itt
And in thesse thoughts, let our souls range
what wonders, we do meet

Of fallen man, thou dost refuse   5
the most, and pase them by
yet out of them, some thou dost chouse,   p. 94
noe reason given why

Thou chousest out, somtimes the worst
to be heirs, of thy grace   10
Whilst better natures, ar acurst
for ever, from thy face

The glorious, angels for one sin
in Chains of darknese ly
Whilst rebels, ar, chouse by their king   15
to be set up, on high

Some thou dost pull back, from the sourse
and torent, of mankinnd
The rest ar left, to take their course
as cast out of thy mind 20

To some thou givst larg doles of grace
to others thou givst lesse
Some towards glory, march apace
having a fivefold mese

Some goe on weeping, all their days 25
as still under thy frown
Some they ar led, with glorious rays
Unto their happy, Crown

Some speand their days, in doupts, & fears
and great anxiety 30
Some tast before hand, heavens Chear
Whilst in Christs arms, they ly

On some much grace thou dost bestow
but no joy, in their race
Some with high joys doe over flow 35
that have but litle, grace

Some att ther first conversion
ar shaken over hell
With sighs, & sorrows, theyr led on
in darknese, they doe dwell 40

Some feell, but few pangs, in their birth p. 95
But ar drawn in by love
And still led on, with joy, and mirth
unto the god above

Great difirence, their is alsoe 45
in the same soull, at times
One while, his faith, & hope is low
anon, on high, it climbs

Let me, by this, learn to adore
Thy holy, sov'raignty   50
Extolling free grace, evermore
henceforth, eternally

59   The voice of faith december 6 71

I know in whom, I have beleiv'd
he shall up for me lay
the Thing, I to him, have bequeth'd
against, the last great day

My soull, thou wilt in safty keep   5
soe that the gates of hell
With all ther crafty, counsell deep
Shall not on it, prevaill.

Jehovahs, everlasting arms
Shall still encircle thee   10
Untill from all dangers, and harms
he set thee fully, free

Engaged is omnipotence
for to cecure my soull
From sin, and Satens violence   15
in its race, to the goall

For why thy love's unchangeable,   p. 96
although my vessell Leak.
This is to me, a strong cable,
of hope, which cannot break.   20

And though, thou somtimes frownst on me,
& sin, doth sorely haunt,
Thou wilt extend thy favour free,
to one, in covenant,

The products of, eternall love   25
cannot prove abortive
Thou'lt safly Lodg thine own above
and with thee, they shall live

Thy love, as a strong torant ran
in sending Christ to dye   30
And gives firm ground, to build upon
Thou wilt not cast us by

I dare not plead, sanctification
yet tis thine image Lord
Wherby we know, we have relation   35
to thine, esentiall word

Though weeping may endure a night
when thou dost hide thy face
Joy shall come in, att morning light
succeeding, sorrows place   40

My soull, up, follow them. who through
beleving patience,
Have now safly, atain'd unto
their Crown, and high defence

My tears shall all be wip'd away   45
by my, mediators hand
His love will nott, make long delay
Till it me comprehand

one smile from Christ, within the gate   p. 97
Of heavens, glorious place   50
Will make me quite, for to forget
the sorows, of my race

Thou'lt shortly Lodg, my weary soull
Within thy sacred arms
Sins scars, and wounds, shall then be whole   .   55
and I free'd, from itts harms

Come sweetest Jesus, come therfore
because thou drawest me
Fecth me, to the angelick Chore
that I may still praise, thee   60

60   the soull tasting somthing of the sweetnese of god. longs to get
neerer and have its fill of him.

Dear god, how sweet art. thou to me
Which makes me neerer; to thee creep
And long, still more, of thee, to see
In, depths of love my thoughts I'de steep

Oh hasten, hasten, my remove   5
that I may, on thee fix mine eye
And be engulph'd in ocean love
To'th ages of eternity

Thou hidst thy face, most times from me
With cloudynesse I'me over-spread   10
How can I chouse, but long to bee
Removed up to'th fountain head

Throw in great, measures of thy grace
Whilst I am in, an absent state
That soe I may grow up apace   15
to fruition, immediate

Oh let me live, in flames of love   p. 98
And also in them let me dye
And on loves wings, let me remove
When I away, from hence shall fly   20

In pleasures, let whose will carouse
And take their fill of vanity
I still will eye. my fathers house
And make towards. it restlesely

This vain worlds, honour, and grandure   25
It is a poor, and empty, thing
Oh that my soull, were once cecure
In the armes, of its Crowned king

Oh blessed souls, now Lodg'd above
Sweetly attending on his throne   30
How ar you drench'd, and drown'd in love
Whilst I'me lefft here, to pine, and moane

Yet seeing, tis thy blessed will
I would be silent, and submit
It is my duty, to be still.   35
And throw my self, down at thy feet

The longest day, will have an end
In time, the prison walls will down
And then the pris'nor, shall ascend
To take posesion, of the Crown   40

61   Concerning judging of others.

Sit thou not on, the Judgment seat
itt dont belong to thee
god, thy cencure soon defeat
When all, shall judged be

Condemne not, least thou be condemn'd   5
god only, knows the hart
Take heed thou dost not discommend
thosse that, in Christ have part

Ther cause he'l surely vindicate   p. 99
acquited they shall be   10
And then, for thee, t will be to late
thy folly for to see

Goe not forth out, of thine own dore
ther work enough at home
On others faults, thou needst not pore   15
till thou, hast none, of thine own

Tis said speak evill of no man
then what hast thou to doe
Any, mans actions for to scan
or to denounce, a woe   20

Though hee be wicked in thine eye
thou knowst not gods decree
He may, from all eternity
elect, to glory bee

If he be truly, gracious   25
though full, of great weaknese
Know that to god, conspicuous
is the, least dram, of grace

And god doth deerly, love his own
theyr pleasing, in his eye   30
If thou deface, & clip, his coin
he will not pase it by

Let god but leave thee to thy self
with the worst, thou mayst vie
Take heed, therfore, & doe not delve35
in others faults to spy

Oh let me always tender be
of cencuring, another
Least if he be, belov d of thee
I should be found, to murther   40

63   experience march 3 71/2   p. 100

I heard of one has got the start
And is to her dear Jesus gone
But ah this word, did break my hart
Fainting, for thy salvation

Shouldst thou fecth home, thine one by one   5
And leave me out, untill the last
Ther is no wrong, in what is done
Though I look on, as an outcast

I have so litle of thee here
Me-thinks I look, like none of thine   10
Thou givst to others, hea'vns Chear
Feasting them in thy house of wine

I have no reason, to complain
Because of my unworthynese
Yet till drench'd, in the ocean main   15
I shall, be always comfortlese

Unworthynese, shall never make
Mee leave off, after thee, to presse
For if that should. att all take place
I may not look, for more, or lesse   20

Oh that I could, by faith espy
ane hole to Look, in att thee still
Till thou removst me, up on high
to have of thee, my joyfull fill

64   The priveledges, & hapinese of beleevers.

Each sainct, is a victorious king
already, in his head
They may with triumph, goe, & sing,
into the grave, ther bed

They ar the Children, of ther god   5   p. 101
he will not, them disown
But will be their eternall lot
when time, and days, ar done

Each sainct, is heir to a crown
that fadeth not away   10
A crown of glory, and renown
that never, shall decay

Each sainct's a member, unto Christ
who is, ther glorious head
One cant be lost, soe strongly ty'd   15
and firmly, united

They ar not only kings, but preists
and dayly they doe offer
Ther praises, and perfum'd, requests
unto ther god, and father   20

All things ar theirs, both things present   p. 102
and alsoe, things to come
Both life, and death, by covenant
and purchase, of the Son

They ar gods Jewels, keept safly   25
however here abhor'd
They shall shine forth, with majesty
in the superior orb

Ther's is the good, of providence
and projects, that ar lain   30
Gods wisdome, and omnipotence
turns each thing, to their gain

They ar a royall diadem
in the hand, of their god
They'r in his Crown a sparkling gem   35
and his peculiall, lot

They ar, the aple of his eye
tender, and delicate
& When afflictions on them lyes,
he doth comisarate.   40

Each sainct's a temple, for the spirit
with them hes pleas'd to dwell
In them, he doth sweetly inhabit
& makes ther Joys to swell

They ar a garden, of delight   45
soe hedg'd, by providence
That neither mans, nor devils spight
can come, to break the fence

Ther names ar written on Christs hart
they cannot, be forgot   50
They'r his by compact on each part
hells rage, cant break this knot

Hee hath stil'd them, his brethren
a brother, neer of kin
Hee took ther flesh, that he for them   55
might bear the weight of sin

They ar a noble, and free state p. 103
redeem'd from slaviry
Their freedome, bought at no meane rate
the bloud, of the most high   60

The blessed angels, them attend
whilst they ar in there way
And when their days, ar att an end
they them to rest, convey

Then now may we make, holy boasts   65
breaking forth into joy
Our God, he is the God of hosts
what then can us anoy

He is a God, omnipotent
a God, mighty to save   70
Tis he that makes, the rocks to rent
and stilleth the proud wave

This God, he is our god, for ever
till death, he'l be our giude
Nothing from us, his love can sever   75
or us, from him devide

Under our feet, he will tread down
each, hatfull enemy
And on our heads, hee'l set the crown
of joyfull victory   80

65   The Mansion.

Arise by faith, my soull be gone
And veiw what Christ has for thee done

Mount up, above the starry, sky
And on thy mansion, fix thine eye

The Mansion, which eternall love   5
Prepared has, for thee above

This mansion is not made with hands
Which in the heavens, for thee stands

Its price, itt was not that of gold   p. 104
But Christs bloud, was for itt down told.   10

It is a castle of defence,
Still gaurded, by omnipotence.

It standeth in a place cecure,
And shall eternally endure.

In it can creep, no enemy,   15
Once to disturb, or come to pry.

The trenches ar soe, wide, and deep.
No sin, can o're them ever creep.

The ayr is wholsome, good, and clear.
No pain, or sicknese, thou shalt fear.   20

It is enlightned, with the rays,
Of him, whom thou shalt always praise.

No sorow, can to itt arive,
But pleasures to excell, do strive,

Ther is in itt, no heat, or cold.   25
Its priveledges, cant be told

The water of life, runeth through
The mansion, thou art going too

In it ther's all variety
For to delight, and please the eye   30

No earthly palace, may compare
For workmanship it is soe rare

It standeth far, out of the reach
Of any, that would thee impeach

The neighbors round itt, they ar free   35
From sin, & of one hart with thee

It hath this blessed priveledg
That itt shall ne're decay with age

God, is the blessed architect   p. 105
That did this Mansion house erect   40

Infinet wisdome did contrive
This house, to which thou shalt arive

Infinet love, did lay the floor
And rear'd it, buy almighty pow'r

Wher wisdome, love, and powr meet   45
The struckture, must be very sweet

Dear Jesus thou art gone before
Oh let me quikly, after soare

Thou art gone, to prepare a place
'Gainst I have run my weary race   50

Then thou hast said, thou'lt come again
And I shall ever, with thee reign

Oh hasten, & compleat, thy work
That in this Mansion, I may lurk

Give in of grace, my fulest dole   55
And then transplant, my longing soull

From this earths barren, durty, soyle
Wher is nought but restlese turmoyle

Unto that city up above
Wher I shall have, my fill of love   60

And learn both to admire, and praise
Whilst on thesse heights, of love, I gaze

66   All wants made up in Christ

Thou draws'd a vaill over my grace   p. 106
tis a created thing
That itt may not take up Christs place
my uncreated king

I see my self needy, & poor   5
I will not therfore starve
Whilst I to Christs abundant store
may freely goe and carve

When nothing, I can see but night
and cloudy all about   10
I'le goe to Christ, who is my light
he will on me, shine out

When I feell, my self dull, & dead
like one without a hart
I'le make out, to, my dearest head   15
life to me, he'l impart

When I see litle grace, within
my stock decreasing low
I'le run to Christ, my constant spring
where grace doth overflow   20

When I find litle life, or heat
and know not how to pray
I'le look unto this mercy seat
and will not turn away

Justise, the law, Saten, and sin   25
I'le turn them o're to thee
All accusations, they can bring
thou'lt answer them, for mee.

When they acuse, I'le say to them
goe to Christ my surety   30
If he cannot, answer you, then,
I am content to dye

But this I know, Lord, cannot be
whatever they can cull
All depts ar satisfied by thee   35
and Justise, to the full.

I'le never seek that, in my self   p. 107
which is not to be found
I will from Christ, my comforts delve
And then, they will be sound   40

Eternity, is litle enough
to praise thee for thy Christ
His macthlese love, & grace, & worth
can n'ere be fully pris'd

67   Unworthynese no let in the persuit of the greatest attainments
because grace is free.

A sence of my unworthynese
shall never be my let
of grace Ile seek the Largest mess
and great things strive, to get

Whatsoe'ver any have atain'd   5
both as to grace, and peace
I will try, if it may be gain'd
while last's, my short lifes lease

Thou hast not set bounds to thy grace
and therfore why should I   10
I will then always seek thy face
For things both great, and high

My own unworthynese I'le take
To make an argument
That thou thy sweet, free grace, mayst make   15
in me more emenent

The best of saincts, have been the worst
of sinners at somtimes
Grace, has this bond asunder burst
and gloriously shines,   20

Ther's nothing that will soe much turn
to thy free graces praise
As to work wonders, on a worm
t'will make others to maize

Then Lord, though nothing I deserve   25   p. 108
yet glorifie thy grace
Unto me, always largly carve
that I may grow apace

Nothing will serve. me but the best
because thy grace. is free   30
I neither can, nor will, take rest
untill I perfect bee

I can but goe without att last
the thing which I doe crave
Yet I will hold the promise fast   35
What you ask you shall have

The stronger sin, the more I'le plead
that stronger is thy grace
Therfore that cant att all impead
but it shall dy apace.   40

What is there then, can hinder mee
from grace, and comforts growth
(Seeing thy grace, is allways free
and unto all held forth)

But unbeleife, take that away   45
and then I shall mount, up
Apace to an eternall day
when fil'd shall be my cup

68   The soulls pleadings to be gone.

How Long oh Lord, holy and true
Shall it be, e're I bid adeiw

To freinds, and earthly vanitys
That I on thee, may fix mine eyes

Doth not a mounth, unto me seem   5
A yeer, whilst I thine absence deem

A greater torment unto mee
Then any other thing can bee

When first I wake, somtimes my hart
Is brok to think, time still doth part   10

And this is that, which doth augment   p. 109
My greif, whilst in the body pent

I cannot know, how long my time
May be protracted, e're I climb

Unto that city up above   15
To veiw the face of him, I love

From sin, I cant, be fully free
which makes me long, to bee with thee

Earths-cumber-ground, whilst here am I
It will not mise me, when I dye   20

When shall I, from it take my flight
To have a soull, delighting sight

Of him who has drawn, before-hand
My hart up, to that holy land

Have I not reason, for to cry   25
To be transplanted, up on high

When out, still, a contrary way
Members are drawn, may I not say

It tis a pain, that is soe great
As throws, into a burning heat   30

The head is there, the body here
And cant find ease, till to its dear

Head, it be firmly Joyn'd and knit
And each togather sweetly meet

My husband, father, and my all.   35
Ar ther, &, sha'nt I cry & call

To be fecth'd from, this irksome cell
With my relations, for to dwell

Oh let thy bowels yearn on me
Extend thou thy compasion free   40

Thou knowst the akeings of my hart
Till fully thou thy self impart

Untill on thee, I fix mine eye   p. 110
I cant sitt down, contentedly

Yet whilst I am, fors'd, here to stay   45
Dart still on me, some gloryous ray

Wherby I may be set on fire
And bend to thee, with strong desire

Oh doe not me, of this bereive
Till of this world, I take my leave   50

To lanch into the ocean wide
Where Christ, and glory doth reside

In thee, in thee, I would expire
That I with the celestiall quire

The sinlese songs, of praise may sing   55
Unto our blessed crowned king

Now sweetest Jesus, come away
My souls impatient of delay

69   Contentation.

A will that's fully swalowed
Up in the will of god.
Is with most sweet contentment Led
what ever is its lot

And what-ere its condition be   5
Whether tis good, or bad
It is from all, repining free
and is not over sad

Its always, in a well pleas'd frame
whatever befalls it   10
He knows, tis god orders the same
and att the sterne doth sit

It dos know no will of its own
in gods will it is lost
What ever is by its god done   15   p. 111
Its will, cannot be crost

Ask such a soull what it would have
what god will give, saith it
Thesse outward things, I will not crave
he knows what's for me fit   20

If providence, doe on it smile
then thankfull it will be
And if it frown, (within a while)
from grudging, it is free

It doth beleive practically   25
and on this it doth rest
It saith god is, wiser then I
and acts all, for the best

Contentment sweetly, fitts the soull
for each condition   30
And keeps itt, that itt, cannot prole
from its fixt station.

Ther, is no sin, makes us soe like
saten as discontent
By it we run upon the pike   35
of wrath, and punishment

Is gods will thine, then thou'rt like to
the angels that doe stand
With bended wills, to run, and doe
all that god, doth command   40

Douptlese, this is the sweetest life
that is under the sun
It frees us, from, all inward strife
whilst in our race, wee run

Wouldst thou then learn, this holy art   45
my soull, then goe to Christ
And beg of him, a weaned hart
from things, and persons pris'd

A hart that's fully set, and bent   p. 112
on any thing below   50
Christ, will not come to be content
When god cals, to lett goe

70   Some few perticular mercy (amongst many) taken notice of
throug the whole course of life.

How sweet it is, to meditate
upon thy love, and grace
And quietly to ruminate
whilst we, thy works do trace

Now from the cradle, I'le begin   5
then I was nurst by thee
From all my freinds, thou dist me bring
and hadst a care of me.

Betimes, thou maydest me to find
and see, earths emptynese   10
Yet thou didst shew, thy self most kinnd
unto the fatherlese

Before I was twelve yeers of age
thy sweetnese, I did tast
But thorow sin, and Satens rage   15
I let time run to wast

Somtimes on duty, I would set
then throw it by again
yet still, thou wouldst not me forget
but laidst a cecreet traine   20

To fecth again my wandring soull
back to thy blessed self
Though many times, my hart was stole
by earths vain, foolish pelf

Thou notwithstanding leavst me not   25
But didst my soull persue
Till my hart, thou hadst fully got
thou wouldst not bid adeiw

With many triels, I did meet   p. 113
thou drewest me therby   30
Making me tramble, under feet
the world, as vanity

Thus I went on, not questioning
once thine eternall love
Thinking I should, to heaven spring   35
when hence, I should remove

But quikly, I met with a storm
which lasted many a yeer
Fearing, I was not yet new born
seeing no fruit, appear   40

The want of grace, was in my eye
the thing I only pris'd
As that I thought would qualifie
me, for to come to Christ

Could I but get inherant grace   45
I thought it no hard thing
For to beleive, & then apace
comfort to me, would spring

Whilst thus, in duty, I went on
and could no comfort get   50
I saw that I was in the wrong
and did encrease the dept

But herein, did the tender love
of god to me apear
In that he would not let me move   55
away from him by fear

But out of self, he threw, me more
and more, still ev'ry day
Untill he brought me, to Christs store
where my hope, and strength lay   60

Thou maidst me, give my self to thee
by a firm covenant
Taking thee, for my god to bee
and guide unto the end

I gave my self to thee, by vow   65   p. 114
and resignation
And am my own, noe longer now
but thine, and thine alone

My soull by cecreet hope thou didst
cary on day, by day   70
Yet from me still, thy face thou hidst
darknese, was in my way

The most thou gavest in to me
was strong enlarg'd desire
That I might be, made more like thee   75
and might in grace, get high'r

Somtimes my hart, was brok, and bent
and on thee, fully sett
T'was sweet to give my soull full vent
(what though the seedtime's wet)   80

Somtimes thou shinest on my grace
then hope, I did conceive
And then again, thou hidst thy face
as though thou wouldst me leave

Of late, thou hast made me to see   85
that it is not in vain
With constancy, to wait on thee
it shall prove ceirtain gain

Somtimes thou dost, sweetly reveill
thy self, to be my god   90
And to my soull, dost fully seall
That none, shall break the knot

My god then take thou all the praise
for it belongs to thee
I could to thee, make no esays   95
untill though drewest mee

Ther is no reason, but free grace
that I should mercy find
And be rul'ed, out from the race
of sinfull, lost mankinnd   100

Oh cary on, thy blessed work   p. 115
in me, with hast. & speed
Let noe cecreet sin, in me lurk
Doe thou it clean outweed

Make me apace, to grow in grace   105
because thy love is free
Oh let me quikly see thy face
and have my fill of thee

And whilst I live do thou make use
of me, to glorifie   110
Thy name, & let me not abuse
thy grace, to levity

71   hope.

A Christians life's a life of hope
My soull without this could not cope
with any single foe
But they would quikly win the day
And sweep my comforts, clean away   5
filling my soull with woe

What have I else, to live upon
In my defer'd salvation
but futerietys
Hope saith, tis but a litle while   10
Er'e I shall all enemies foyle
and gain the happy prize

When I fear, the length of my race
Hope, spurs me on, to run apace
that it may sooner end   15
Hope saith, it is the surest way
To hasten my desired day
when I shall hence ascend

When I through fear, & sloth sit down   p. 116
Hope then takes up the glor'ous crown   20
and holds it to my veiw
That I may up, again, and climb
To win the hill, beyound times line
thus hope, doth strength renew

When god dos frown, and I do tire   25
Because I cant, have my desire
nor come to have my fill
Tis but a litle while, and then
(saith hope) thou shalt be filled when
thou getst, to Zion hill   30

Hope in the soull, doth put new life
When grace, and sin, ar att a strife
and sin, doth seem to strong
Hope, will not let us drouping lye
But prompts us on, with victory   35
we shall have, ere't be long

Hope in the sadest stat of all
Doth keep the soull, it cannot fall
into finall despair
Hope in the worst extremity   40
Doth fecth down cordi'als, from on high
to free the soull from care

If hope, did not beyound time look
Wee never were able to brook
the bitternese we meet   45
But hope is to the soull, a wing
To mount it to an higher spring
where stremes, be pure, & sweet

Hope makes us run unto the goal
And is an anchor, of the soull   50
entring within the vaill
Tis fastned on a rock, soe strong
wee cannot come to suffer wrong
whilst on this sea we sayl

If in this life, only we had   55   p. 117
Hope, our condition were so bad
as none might with us vie
By faith, and hope we come to stand
Till entred in the holy land
then they, from us, shall fly   60

We need them not, but in our race
To fruition, they both give place
When they to this hath led
They will then to us, bid far well
Leaving us ever, for to dwell   65
att the sweet fountain head

72   A veiw of the vanity of the world, and the sweetnese of Christ
makes the soull long after him

Thou art in the abstract, most dear
to me my only one
I can find sweet, and blessed chear
in thee, and thee alone

All cretures ar, to mee as Chaff   5
to smoak, they doe evanish
But when on me, thou dost once laugh
all sorrow it doth banish

The world's an outside painted fire
att which poor fools doe sport   10
Tis Christ, that I will still admire
and his love, I will court

When I compare this world with Christ
I find it bear no weight
Here's nothing like him to be pris'd   15
all cretures, ar deceit

The meat, & drink, this world dos give
it is not worth our toyle
I cannot tell, how on't to live
the world's a barren soyle   20

Its sweet for to be throughly wean'd   p. 118
from this worlds vanity
Our harts, ar then, by Christs love chain'd
and knit to him firmly

Christ he is alltogather sweet   25
a rose, without a thorne
On earth with briers wee still meet
wher by our hearts ar torn

Christ is most pleasent, to the tast
when we with bitternese   30
Doe meet in this unkind worlds wast
and howling willdernese

It is comunion with thy self
in duty, I doe prize
Beyound all this worlds durty pelf   35
without this, my hart dyes

Oh fill me up, unto the brim
with thy love, whilst I'me here
In ocean love, I long to swim
in heavens highest sphere   40

Oh fecth thy conquer'd captive home
taken, in chains of love
Draw me, by them, untill I come
unto the god above

73   the soull weary, & tired, with the world, makes out ernestly,
after that, which can give satisfaction.

I cant endure, this world, tis poor
and empty, unto me
Oh that thou wouldst, break ope the door
that I to thee, might flee

When on loves wing, I get to Christ   5   p. 119
and take a veiw of him
Tis he thats by me, only pris'd
the world looks very dim

I care not then a rush, a straw
for its smiling aspect   10
All things in it, to me tast raw
to my eye, they'r abject

Fain I would get, the holy art
whilst I'me forct to live here
To win, and wind, into the hart   15
of my redeemer dear

When I doe get, upon this hill
I can look with disdaine
Apon the world, which cannot fill
my soull, with all its traine   20

Somthing faith spys, (what it cant tell)
which fain, it would be att
I cant enter; that citydell
till thou lay the wall flatt

Ther dwells within that cyty wall   25
a prince, that's dear to me,
My only one, my all, in all.
whom I doe long to see.

I must pase through, deaths black entry
before I come to thee   30
Oh that thou wouldst, the knot unty
that I, from hence, may flee

p. 120

Thou drawest me, by a strong pull
of omnipotent strength
Ther's nothing that can fill me full   35
but love, which hath no length

I hunt, and hunt, but cannot find
that which I seek for here
perfection, that doth ly behind
reserv'd for heavens chear   40

I pine, but cannot have my fill
of thee, on this side time
Oh fecth me, quikly to that hill
which lyes beyound, times line

That litle tast, thou givst me here   45
it will not serve my turn,
I must to thee, get close, and neer
or else I ly, and burn.

It is a sweet, tormenting pain,
to burn in strong desire,   50
Whilst my afections, run amain,
and after thee aspire.

I cannot have, my fill of this,
whilst in a tent of clay,
Which makes me long, for future blisc   55
and an eternall day.   .

that day, wherin no cloud shall be
my comforts, to eclips
The spring of life, shall flow to me
I sha'nt be fed with sips   60

Thoughts of long absence, I cant bear
I find no true content,
But gasp after the open ayr,
as one stifled, and pent.

Give patience, to me in my way   65
tis but a litle, while
And thou'lt abundantly repay.
me, for each weary mile.

Come look, & see, what thou hast wrought   p. 121
thy workmanship Lord, own   70
And fecth me to the purchase bought
to stand, before thy throne

Thesse breathings did from thee first spring
thou art the blessed authour
Then own them Lord & quikly bring   75
my soull, to its sweet harbour

74   The soull under a sence, of gods hiding his face.

Lord let me have
That which I doe desire
I cant but crave.
to be sett, all on fire
I cannot rest   5
Lord what is this
the way to blise
and to that nest
Of sweetnese, where I hope to ly
Secure, to all eternity   10

Tis far from well
when thou thy self dost hide
It is a hell
whilst in the world I bide
Oh pity me   15
I am distrest
Open thy breast
and let me see
The stremings, of eternall love
And then my sorrows will remove   20

I clearly see
without a deity
Heaven would be
a hell of misery
It is thy face   25
and that alone
For which I moane
let me apace
March through this region of sin
To veiw my uncreated king   30

Quench not my coal   p. 122
let thy love sweetly burn
And scorch my soull
as pledg, of thy return
Ther's no releif   35
except thou shine
by rays devine
I sink in greif
Oh cast a favorable eye
Upon my soull, or else I dye   40

This world of woe
thou knowst, I love it not
It is my foe
I'le none of't as my lot
From its vain pelf   45
upon the wing
Let me still spring
unto thy self
All's but a dream, A short liv'd sceane
Doe thou me, from it throughly weane   50

My freinds ar few
yet thosse few, through thy grace
I'de bid adeiw
so I might see thy face
And have my fill   55
thou hast my hart
By holy art
Preserve it still
And keep it safe, till get I shall
To'th vision beauatificall   60

75   fear conquered, by faith.

Somtimes with David, I doe say
that I shall one day fall
And be ensnared, in my way
by the hand of this Saul

Saten doth Joyne, his force with sin   5   p. 123
my soull for to undoe
Using all meanes, that he may bring
it into dismall woe

Somtimes he doth, soe hard oprese
I'me ready to recoyle   10
Leaving the feild, as weaponlese
thinking he will me foyle

But faith gets up, & doth espy
A Christ within the feild
And then crys out, my sin shall dye   15
I will not, to it, yeeld

For shame my soull, doe not draw back
nor from thy coulours flee
Thou needst not let, thy courage slack
worsted thou canst not bee   20

The Captain of Salvation
for thee the sword doth weild
do thou but stand, & look upon
him. he will clear the feild

Christ has wrought out, the victory   25
For thee before-hand
Fight on, for now thou canst not dye
if thou thy ground doe stand

Hold out, my soull, a litle while
and thou shalt win the day   30
Whilst fighting, Christ will on thee smile
and for thee, clear the way

Christ hath triumped over sin
already on the crose
From thence, my faith, and hope, doth spring   35
hee'l purg away my drose

The promise of the holy spirit
is mine, to mortifie
Sin, and quite for to disinherit
of its authority   40

thers nothing then imposible   p. 124
to him that doth beleive
Doe thou, by faith, me inable
great things, for to acheive

Cov'nant priviledges, ar great   45
could we but sue the bond,
By faith, we might, our foes defeat,
and make them all, abscond

76   Eternity

Eternity, eternity
what a vast thing, thou art
And shall I once, regardlesly
put thee out of my hart

Eternity, is like a ring   5
in which we may look round
T'has no begining, or ending
tis that which has no bound

Tis an unalltarable state
of joy, or misery   10
when in't engulph'd, tiwll be to late
to wish, for time past by

On this short inch of time, this now
depends our woe, or weall
We ther, shall reap, as here we sow   15
from thence ther's no appeall

Could we count, all the piles of grase
to this day, that have been
Since the creation, on the face
of the earth, to be seen   20

Could we count all, the drops of rain
Since the creation
And could we tell, each seed, or grain
that from the earth have sprung

Could we reckon, up all the sands   25   p. 125
that ly on the sea shore
Or ev'ry dust, in all the lands
on earth, t'would be great store

All this is nothing, when we doe
look to eternity   30
when soe ma'ny, ages ar past through
tis no lese to the eye.

When milions of ages, ar past
our stat, shall not wax old
Ther's no arithmetick so vast   35
wherby its number's told

The miserys, of the damned
shall never have an end
The joys, of the, glorified
shall ne're decay, or speand   40

What mad & sottish fools, ar we
to minde that by, the by
Though we see time, with hast to flee
into eternity

What is the longest age of man   45
to an eternall day
Tis but a shadow, a short span
which soon doth pase away

What need have we, to redeem time
and idlenese to flee   50
Wee know not how soon our lifes line
may snapt, asunder be

Ther is not one, can truly say
to morrow is my own
then work while, itt tis cal'd today   55
thy time to come's not known

How carfully should we redeem
our time from meat, and sleep
And all things, that, doth not beseem   p. 126
One, that knows, life is fleet   60

As knowing that, we must be gone
whether we, will or noe
Into a state (e're it be long)
of endlese Joy, or woe

Oh let me still, be drawn by love   65
to act for thee, whilst here
That soe when I, from hence remove
I may with joy apear

My time, my God's a precious thing
help me it to improve   70
That my acount, I may givc in
with joy, when I remove

Then shall I rest eternally
reaping the fruit of grace
Which shall to all eternity   75
yeeld new matter of praise

77   longings to be gone.

Oh when shall I, hoyst sayll, and goe
Out of this world, of sin, and woe

To my redeemer, and my king
His praise eternally, to sing

Among the spirits, up above   5
Who allways, move, and act, in love

That in thy praises, I may soare
And with them, learn how to adore

Oh be not angry, cause I cry
To be transplanted up on high   10

It is thy love, that draweth me
And makes me long thy face to see

Those that ar parents, will pase by   p. 127
Thosse faults, they in, ther Children spy

When they do know t'was only love   15
That did iregularly move

Making them ayme, att things not fitt
As yet for Childish, unripe, wit

Thou art Lord, more compationet
And surely wilt comiserate   20

Nott Charging that on me, as sin
Which thou dost see, from love to spring

Lead me, through, this imperfect state
That I submisivly, may wait

The days, of my apounted Change   25
Then in thy love, I still shall range

78   The fruit of sin, or a lamentation for england.

What cause have we, asham'd to stand
when we doe seriously
Veiw, what sin has, brought on our land
within our memory,

Wee were a terrour far, and neer   5
unto the nations round
Thou maydest us, to them a fear
when they did hear our sound

But now wee ar, become a scorne
And byword, round about   10
With durt, thou hast defil'd our horn
and seemst to cast us out

Thousands in one yeer swept a way
By'th plauge att thy command
Thy dreadfull wrath, thou didst display   15   p. 128
by empting our land

Thy Judgments, they have been abroad
when on the sea, we fought
Within we are, full of discord
which makes our foes to shout   20

A dreadfull, conflagration
has laid our houses wast
Our statly metripoliton
By fire, was quite defac'd

Yet have we, not return'd to thee   25
but still we are the same
Prodigiously wicked, are wee
dishonoring of thy name

The glory of england is thin
her beauty, waxen leane   30
And yet we act, as if by sin
'to undoe our selfs, wee meane

Great Judgments, o're our heads impend
to think this, we have ground
The quarell is not att an end   35
whilst sin, doth thus abound

We dayly dare, omnipotence
and stand it out with god
As if we meant by violence
to pull on us, his rod   40

Thou standest now on the threshold
as if thou wouldst be gone
And yet how stupid, and how cold
are we, like to a stone

Remember Lord thy covenant   45
thy glory, and thy name,
And let it not be made, the taunt
of'th wicked, & profane

Take not away thy gospell Lord   p. 129
though thou aflict us sore   50
Give us thy presence, with thy word
till time shall be no more

A gospell, in its purity
when we cease, to live here
We beg that thou, wilt not deny   55
unto our Children dear.

79   The Child in a strangers arms.

Oh world, what means thy tempting charms
I'me like a litle Child
Infolded in, a strangers arms
whilst in thee, I am held

If the Child doe, its father spy   5
it then can take no rest
But will strecth out, its arms, and cry
in'ts fathers arms to nest

Whatever you. to it can give
it will not satisfie   10
Nothing can to it give releife
But still t'will moane, and cry

Untill its father, do it take
and then its crys, doe cease
Its fathers arms can only make   15
it still, & be at peace

Oh pity Lord, my weary soull
still reaching after thee
And cannot rest, till thou condole
and strecth thine arms, to me   20

My soull cannot be quiet sung
with this worlds luluby
somthing There is that from thee sprung
that makes mee restlesly

Desire, and long, once for to be   25   p. 130
in thy sweet arms entwin'd
I cannot come, to reach att thee
whilst I am here confin'd

Thou hast more pity in thee Lord
then fathers, on the earth   30
I shall not then, be long in word
where is nought else, but dearth

Thy meaning's hid, I know it not
but surely thou wilt own
Thy own desires thou'st in me wrought   35
and fecth me, to thy throne

80   The souls suport and comfort in the worst times, & under the
greatest stormes.

Tis time, my soull to exercise. thy faith
The day cals for it, in its strength, and height
The enemys, grow proud, and insolent
Ther rage, & malice, fain would have, a vent
But hast thou not, a god to glory in   5
Though from below, no comfort to thee spring
He is thy father, which att stern doth sit
Who wisly governs all, as he sees fitt
His preditermin'd counsels they stand sure
No anxtious thought, can for thee this procure   10
To lessen to thee, one affliction
Upon thee, twill a greater load lay on
But on thy god, as on a rack most high
Thou mayst look down, with great security
Upon the raging billows, here below   15
When roaring, as if they would overflow
Unto thesse bousterous waves, he sets a bound
The wrath of man, shall to his praise redound
But come my soull, and let us veiw the worst   p. 131
Faith can all bonds of fear, asunder burst   20
Should thy estate, by foes, be snach'd away
Can not thy god, abundantly repay
Both in this life, if he see fitt in kinnd
How e're in him, thou wilt abundance find
Should thy relations, by them, dye, and fall   25
Is not thy god, and father, all, in all
Once more, suppose, thy life, from thee they take
What hurt is this, that they shall sooner make
Thee take thy flight, unto that place of rest
Where thou dost dayly long, to make thy nest   30
I grant to nature, death by violence
Seems worse, then quietly to goe from hence
Yett god has promised, what he cals to
Hee will stand by, inabling to goe through
What cause hast thou, my soull to be afraid   35
To heaven, in a sea of bloud to wade
If thou wilt take, this course, thou shalt not faint

Still more, & more, thy self with god acquant
Acquant thy self with him, & be at peace
And then all anxtious, fears, & doupts shall cease   40
And thou shalt quietly both live, and dye
In spight of hell, with all its enmity
Oh fear not them, which cannot reach the soull
But shorten its race, to the blessed goall
To take possesion of that massy crown   45
(Laid up for thee) of glory, & renown
Can any in a better quarell dye
Then for the honour of that sweet & high
Exallted prince, & ever blessed one
Who in the highest heavens, has his throne   50
And if thou suffer with him, thou shalt reign
Whilst ages of eternity, remain.

81   Questions of a restlese disatisfied soull   p. 132

When shall this black night disapear
and the day, giv to dawn
When shall the sky from clouds be clear
by'th bright beams of the sun

When shall the prison walls decay   5
and be quite pulled down
That soe, the soull, may have its way
made clear, unto the crown

When shall the battell have an end
and the war, fully cease   10
When shall the combatent ascend
where is no war, but peace

When shall the rafer, win the goall
and have the prize, in hand
When shall the reslese, lovesick soull   15
thy sweet love comprehand

When shall the pained, and the sick
attain to health, and ease
And get unto, the highest nick
of holy nese, and peace   20

When shall the weary travilor
get to his fathers court
When shall the seasick pasenger
land, in his happy port

When shall the pillgrim home retire   25
and sitt him down to rest
When shall the soull that doth aspire
on high, still make its nest.

When shall the hungry, have its fill
and never once, more pine   30
After a draught, on Zion hill
Of Christs sweet, love devine

When shall the feavorish burning soull
in ocean love be drench'd
When shall the soull, that doth still prole   35   p. 133
to thee, have its thurst quench'd

When shall boundlese desires be filld
and fully satisfi d
When shall the soull, come to be skil'd
in knots, not here unty'd   40

Ther's none my soull, can thee resovle
But god, who knoweth all
Thy longing whens, doe thou revovle
on him, who shortly shall

Thy questions, fully satisfie   45
when thou art ripe for him
Hee will transplant thee up on high
and fill thee, to the brim

If itt be soe. Lord, ripen mee
by thy warm rays, of grace   50
That I may always, thriving be
and growing up apace.

82   Worldlings folly

Mad world, why dost thus mistake
To think that true. religion
Doth soe unman us, as to make
Us lumps of stupifaction,

Wee must to pleasures. bid adeiw   5
And say to Joy, and mirth be gone
And this is all, that doth acrew
If th' world may be the Judg alone

But wisdome, is, Justified,
of all her Children, which doe mind   10
Her. they find, they ar by her led
To pleasures, unmix'd, & refin'd

Goe on, my soull, goe on, I say
In the strength of thy dearest Lord
And in that strength, sweetly obey   15   p. 134
And still his love, & praise record

What though this purblind world should still
Laugh thee to scorn, and vainly think
That better is ther brutish swill
Then thy deviner nobler drink   20

Shall not thy sweet experience
Bring joy, & comfort, unto thee
Whilst worldlings, sottish ignorance
Thou shalt with greif, & wonder see

What though they brave, it out a while   25
Speanding their days, in vanity
And all things on them seem to smile
Lulling them, in cecurity

Stay but a while, the scene will chang
And tragicall, will be their end   30
In helish darknese, they shall rang
Whilst thou to glory, shalt ascend

I would not have, their cecreet nips
And stings of conscience which they feell
For all the world, which is but snips   35
Of vanity, upon the wheel

Whilst wicked men, have not the least
Of solid comfort, Joy, or rest
Thy people live, upon the feast
Of a good conscience in their breast   40

The tears of those, that doe belong
To thee. more sweetnese have in them
Then all the pleasures which doe throng
And flow in upon wicked men

What ere thou hast, vain world hold fast   45   p. 135
I will not covet, what is thine
I shall insult o're thee, att last
When I in glorys, orb shall shine

83   The best Cordiall

A cordiall, in a fainting hour
When all things, doe, on me look sowre

Thou art still unto me, my head
And everliving advocate

Bee thou to me. a constant spring   5
That soe I may thy praises sing.

Both whilst I am forct to live here
And when I'me fixt in heavens sphere

When under fainting fitts, & pain
Because of sin, which doth remain   10

Thy bloud's a cordiall unto me
When I, by faith, can to it flee

When I this world, doe dayly find
To be deceitfull, & unkinnd

This cordiall doth refresh my soull   15
Whilst in its race unto the goall

To think tis but a litle while
And Christ will ever, on me smile

When into heaven, I am let
My sorows, I shall quite forget   20

When I in that imperiall ayre
Breath, I shall need no cordiall their

Because I then, shall perfect bee
And free from all, infirmity

I then shall bee att a full growth   25   p. 136
And Christ shall still, new life give forth

84   The souls complaint from a sence of its inntabilyty, and
unconstancy, in this imperfect state.

Oh who will help me, for to moane
Whilst in a tent of clay
'th body of sin, makes, me to groan
And long, to get away

That which is now before mine eye   5
And makes me stand, & maize
It is my great unconstancy
relapses, & decays

Somtimes in duty, I delight
and tast how sweet thou art   10
Somtimes, I cannot get a sight
of thee, not for my hart

Somtimes, to heaven, I doe get
anon to hell I fall
And am with darknese soe beset   15
as that I question all

I'me constant here in nothing but
A vain inconstancy
My hart doth still open, and shut
to sin, and vanity   20

Somtimes, my faith, is strong, and bold
And will not daunted be
But will on any thing lay hold
that's reached out by thee

Anon it is so weak, and low   25
as that it cant scarse creep
Tis trambled on, by ev'ry foe
and lyes as t'were asleep

Somtimes I feell, sweet acts of love   p. 137
seting my soull on fire   30
Drawing my hart to god above
the object of desire

Somtimes, I cannot feell a cole
of love, left in my hart
Nor any spark within my soull   35
that can true warmth impart

Somtimes, repentence that runs free
sin makes my hart to melt
Again such hardnese, I doe see
that nothing else is felt   40

the sin of which, I do complain
doth seem to lye as dead
Within a while it starts again
and gets a greater head

Somtimes my hart, is put in tune   45
and mounting up on high
But quikly tis let down and soon
upon the earth doth lye

Enlargment somtimes, I do find
when unto god I seek   50
Anon soe streightly pent, no mind
I have att all to speak

Somtimes thy love, I can beleive
and sweetly doe aply
Anon their's nothing can releive   55
my hopes, they seem to dye

My will somtimes, seems to be brought
quite over to thy will
But soon with discontent I'me fraught
and what thou dost, I vill   60

Somtimes a great afliction
doth seem unto me light
Again a small crose makes me wan   p. 138
when it appears in sight

Somtimes, a small sin, like a moat   65
will make the eye to weep
Anon, a greater comes afloat
and I ly as asleep

And thus t'will be, I know alway
whilst on this sea I sayl   70
Each will contend to win the day
till grace, att death prevaill

If thus it must be always then
that here, I cant have peace
Oh give, me leave, to cry out when   75
shall thesse days of sin cease

Thou wilt Lord. stand on graces side
tis thine, thou makst it mine
Thou wilt not let sin long abide
thy grace shall fully shine   80

85   the soull longing for death, eyes the resurection, and future
hapynese of the body.

Oh death come, come
And fecth me home
The days, and hours, to me seem long
Ere thou these sinfull fetters strong
Break of from me   5
and set me free.

When in the grave
A place I have
To me twill be a bed of rest
A pleasing, sweet, perfumed nest   10
'cause Christ when dead
their laid his head

How can it be   p. 139
but sweet to me
To be for some short time confin d   15
Where Christ, such sweetnese left behind
As still doth smell
in each dark cell

My head, & king
took out the sting   20
When on the crose, he triumphed
Death was by him, then captive led
and he a rose
in spight of foes

And so shall we   25
unto him flee
Out of the grave wherin we dwell
By the voice of the archangell
when he us shall
out of them call   30

The body then
shall be ag'en
unto the soull reunited
All drosinese b'ing from it fled
it then shall fly   35
above the sky

At gods right hand
ther it shall stand
The sentence of absolution
And pardon for what here t'hath done   40
it then shall hear
with its own ear

Then it shall reign
and still remain
With Christ pertaking of his blise   45
Folowing him, where e're he is
delighting still
to doe his will

Eternally   p. 140
we then shall eye   50
The beauty of our Crowned king
Whilst we, his love, and praise do sing
and still adore
him ever more.

86   The soull veiwing Christ in his humiliation, rejoyces att & longs
for a sight of his now glorious exaltation, & his second apearence.

Come now my soull, behold thy king.
both in his low estate
And then by faith, to heaven spring
and veiw his glory great

Thou seest him born of parents poor   5
and in a manger laid
This world will scarce open its door
to him that all things made

When thou shalt see him come again
atendants he will bring   10
The saints, shall be his blessed traine
and angels on the wing

His visage here, was marred more
then the sons of men. – yet
Thou'lt see heaven, and earth adore   15
when on the throne hees sett.

His beauty shall be as the sun
whose reflect beams shall dart
To warm, refresh, and overrun
Thy soull, & ev'ry part   20

Thou seest him in the garden now
sweating great drops of bloud.
The weight of sin, did make him bow
gods wrath, came as a floud.

Thou'lt see, him shortly triumphing   25   p. 141
as having paid the dept
And fully satisfi'd for sin
b'ing o're all as head

Thou seest him now, at pilats bar
acus'd by enemies   30
Thou shalt see him exalted far
above the earth, and skys

Thou seest him crown'd with thornes, & led
unto the high preists hall
And ther unjustly condemned   35
and flouted att, by all

Thou'lt see him next with glory clad
Sitting in majesty
His glory shall thy hart, make glad
and still delight thine eye.   40

Thou seest him now, my soull by faith
upon mount Calvary
Crucified and in the height
of soull perplexety

Thou'lt shortly see him, set upon   45
the top of Zion hill
Mounted as king upon his throne
his foes, to crush, and kill

With sound of trumpet he will come
to Judg both quik, and dead   50
To fecth his own unto his home
and to ther dearest head

Oh hasten Lord, this blessed day
the joy of ev'ry saint
When thou, shalt fully bear the sway   55
and we with thee, shall haunt.

87   The soull encouraging it self with the hopes of the speedy
satisfaction of its desires in the full enjoyment of god. p. 142

What meanst thou poor. impris'ned soull
Thus day, by day, to cry, & moane
Thy god will surely, thee condole
And fecth thee hence, unto his throne

The argument from whence, I doe   5
Draw forth this sweet conclusion
That I shall soon, attain unto
My longed for salvation

It is not any thing I see
within my self to grow, or spring   10
But only from the love, and free
Boundlese compasions of my king

Who cannot will not. long delight
To see me, pine, in misery
Because I cannot take my flight   15
Into a blest eternity

Hee'l surely fill, and satisfie
The mouth that he hath opened
And made. to gape soe gredily
With heavens daintys to be fed   20

Tis he, and only he alone
That knows the workings of my hart
Whilst after him, it still doth moane
And he it is, will take my part

Hee will unto his own lay claim   25
Least I should be discouraged
Hee will bring glory, to his name
And fecth me, to, the fountain head

88   more to the same purpose

He that hath said, it is but yet   p. 143
A litle while. & then I come
He will not soe his word forget
As not to fecth his banish'd home

Although to thee, a thousand yeers   5
Ar in thy sight, but as a day
Yet thou dost know a day apears
To me a yeer, in the delay

Of that which I, doe still desire
The full enjoyment, of, thy self   10
The only, object, I admire
My god, my rock, and saving health

Oh that thou wouldest march apace
Over the ruged coasts of time
That I with joy, may see thy face   15
And bath in seas, of love devine

89   longings to be in heaven.

When shall I leave, this world unkind
And trecherous, sinfull hart behind

Me whilst I leap beyound the bound
Of time, thy praises, to resound

I cannot come. to dwell in love   5
Till climbed up the hill a-bove

Love is the ayr, I shall breath in
Love misterys, I then shall sing

Thy love, I cannot comprehand
Till thou away, for me doe send   10

Then it shall comprehend me still   p. 144
And I shall have my blessed fill

Whilst I those knots of love unty
New misterys, I shall espy

I cannot but desire, with speed   15
that book of love to see and read

That book which from eternity
Lay hiden, to each mortall eye

But was made manefest in time
Unto the sons, of Adams line   20

What emulation, doth me fill
When I by faith, climb Sion hill

And see the spirits up above
Emplo'd in their sweet acts of love

Whilst I in sin, and mire doe lye   25
And cannot up, unto thee fly

My times ar in thy hand oh Lord
Yet fain, I would thy praise record

Among the saincts glorified
And drench'd in love at fountain head   30

90   The soull patienetly longing after satisfaction in the full
enjoyment of god.

I Long, I thurst, I cannot rest
I feall a constant fire
Which burneth always, in my breast
whilst to thee I aspire

I cannott here, be filled full.   5
with'th fullnese of a god
My emptinese, my soull doth pull
and is its weary lott.

This makes me long. most restlesly   p. 145
thy blessed face to see   10
Ther shall be no vacuety
left.   when engulph'd in thee

Tis after thee, that I do pine
and cant be satisfi'd
I long to be, beyound times line   15
where fullnese doth abide

My thurst, is so far, from b'ing quench'd
thesse sips doth it encrease
Till in loves. ocean I am drench'd
I look not to find ease   20

My soull doth tose, and finds no rest
it cannot be content
Till in thy bosome, it doth nest
on thee, tis fully bent

Because I cant here have my fill   25
its makes me cry out, when
Shall I get up to Sion hill
I shall be filled then.

91   Abought thoughts.

When shall it once, be naturall
To have my thoughts, on thee. still fall
as Adams e're he fell
With fresh delight
To take their flight   5
and always, on thee dwell

It never is, soe well with me.
As when my thoughts, ar fixt on thee
But Lord, how doe they flee
And run a drift   10
Except thou lift
And draw them up to thee.

Tis thou that must atract, & draw   p. 146
My thoughts from objects. leane, and raw
And make me to espy   15
by faith what is
in future blise
And an eternity

Experience, doth me, dayly teach
Ther's nothing here, which I can reach   20
that is before me set
Can fill the hole
made in my soull
but that that's infinet

Thou hadst from all eternity   25
Us on thine hart, and in thine eye
oh what a spur is this
to fix upon
our only one
The centor of our blise   30

Oh let my thoughts, no more henceforth
To fix on thee, seem. to be loth
But draw thou constantly
thesse thoughts of mine
by pow'r devine   35
To objects, pure, & high

92   The soull expostulating with god under a sence, of the hiding
of his face march 11 71/2

My god, why hidest thou thy face
my soull within me dyes
When thou witholds, the rays of grace
it breeds anxietys

Oh give me leave, with thee to plead   5
and ask the reason why
Thou dost in paiths of darknese lead
and sorrows multiply

If thou wilt not upon me smile   p. 147
I sink and dye apace   10
Each step will seem to me a mile
in this my weary race

But whether I have this, or no
I cannot be deny'd
Thy grace whilst here, on me to flow   15
and pleantuously reside

To thee my god. I dare apeall
will this world fill my soull
If thou shouldst of it, to me deall
A larg, eternall dole   20

If thou shouldst in it, let me live
to an eternity
And all its wealth, & tresure give
would that me, satisfie

If thou shouldst say here take thy part   25
I can afford no more
Would it not break, my very hart
as if asunder tore

Nay yet I'le goe another step
and once more, ask of thee   30
if I from hence, to heav'n might leap
and ther I might not see

Or ever find, a deity
or have my fill of Christ
Would not his presence, in my eye   35
in hell, be more pris'd

Was this the bargain, that was made
between thy self, & mee
Has not my god, in cov'nant said
I'le give my self to thee   40

Did I not then acept, and take   p. 148
thee on thy tearms, of grace
Oh doe not think quiet to make
my soull without thy face

I'le leave thy promise, free, and full 45
before thee for to stand
Thou canst, not, wilt not disanull
what giv'n under thine hand

93   About spirituall discourse June 13 72

What means this sinfull. modesty
Which maketh me, most times, soe shy
To speak how good thou art
when soe I might
others envite 5
To come, and take a part

Who wilt thou speak for, oh my soull
If not for him, whose thou art whole
why then art thou so loth
for to begin 10
to speak of him
And set his glory forth

Canst thou another. object find
More sutable unto thy mind
That thou dost not delight 15
of him always
To speak the praise
Unto thine utmost might

Is this the reason. 'cause thine hart
Within, is the most baren part 20
If that with god weare fild
thou wouldst alway
from day, to day
To speak of him be skild

Canst thou pretend, to be the freind 25   p. 149
Of Christ, and not still att one end
Of thy discourse find place
to speak somthing
of that sweet king
And of his love, and grace 30

Somtimes thou fearst hipocrisie
When cecreet prid, thou dost espy
And soe to speak art loth
resovlving wroung
to hold thy tounge   35
And silent, be hencforth

Wherby thou dost but gratifie
The devill thy grand enemy
Before thou art a ware
therfore goe on   40
through grace alone
And break thou, through this snare

Tis thou Lord, must open my lips.
That I may not, thy grace eclips
And make me readyly   45
to speak of thee.
As I shall see
Fitt opurtunity

94   Emulation, and desire June 18 72

Oh blessed souls now sweetly lodg'd above
How ar you always drench'd & drown'd in love
What plesure, doth unto you still arive
Whilst you in boundlese, seas of love doe dive
Love is the book, in which you always spell   5
Such wonders, as none else can paralell
Whilst you into love misterys, doe pry
What heights, and depths, of love doe you espy
You allways sing, the songs of love, and praise   p. 150
From whence, your halalujahs you doe raise   10
The work is love, in which you ar employ'd
A work so sweet, you cant in it be cloy'd
Love is the ayr, in which you breath, and live
And that unparaleld pleasure doth give
love is the object, on which you still gaze   15

Whilst sweetly you'r enlightned from its rays
In arms of love, you alway, lye, & rest
Making your nest, in that sweet, sacred breast
From princeples of love, you act and move
And always reap, the blessed friut of love   20
To all eternity, you gather in
The crop, & harvest, which from love doth spring
Since yet unto this life, I cant atain
Whilst in this tent of clay, I doe remain
Oh give me leave, to prese after this tresure   25
That I may have of it, a fuller measure
And come to live upon the borders of
That other land, that land, of perfect love
That I of that angellick life may come
To have a sweet fortast, ere I get home   30
Whilst here let me, still restlesly aspire
And after thee, reach forth with strong desire
Till over head, and ears, I shall be drenc'd
I dayly thurst, but cannot have it quench'd
I somtimes feell such pain, and misery   35
(Because I cant, this mesenger espy
As should convay my soull, into this land
Where thy love shall me sweetly comprehand)
As that I know not how, nor where to rest
Because of dubious thoughts which fill my breast   40

95   The soull under a sence of Christs hiding his face, &
suspending influences makes its complaint.   p. 151

How mutable is this my state
somtimes thou shinst on me
Somtimes it is my dismall fate
thy face, I cannot see

Former experience. I doe call   5
in question as not true
Whilst thus my spirits sink, and fall
to peace, I bid adiew

With darknese, I am wrapt about
and covered all o're   10
Soe that no paith, I can find out
Though I doe seek, and pore

The influences of thy grace
thou dost from me suspend
No quikning rays, from thy sweet face   15
doe on my soull descend

I am as one bewildered
and got into a maize
My graces, they ly as t'were dead
untill thy spirit raise   20

Now doe I long, for to be gone
Thinking it cant be worse
Then thus to live, as one alone
that's left to take her course

Yet some relief, in this I find   25
in pouring out my soull
Justifiing, thee, in my mind
whilest I my state condole

Thy covenant, I wil hold fast
for thy return I'le wait   30
Veiwing thy loving kinndnese past   p. 152
which cant by sin abate

Their s nothing, that will satisfie
whilst thou dost hide thy face
Therfore thy self, let me espy   35
and draw thou neer apace

96   Spirittuall Prid. June 20 72

Wouldst thou my soull, a monster see
Of dismall, strang, deformity
Then look, and search about
Untill thou find pride out
That which we call   5
spirituall

Ther's no sin soe rediculous
As this which dayly haunteth us
I meane the sin of pride
which in the hart doth hide   10
and slyly lurks
whilst ther it works

Thosse that have, the greatest measure
Of true, saving graces tresure
May clearly find, and see   15
most cause, humble to be
Because they are
in dept farther

Then other men, in graces book
Which while in itt, they read, and look   20
They may with wonder stand
'cause they cant comprehand
The reason why
god should them eye

And upon them, should more bestow   25   p. 153
Then upon others, here below
Cut out of the same stone
with them (tis grace alone)
Which should us lay
in dust alway   30

What hast thou, that is not receiv'd
Wilt thou be soe, of sence bereiv'd
The giver to forget
whilst thou dost proudly set
Self in the place   35
of gods free grace

Is'th sun beholding to the earth
'Cause by its rays, tis keept from dearth
And by its heat, doth spring
and pleasent fruits, forth bring   40
For to delight
the tast, and sight

Prid is a vain, and foolish sin
though whilst in acting pleasure spring
Yet ceirtain greif, and pain   45
Doth after it remain
When god doth come
to sett it home

Without influence from above
We cannot ether stir, or move   50
So dead, at root are we
noe sap apears 'cept he
Apon it shine,
by rays devine

Wilt thou by prid, that grace abuse   55
Wher by he is, pleased to use
Thee for to glorifie
his name, & bring thee nigh
Unto himself
thy only wealth   60

This seed will grow, in graces soyle   p. 154
And will not out, without turmoyle
But ther it will remain
and spread, & come, to reign
Except with heed,   65
thou wacth, this weed

Prid is the greatest enemy
Unto the soull, because therby
It is att distence sett
from that god, infinet   70
Whose only hand
can make it stand

Pride is a weed, that smels soe strong
That god will not, endure itt long
But will goe far away   75
And then we soon decay
but woe, to us
when it is thus

Oh give me that humility
Which is soe pleasing, in thine eye   80
And makes me heir unto
thosse rich promises, through
Thy dearest son
my only one

The humble soull, thou wilt revive   85
And make it still to grow. and thrive
Thou'lt guide it with thine eye
And keep it carfully
soe that it shall
not catch a fall.   90

As I from thee, receive each thing
Let me, to thee, the glory bring
And lay all at thy feet
as it is still, most meet
That glory may   95
be thine all-way

97   the soull having a litle glimps of god afar off. wonders what it
shall have, and longs, for full enjoyment   p. 155

If thy back parts soe lovly be
what is thy pleasent face
Oh what hast thou, laid up for me
in thy prepared place

Oh if a glance far off be sweet   5
and yeelds the soull soe much
What joy, & comfort, shall we meet
when we draw neer, & touch

If in a duty painfull thurst
yeelds daintys to the soull   10
What fulnese, flow to us, needs must
when fil'd shall be our bowl

If in boundlese, desires which here
cannot be satisfi'd
Wee find such sweet, & blessed chear   15
we would not be deny'd

what then, shall the enjoyment be
of that we doe desire
When we shall fully tast, and see
how then shall we admire   20

If in pouring out of the soull
& moaning in thy breast
Thou canst give in soe sweet a dole
as cannot be exprest

What shall we find when all the day   25
we shall before thee stand
Hav'ng all our tears, wip'd away
by the mediators hand

When we shall bee, still fraught with joy
and never more complain   30
Of any thing, that may anoy   p. 156
or trouble us again

My hart is overwhelm d in me
I cannot have my fill
Of that fullnese that dwells in thee   35
till I climb Zion hill.

98   Heaven upon earth   June 21

How sweetly this the soull, doth animate
When we on future glory, ruminate

And come by faith, to take a livly veiw
Of'th glory that shall unto us acrew

When we have run our race, & finished   5
Our course, & got up to the fountain head

It makes the soull grow, boundlese in desires
Whilst after full perfection, it aspires

The thoughts of fruition, immediate
Doth make the soull, whilst here, take holy state   10

Living as heir, unto a glorous crown
Still scorning, unto this world, to stoop down

Walking whilst here, acording to the port
Of one, that dost belong to heavens court

Could we come, to live in the practicall   15
Beleif of future glory, which we shall

Enjoy with god, to all eternity
How worthlese would, this world be in our eye

How light, & vain, is this worlds frothy fame
Whilst we at high, sublime, enjoyments ayme   20

When the, soull, is drawn up, to some high nick
Of joy, and peace, how is it even sick

Of cretures, and enjoyments here below
longing its self, into Christs arms, to throw

When on the borders, of that other world   25   p. 157
Wee come to live, how ar thesse meane things hurl'd

Out of the hart, with scorn, and high distaine
Counting them all but dung, so we may gain

Christ, and him crusifi'd & come to know
The power of his death, wherby we grow   30

When we somtimes ar taught, neer him to creep
We ar acquanted, with things high, & deep

And whilst we ar thus nestling, nigher him
We strangly, long to be fil'd to the brim

The more boundlese, the souls, desires do grow   35
The more of heaven, doth upon it flow

This is to live, in the suburbs of heaven
And with that blessed proto-martyr Stephen

To have a sight of Christ beforehand
And veiw the glory, of that other land   40

Thou hast not (Lord) unto thy grace set bound
Oh let no bound, for my desires be found

But let them always, more enlarged grow
Untill thou shalt, be ples'd, to take & throw

My soull, into that ocean of thy love   45
Which is in the Herusalem above

Let me still grow more restlese in desire
Untill the time, they shall in thee expire

And I shall come, to have my joyfull fill
Of love upon, the top of sion hill.   50

99   Concerning the good opinion of men

What is the vain aplause of man
Who cannot actions, throughly scan
Or what will ther vain breath
Stand thee, in steed at death
let me not care   5
for this fond ayr

Let me aprove, my hart to thee
In truth and in sincerity
And then a straw for men   p. 158
I'le ne're desire their ken   10
provided I
may glorifie

Thy name, whilst I am here below
And may not give, them cause to throw
Durt on thy holy ways   15
And soe eclips, thy praise
Oh rather I
would chance to dye

Could men unto the Judgment seat
Goe with thee, & for thee defeat   20
The sentence pronounced
By Christ, the king, and head
and Judg of all,
both great, & small

Then somthing might be said, by thee   25
Which might excusive, seem to be
Why thou thine ear shouldst bow
To mind, what they say now
but tis not soe
Oh no, oh no   30

They must on even ground then stand
With thee, when in that other land.
and Judged they shall be
By Christ as well as thee
appeall theirs none   35
to any one

What need we care, though man defame
If god, who only knows our aym
pronounce upright at last
His voice, must give the cast   40
and if he clear
what need we fear

Men Judg acording to the eye
But god, into the hart doth pry
Acordingly needs must   45
his Judgment still be Just
because that he
all things doth see

What is the good opinion   p. 159
Of all, or any single one   50
It will apear but light
and vain, in our eye sight
When we draw nigh
eternity

Those that speak well, of thee to day   55
To morrow, they may quit unsay
All that which they have said
and why, cause they are led
More by the eye
then verity   60

Ther's nothing then, soe vain endeed
As this, oh why should we give heed
Or listen with the ear
what we, of self can hear
From others when   65
they ar but men

Give me thy love, and thy esteem
And what care I, what others deem
This is the thing I chouse
for which I will refuse   70
The world as vain
with all its traine

Oh let my nobler mind aspire
To gain those things, that have far high'r
Excelency in them   75
then what can spring from men
Though good, & Just
they ar but dust

Oh let me always, through thy grace
Esteem the praise, of Adams race   80
As worthlese vanity
and soe contemptuously
Let me tread it
still under feet

When on a death bed I shall lye   85   p. 160
Drawing neer to eternity
Such thoughts as I have then
of the esteem of men
Let me now have
I humbly crave   90

The way to get a blessed name
And glorious, eternall fame
Is for to glorifie
God here, and when we dye
he will us crown   95
with true renown

100   The soull pleasing it self beforehand with its last farwell at its
departure

Farwell vain world, from thee I flee
again, I say farwell
Lord Jesus, I now come to thee
in ocean love to dwell.

Adeiw Saten now for ever   5
thou shalt me no more tempt
From thy strong, subtle, endevour
I shall be now, exempt

Farwell you cords, of misery
I meane, in dwelling sin 10
Farwell, to all eternity
I goe to Christ, my king

Farwell relations, & freinds
With joy, I take my leave
Sweet Jesus, shall make me amends 15
Though death of you bereive

Farwell dear freind, thou tent of clay
in hope ly down, to rest
I shall meet thee, another day
more gloriously drest 20

Far well my doupts, and dismall fears p. 161
I shall know you no more
farwell my sorrows, & my tears
to constant joy, I soare

Now farwell faith, and welcome sight 25
farwell pray'r, & wellcome praise
From this world, I now take my flight
to sit under Christs rays

Now deerest, sweetest Jesus I
commit my soull, to thee 30
Hoping in thine armes, I shall ly
and thy face always see

Come Lord Jesus come quikly
   Amen.

The Second Century

Oh let thy spirit me direct   p. 162
And let me, back again reflect
That love which from thee, still doth flow
Whilst I do sojourn, here below

Whilst here I dwell, let me soe shine   5
Enlightned by, thy rays devine
That I to others, still may be
A light, to lead them unto thee.

2   Satens polycy and enmity.   June 22   72   p. 163

Oh what a subtle enemy
Is Saten, who doth alway pry

About to see wher he may lurk
And cuningly his mischeif work

He still doth search, & hunt about   5
If he can but, a hole find out

He will at the ungaurded part
Be sure to creep, into the hart

And if possesion he doe get
Hee doth soe strongly, us beset   10

That out he'l not be, got again
But more, & more, he strives to reign

Wee may of him truly foretell
Give him an inch, he'l take an ell

If in our thoughts we once admit   15
The least of him, down he will sitt

And draw the soull on by degrees
Untill he fill it with the Lees

Of sin, and frothy vanity
except with heed, wee speedyly   20

Cast him out of the hart att first   p. 164
He'l never leave, untill he thurst

All that is good, out of the hart
And fill with vanity, each part

If he can come, to wind into   25
Our words, he will by them break through.

By thesse he gets, a litle hold
And soe by that, he grows more bold

In duty, he will not stand out
But cuningly, he lurks about   30

To see if he can steall away
The hart from god, then he'l esay

To rob us of the comfort which
Might flow unto us, from the rich

Incomes of grace, that soe therby   35
He may make us, in grief to lye

And if he cant, our thoughts from god
Draw off, then he will subtly plod

Which way, he may our thoughts unfix
By throwing in, that which may mix   40

That soe he may, come to entwine
And cacth us, with his hook and line

That which he dos aym at hereby
It tis to fill, with Jelousie

Concerning our eternall state   45
Whilst we on sin, do ruminate

Then he rejoyceth when tis thus
And he such fools, hath made of us

Somtimes he slyly, steals away
Our time from duty, by delay   50

That whilst we foolishly doe Joyne
With him, he may from us purloyn

The comfort, which to us, might spring   p. 165
From duty, whilst imployd therin

No duty we can goe about   55
But he will find, some crany out

In which he creeps, to rob the soull
Of joy, either in part, or whole

Hee'l suffer us, in good to be
Employ'd somtimes, if that way he   60

May keep us off from that which will
our soulls with greater profitt fill,

My soull, oh Lord, I doe commit
Into thy hands, see thou to itt.

That it from him, receive no wrong   65
Because to thee, it doth belong

Let evermore, thy wacthfull eye
Safe-gaurd me from this enemy

Tis only thine omnipotence
Must be my strong, and sure defence   70

Untill transplanted up on high
Out of his reach, eternally

Oh hasten Lord, that blessed day
And fecth me up, out of his way

3   The soull desiring still to have that presented to its eye. as may,
make it swiftly towards heaven.

An ernest peny give me still   p. 166
of the inheritance
That I with joy, may climb that hill
and speedily advance

Let me by faith, discern the goal   5
for an encouragment
Unto my tired, weary, soull
in its craky, ascent

Hold forth, to me, the glor'ous crown
that I may restlese be   10
And never stand still, or sit down
untill thou give it me.

But above all, still let me veiw
The beauty, of my king
That I this world, may bid adeiw   15
still mounting on loves wing

Let me not live, once to decline
in the actings of grace
But let me, by, thy rays devine
grow up to thee apace.   20

Present perfection to my eye
that I may swiftly move
Till Joyn'd with the society
of spirits, up above

The glory of heaven unveil   25
that I such sights may see
As I with speed, may swiftly sayl
through this rough sea, to thee

4   Our dependency upon. and beholdingnese to free grace.

When'th Sun removes up from the earth
On hearbs, and trees, ther is a dearth
The sap, to the root, descending
no nourishment, from thence doth spring
And speedyly   5
the branches dye

Thus is it Lord, with my poor soull
When thou, on whom, it hath its whole
Dependance, goest away from it
And tak'st away, thy sweet spirit   10
I soon decay
and fade away

I am like unto one, that's dead   p. 167
When thou away, from me. art fled
I neither can, stir foot, or hand   15
At all to thee. but I do stand
As one bereft. / of life, and left.

When the soull, from the body flys
A lump of clay, the body lys
So is my soull, if thou suspend   20
Thy grace from it, & doth not send
forth speedily
A fresh supply

Without influence, from above
I cannot either stir. or move   25
My grace, that suffers great decays
When thou from it, withdrawst thy rays
I strive in vain
strength to regain

I cannot (Lord,) think one good thought   30
Or speak a word, but I am brought
Unto the brink of misery
And filled, with perplexety
when thou from me
away dost flee   35

Here by tis thou art pleas'd to hide
From man, occations of pride.
Whilst thou by this, dost let him see
His own strength, meer weaknese to be
Thus thou dost throw   40
proud self down low

I never am so strong endeed
As when out of a sence of need
And spirittuall poverty
I run out of my self, & fly   45
to Christ alone
my only one

Then may I say, and not say wrong
When I am weak, then I am strong
Not in my self, but in my head   50
When I by faith, to him am fled
And can depend
Strength, he will send

Upon thy grace, I do depend
Strength I have none, except thou send   55
Down from above, a fresh suply
Of quikning grace, continually
it is thy hand
must make me stand

Turn not a way from. me thy face   60   p. 168
Whilst I am runing, in my race
For I doe stand as one afraid
My soull in me, is sore dismaid
when ever thou
dost bend the brow   65

Oh let thy grace, my strength renew
Till this vain world, I .bid adeiw
And shall above, the clouds mount up
When filled full, shall be my cup
and I shall bee   70
perfect in thee.

5   The soull expostulating with it self because of anxtious
thoughts.

What meanst thou thus my soull to rove
From god, by vanity
Who is the object of thy love
wher thou mayst fix thine eye

Why porst thou on afliction   5
before itt come att thee
Why dost tormentingly, think on
thosse things, that nere may be

Do but beleive, and thou art safe
all things ar for thee best   10
Art tossed by a bousterous wave
t'shall waft thee, to thy rest

Why dost thou take up one hard thought
of god, as if he would
Forsake the work, that he hath wrought   15
or prove unfaithfull, could.

Why then dost thou, soe terifie
thy self, with this sad news
Time will be long, before that I
of Crist, shall take full veiws   20

How knowst thou that, who told thee soe
thy day may quikly end
When grace is ripe, he'l strik the blow
and then, thou shalt ascend.

Why dotst thy sin. soe much affright   25   p. 169
and make thee quite, to sink
As if thou wert, cast out of sight
and now, on ruines brink

Is not the cov'nant firm, and sure
why dost thou not beleive   30
His love, it doth, and shall endure
he will from sin, repreive

Why drawst thou sad conclusions
from sin, because not dead
And when temptation, on thee throngs   35
forgeting Christ, thy head

Why dost torment thy self, my soull
with future sad events.
Ar thou not bid, on god to roll
thy self, & concernments.   40

What if he should, dear freinds hence call
and leave not one, to thee
If thou hast him, then thou hast all
and mayst, contented bee

Thy god's a god, of tender love   45
hee'l not on thee, lay more
Then thou canst bear, but will remove
thee to a fuller store

6   From dark, and cloudy providences, upon the church, & people
of god. June 25   72

Shall wee, our father angry see
And shall we, unconcerned bee
Oh shall we not, be sore afraid
When we doe see, the rod is laid
On others, whilst we ar as much,   5
Or rather more, in fault then such

Who have already smarted by
The hand of him, who dwells, on high
Whilst we doe know our selfs as deep
In giult, shall we not att thy feet   10
Throw our selfs down, and lye prostrate
Untill thou shalt comiserate
And take away, the guilt of sin
In which we have walowed in
How should we wrastle, with thee now   15   p. 170
By faith, and pray'r, least thou shouldst vow
The vialls of thy wrath, to poure
And all thy Judgments, on us showr
What arguments should we now use
That thou mayst not our pray'rs refuse   20
Wee can out of our selfs draw none
But what we fecth from thee alone.
And from the glory of thy name
Which wicked men doe now profane
Oh wilt thou on, the wicked shine   25
whilst thou dost seem, to cast of thine
Thou smilst upon their eterprise
And wilt not hear thy peoples crys
Oh wilt thou favour their design
Whilst they against thee, doe combine   30
And plot how they may doe their best
For to destroy, thine interest
And from the earth cut off the race
Of thosse that love, and seek thy face
We don't deserve that thou shoudst hear   35
Or to our crys, shouldst bend thine ear
Yet (Lord) thy people ar thine own
And here, thou hast set up thy throne
They ar the deer bought price of bloud
And shall thy foes, that swelling floud   40
Arise, and sweep, them all away
Let this not be, we humbly pray
Least thy great name poluted be
Among the heathen, when they see
Thou sufferst them their wills to have   45
And say t'was cause thou couldst not save

Wher ar thosse former victorys
We have had o're our enemies.
Wher is that spirit, of faith, and pray'r
That it is now, become soe rare   50
Among thy people, to be found
Which then did to, thy praise redound
Wilt thou not pour it forth again?
And gloriously amongst us reign
Thoult surely make thy pow'r to shine   55
In the deliverence of thine
In thy due time. thou wilt arise   p. 171
And sudenly, thy foes surprise
They shall be taken. in the net
Which for thy people they have set   60
Thou wilt exalt thy Christ alone
And he shall be, set on the throne
And then thy people shall rejoyce
And praise thy name, with chearfull voice
Delighting the high acts, to sing   65
Of ther victorious, crowned king
Oh hasten Lord, this blessed day
And succour thine without delay

7   The soull reaching out after an neerer communion, & higher
atainments. June 26   72

It never is so well endeed, with me
As when I can be creeping neer, to thee
Thou knowst my god, I can but creep at best
yet till I am with thee, I find no rest
It is my Leasurely, dull, creeping, pace   5
That is my greatest trouble, in my race
Great measures of thy grace, I would here gain
And unto high degrees. I would attain
I would have heaven always shine in my
Converse, & dayly walking, to each eye   10
To heaven I would always take wide steps
And towards thee, I would still fecth larg leaps
I would into thy bosome neerer creep

And come to pry, into thosse misterys deep
I would know what it is, into the hart   15
Of Christ, to win, and wind, by holy art
I would live like a sainct that's dropt from heaven
Whilst I am here, and by a close, and even
Strickt, holy, humble, circumspect, walking
Much glory, to thy holy name, I'de bring   20
In that frame always, I desire to be
Which is most sweet, and pleasing, unto thee
I would have the faith. of an Abraham
How from his countrey, and his kindred, came
To folow thee, at thy command into   25
A land, which yet, he had not pased through
He did not att the promise stager by
His unbeleife, but still did glorifie
Thy name, by his victorious faith, through which
Hee did himself, and all his seed enrich   30
I would the patience of a Job desire
And to the, meeknese, of Moses aspire
I'de have a hart lift up in thy ways high   p. 172
with good Jehosaphat, continually
I would the love, of thy desciple John   35
Still crave, who here, was in thy bosome lain
I would have Davids frame of hart to praise
Thy great, and holy name, whilst here always
The zeall of that sweet chosen vessell Paull
I would desire, & to thee, for it call   40
But none of all thesse coppys were exact
In Christ, thesse graces met, and nothing lackt
Let me after this coppy write as neer
As it is posible, whilst I am here
In this imperfect state of misery   45
Surounded, always. with infirmity
My ayms ar high, but my attainments low
Tis thou that must on me, more grace bestow
That I may dayly come to mend my pace
Through this my pilgrimage, & weary race   50

8   Temptation vanquished

Doth Saten tell thee, that thy god
rejects thy confidence
Beleive him not, he still doth plod
To take away thy fence

That he may have, a free egrese   5
to doe thee greater harm
And thee, of comfort disposese
by this, his subtle charm

Thou mayst tell Saten he doth lye
the god of truth hath said   10
Hee that beleives, shall never dye
or have his hope, frustrate

Thosse that doe in Jehovah trust
shall as mount Sion stand
Which cant be removed but must   15
and is keept, by gods hand

The god of peace, shall shortly tread
Saten, under thy feet
When into heaven, thou art led
thou shalt him noe more meet   20

Goe on my soull. couragiously
thou mayst with Saten cope
God will give thee the victory
if thou beleive, & hope

9   spirituall sloth the souls ruine

What cause have we, for to bewaill   p. 173
Thesse slothfull harts, which we do traile
About with us, whilst we ar here
Were it not for our listlesnese
wee might enjoy, a fivefold mese   5
Of heavens sweet, and blessed, chear

And come, to have a tast, and sight
Of that angellicall, delight
And thosse seraphik joys above
which we shall have, when get we shall   10
To'th vision beautificall
When we out of this world remove

How might the soull most sweetly spring
In meditation, to its king
And on his glorious beauty gaze   15
But that our harts, ar dull, and slow
And apt to fix, on thing below
Because they ar sick, of the laze

In cecreet pray'r how might wee see
Heaven as t'were, open to bee   20
Could we our harts, from sloth once court
We might in it tast such delights
And have of god, such clear forsights
As would with joy, our harts transport

Oh what mights thou atain unto   25
My soull, if thou couldst but break through
This let of spirittuall sloth
To what degrees, shalt thou atain
Of grace, and spiritual gain
If thou wilt but, thy self put forth   30

How canst thou bear it thus to creep
And slowly climb, the hill so steep
Whilst others of thee, get the start
And take posesion, of their crown
And in their kingdome ar set down   35
Whilst thou lookst on, with akeing hart

Cold wishes, will not bring thee thither
Ther must be joyned, strong endevour
Gird up thy loyns, therfore, & run
If thou with speed, the crown wouldst gain   40
No slothfullnese, thou must retain
Untill thy work, and day, be done

Do thou deer Lord, my sloth remove
By the atractive pow'r of love
Give my dull hart, to thee a lift   45
Let love constraine, to run apace
To the fruition of thy face
And then my motion, will be swift

10   Motives to quiken the soul to diligence, June 26   p. 174

Let not thy sloth, thy hopes defeat
Shall any labour, seem to great
To win, to the imperiall seat
where god immense,
Keeps residence.   5

Is not the beauty of thy king
Enough, to set thy soull on wing
And make it always, to him spring
who is alone, thy only one

Is not the blessed three in one   10
Enough to make thee swiftly run
That thou mayst feast thyne eyes upon
that mistery
the trinity

How canst thou chouse, but long to fly   15
Unto that sweet, society
Of spirits who doe dwell on high
where they ar all
Saraphicall

Whilt thou not labour. till thou sweat   20
That crown of glory, for to get
Which shall upon thy head, be set
tis all free grace
yet run apace.

Wilt thou not for that kingdome strive   25
And studiously, still contrive
How thou mayst speedyly, arive
And come to it
down their to sit.

Shall others hazerd life, & health   30
To get a litle worldly, pelf
And wilt not thou strive for that wealth
That is cecure.
and doth endure.

Shall others strive, with more delight   35
For bits of clay. for which they fight
Then thou wilt doe, to take thy flight
to Christ who is, thy only blise

Or canst thou thy time better speand
Then in conversing, with this freind   40
And making him, thy only end
who shortly shall
thee from hence call

Gett hence away, yee bitts of clay
I will not set mine hart one day   45
Upon you more, away, away
Lord thou art mine
And I am thine

Oh quiken me, soe with thy rays   p. 175
That I may bend, to thee always   50
Untill I come, to sing thy praise
In heaven high
eternally,

Tis after thee, that I will presse
Thou art, my only happynese   55
Let my desires, grow more boundlese
Untill they bee
filled, with thee.

Oh make me active, in my place
Still runing onwards, in my race   60
That I with speed, may see thy face
and have my fill
on Zion hill.

11   from thosse words in luke 2 7 & laid him in a manger because
there was no room for him in the inne

How strange this word, sounds in my ears
(ther was no room for him)
Who was above created peers
but in a sorry Inne

Nay worse then this, was yet his doom   5
Ther's no room in the Inne
But in the stable, was his room
though Zions crowned king

He did att first. the world creat
yet in it could not find   10
A room, to Lodg his weary head
t'was soe hard, and unkind

He who commands both sea, and land
the world, with all its traine
Hee whom we cannot comprehand   15
was in a manger lain

Hee came down here unto his own
and they recevi'd him not
Though he had left, his fathers throne
room they'd not make one jot   20

Well world, I'le never wonder more
att all thy usage bad
My deer Lord, whom angels adore
no better usage had.

Come take a lodging in my hart   25
and ther erect thy throne
Do not distaine, to fill each part
deer Lord, tis all thyne own

12   Apon this question how doe, you doe.   p. 176

Who can be well
Whilst here they dwell
In an imperfect. sinfull, stat
Stilling, bowing down under the weight
Of Sin, which dwells within   5
And ther doth sprout, & spring

It cannot be
heare, well with me
Whilst I am absent from my king
My joy, my comfort, & my spring   10
and fountain of delight
to whom I'de take my flight

I cannot say, / I'me well one day
Because I am imprisoned
And in times net entangled   15
So that I cannot fly
into eternity

Saten doth vex / and still perplex
Whilst I live here, he will not rest
but by temptation, still molest   20
How then should I be well
whilst in the world I dwell

But it may be
you'l say to me
That I do wrest, by violence   25
The question this is not your sence
you meane my health, & ease
I'le answer you, and cease

Tis true that healths, good in it self
But'th more I find of health & ease   30
the more I find my pain encrease
and inward, restlese strife
for fear, of a long life

Tis you then must
resovle me first   35
Which way, I may, speak truth when you
Do say to me, how doe you doe
Till then be silent, and
put me not to a stand

Ask me noe more   40
till hence I soare
Out of this world, of misery
into a blest, eternity
then you may know I'me well
though I cant come to tell   45

13   June 28 '72   p. 177

Thy ways, ar ways, of pleasentnese
And all thy paithes, ar peace to me
This I must say, and will confese
Oh what will glorious heaven bee

When somtimes, I can get to this   5
To have but only some dark sights
Of heavens future joy, & blise
And thesse angellicall delights

How can I trample, with contempt
Upon the world, as vanity   10
From this I would, not be exempt
For all its spleanded, braviry

Such reall, true, gainfull, commerse
Ten thousand worlds cant to us bring
As doth one half hours sweet, converse   15
With god, unto the soull bring in

Let whose will then, this world esteem
And take ther portion, here below
Those comforts I will only deem
Worth having, as from thee doth flow   20

14   Experience working in — soull encouragment (to hope & wait
for greater mercys) and thankfullnese.

In my distresse, to thee I cry d
and made my wofull moane
Then comfort to me was aply'd
thou heardst me, from thy throne

My spirits were in me confus'd   5
my hart, strangly opprest
My soull was in me sore amus'd
but thou, hast me refresh'd

Thy love in question, I did call
I said thou wouldst not hear   10
My spirits they did sink, and fall
my sins, did make me fear

Thou didst give unbeleif the ly
whilst I did seek to thee
And didst in mercy, pase it by   15
makeing me it to see.

Thou didst convince me, t'was a sin
Soe anxious to be
Seeing, I had, a crowned king
who orders all for me   20

That life, & death, was in thine hand
and thou hadst all things wrought
If thou sawst fit, thou wouldst command   p. 178
life, for him, whom I sought

Thou didst cecreetly, then distill   25
A sence of love devine
And then, thou broughtest up my will
unto that will, of thine

Though I by unbeleif offend
yet thou dost pardon all   30
And graciously, condesend
to hear, when I doe call

My god has granted unto me
the thing, I did desire
It shall to me, an ernest be   35
of things, greater, and high'r

This mercy shall. not come alone
thou'lt greater things throw in
And more for me shall yet be done
that I thy praise, may sing   40

Oh now my God! what shall I say!
Thy mercy is so great
That thou shouldst look, on worthlese clay
From thy high, glorious, seat

Oh that, I might, make others fall   45
in love with thee, and take
Thee, for their only all, in all
and vanitys, forsake

Oh that I could, thy praises sound
through heaven, earth, and skys   50
That each mouth might, with songs abound
of thine excelencys

15   Christ only excelent, only desirable.

The Sun, & moon ar glorious
Which in the heavens, run their course
but whats this to compare
With one bright ray
which doth display   5
It self from Christ, the heir

The heir of all things, & the sun
Whose beames of glory, still doe run
Through the creation
Warming the hart,   10
filling each part
Of th heirs of sallvation

This glorious, sublunary world
When it is bravly deck'd and curl'd
Compared with this face   15   p. 179
tis to the eye
deformity
With all its outside glaze

Each coppy here, is full of blots
The moon, is not without her spots   20
But in Christ ther is none
for he it tis
that spotlese is
And only, he alone

This Lord, the mighty god is stil'd   25
The everlasting father, (mild)
And the sweet prince of peace
The wounded soull
he maketh whole
and gives in joy, and ease   30

Of him, it is most truly said
He is the sweet, and pleasent, shade
Of a great rock, whilst in
this weary land
we meet with grand   35
Storms, and discouraging

His name is called wonderfull
When enemies, would us down pull
He dos with succour meet
giveing them cheak   40
and on their neck
He makes us, set our feet

He is the only rose, without
A thorne, which spreadeth all about
The new Jerusalam   45
Wher he doth dwell
and sweetly smell
who sprang, from Davids stem

Tis he is called the true vine
Which yeeldeth that delicious wine   50
Wherby we ar strength ned
Whilst here below
but it shall flow
to us att fountain head

He is the way, the truth, the life   55
For which we should, with eager strife
Contend still ernestly
Runing apace
our weary race
till in his armes, we ly   60

He is most lovly, to the sight
A springing, fountain of delight
Which still shall flow upon
our souls when we
transplanted be   65
from hence unto his throne

Oh let me run with hast and speed
That on his beauty, I may feed
And always fix mine eye
upon that face, 70
so full of grace
to all eternity

16   Infinet love of Christ

What love is this, that bouled in
The breast of our sweet, sacred king

From ages of eternity
He did resovle, to come, and dye

That he might fallen man regain 5
And bring him back, with him to reign

Oh how this love should make us blush
Thou hadst (deer Lord) no need of us

To thine esencyall glory we
Could adde nothing, at all to thee 10

thou couldst in thine alfullnese dwell
had we been, in the lowest hell

This Justice might have always shone
In our deserv'd, damnation

The couldest in, the blessed sight 15
Of thy perfections, still delight

And needest not to stoop so low
As on us rebels, love to throw

T'was love, and purely, that alone
That rays'd thee, from thy statly throne 20

p. 180

Whilst thou thy robs, didst lay aside
To purchase, such a worthlese bride

This love, this love, unpara'leld
Could not in heavens, bounds be held

But down he came, love runs apace   25
To save the sons, of Adams race

Love drew a veill, o're the devine
Nature, that here it might not shine

For why, the glory therof we
Could not in this state, bear to see   30

Love ran through ev'ry action
That was by our dear Jesus done

T'was love in him, that sweetly smil'd
When he became, a litle Child

T'was love that made him not distaine   35
To be here, in a manger lain

Love made him att twelve yeers of age   p. 181
With the great doctors, to engage

Entring with them into dispute
Whilst he their answers, did confute   40

T'was love, that sent him for to preach
And still both day, and night, to teach

Which way our souls might find a rest
And be, of hapy nese possest

The godhead, did it self reveill   45
When all diseases, he did heall

Whilst mortals mad, did shew their spight
In seeking to eclips this light

Yet n'erethelese thy love, went on
In healling all, leaving out none   50

That came to thee, with malidys
Thou curest ther infirmitys

Thou didst not make, the body whole
Alone, but love did reach the soull

Ther's few that came to thee for ease   55
And cure, of bodily disease

But thou ther souls didst also heall
And pardon of their sins, reveill

So meane a boon, thou scornst to give
Thy love, would make the soull to live   60

The cabinet thou knewest well
Was nothing worth, to the Jewell

In itt so excelent, & rare
Whole worlds, could not its lose repair

But whether do, I start aside   65
Thy love is broad, & deep, & wide

T'were infinet for to goe through
Each pasage, of thy love unto

The full dimention of itt
Till down in glory, we shall sitt   70

When on this love, my thoughts I bend
I know not how, nor where, to end

yet here I cannot leave off yet
A litle further, I would get

And see how love, did flow, & spring   75
Both in thy death, & suffering

As in a garden. sin begun
So ther thosse drops of bloud, did run

From off thy face, upon the ground
Oh how thy love, did here abound   80

Each drop of bloud did loudly say   p. 182
That love, in thee bore all the sway

Thy love did rise, exceeding high
When thou wert in an agony

And needst help from, thy menn all   85
servants, which still atend thy call

before that thou didst bid adeiw
to earth, thou lefts with us, a new

To ken of love, that always we
Seeing it, might remember thee   90

When this was done, still love went on
From step, to step, till in the throng

Of those that sought his life, he fell
Though with a look, he could them quell

Hee caus'd them backward for to fall   95
To shew he could, escap them all

If he had pleas'd, but he would give
His life for us, that we might live

Love led him, to the high preists hall
To be derided ther by all   100

Scourged, spit on, & buffeted
And att the last, their condemned

Love made him bear away his crose
On which he purged out our drose

His life on it, he then laid down   105
That soe we might atain that crown

Of glorious, immortality
When we shall, with him, reign on high

Love rays'd him up, out of the grave
That we a firm, support might have   110

When he ascended up on high
Hee led captive, captivity

And though in heaven he be set
Hee doth us not, att all forget

Our names ar written, on that brest   115
Which is the sinners, sacred nest

By his atractive pow'r of love
Hee still doth draw, till up above

He hath got his redeemed ones
And plac'd them on, ther glor'ous thrones   120

What shall we now return to thee
For this most wonderfull, & free

Love which thou dost on us bestow   p. 183
And make, plentifully to flow

Nothing but love, thou dost require   125
Oh let me, answer thy desire

Wilt thou acept so meane a thing
then give it me, that I may bring

Such love, enflamed, strong, & quik
As may reach, to the highest nick   130

As any soull, can here atain
Whilst in the body, they remain

Let love grow up, to such a flame
As may reach that, from whence it came

And terminate, still in that breast   135
Which is of love, the sacred nest

Let love, in me soe much abound
That I may know, what tis to sound

Away, into thine armes for love
Whilst my afections, strongly move   140

And bend to thee, with such desire
As may not rest, till they expire

in thee, and shall be swalowed
Up in thy love, att fountain head

17   the soull from a sence of its unworthynese of the least mercy.
expostulateth with it self, for it discontent; because it has not greater
mercys, yet gathers suport from the freenese of gods grace.

How darest thou my soull, thus to
aspire on high, & think
That god should great things, for thee doe
and to himself, thee link

With shame, my soull, doe but look down   5
Upon thy guiltinese
Thou art unworthy, of his frown
much more, of neer accese

The crumbs that from his table fall
thou art unworthy of   10
How darest thou to cry, & call
to be drench'd in his love

That he should on thee, cast an eye   p. 184
how canst thou it expect
Yet seekst thou in, his arms to lye   15
and their thy nest erect

The leavings of his Children deer
ar, to good for thee to have
yet seekest thou, the chousest chear
and a full mese dost crave   20

Thou art unworthy, for to look
that hee should on thee shine
Why sullen then, because not took
into his house of wine

Thou art unworthy once to tast   25
how good, and sweet he is
Yet discontent, cause not imbrac'd
in those sweet arms of his

Thou art unworthy, for to have
the least dram of true grace   30
yet nothing will content thee save
th' enjoyment of his face

Thou art unworthy, to know that
in which all have interest
How darst thou seek, thosse intricate   35
things, hid within his breast

Thou art unworthy once to spy
his glory, far off, yet
Thou wilt be nestling still so nigh
as to his throne to get   40

If thou wert in the lowest hell
no wrong were done to thee
Yet, cause, thou canst not with him dwell
thou'lt discontented be

Now art thou not asham'd, my soull   45
thus dayly, to aspire
And in thy thoughts, for to controle
him, whom thou shouldst admire

Yet loth I am, to leave thee quite
without encouragment   50
Least thou shouldst think, out of his sight
and presence, thou art pent

Let not thy sorow to high swell
God promises to teach
The humble soull, & in't to dwell   55
who dos it self impeach

Though this be true. thou art the worst
of sinners & the cheif
yet grace is free, and that can burst
this bond, & give releife   60

The more unworthy that thou art   p. 185
the more free grace shall shine
When it shall gloriously, dart
On thee, by rays devine

The grace of god, shall bear thee out   65
Whilst thou dost always creep
Neerer to him. & search about
for those things, which lye deep

Then search my soull, and always crave
though thou shouldst dye, for why   70
Thou shalt att his feet make thy grave
and by his sweet hand dye

This is the death, I would desire
if I must dy, endeed
That by the hand, whom I admire   75
I might both dye, and bleed

Goe on my soull, now chearfully
thou knowst this cannot bee
The faithfulnese, of god doth ly
as pledg, and pawn, to thee   80

That thosse that seek, and wait for him
they shall be satisfi'd
And filled up unto the brim
if constant they abide.

18   The soull expostulating with god, upon perticular occations, &
sad aprehandtions.

Wilt thou lay the foundation
of a sweet and glorious structure Lord
And not put on, the topmost stone
acording, to thy faithfull word.

Ar not thy gifts, & calling said   5
without repentence, for to be
Shall not thy word then good be made
Whatever thou in us, maist see

Wilt thou bring any soull neer to
thy self, & throw it off, again   10
Wilt thou thyne own work thus undoe
because of sin, which doth remain

If into self, wee look tis true
we may see cause enough why thou
Shouldst to thine own work, bid adeiw   15
and on the soull, should bend the brow

But when on thee I cast mine eye   p. 186
and veiw thy sweet free, love, & grace
Encouragment I then espy
and fear, to hope, seems to give place   20

Thou wilt not sure, my hopes defeat
but what in me, thou didst begin
Thou wilt most perfectly compleat
that I thy love, and grace, may sing

From my unworthynese, erect   25
trophys of honour, to thy name
What thou hast wrought, in me perfect
and take thy glory of the same

However thou mayst deall with me
let me not live, once to decline   30
But let me always, thriving bee
by influencyall, rays devine

19   the soull expostulating with it self for its restlese, impatient
desires to be gone, revived by mrs Sl- death. July 6 72

What dost thou ayl, my soull, what dost thou ayl
Why thus impatient, cause within the vaill
Others are taken, and thou left behind
wilt thou therfore, conclude, Christ is unkinnd
Because thou art not taken yet so neer   5
To him, as others of his Children deer
Whom he has cald from sin, and misery
Have to himself, in his arms for to ly
May he not what he please, do with his own
Who of his actions, gives acount to none   10
Why sufers't thou, tumultious thoughts to rise
And filst thy breast, with fears, and Jeloysies
Wher then, dost thou, his work in question call
Because at once, he doth not perfect all
And stop the mouth, of thy desires, as soon   15
As ever they, ar formed in the womb
Before they ar come, to maturity
Thou wouldst be streight, transplanted up on high
Dost thou know better then thy god, whats best
Or teach him when, to call thee home to rest   20
Wilt thou a quarell pick, with thy best freind
Because he puts not, to thy days and end
Doe but look round about thee, thou shalt see
Thou hast yet company along with thee
Thou art not left out, to the last as yett   25
But mayst yet, before many others gett

Have patience then, tis but a litle while   p. 187
And Christ will come, and for each weary mile
Hee will thee recompence abundantly
And thou shalt still, in his embraces ly   30
Thy weary race shall shortly have an end
And then the blessed angells, he will send
To fecth thee to himself, where thou shalt have
More then thou here, couldst wish, or think to crave
Envy not thosse, that do before thee get   35
Remember alsoe, that thy time is set
Thy days, & hours, ar numbred, & when they
Fullfiled are, thou shalt no longer stay
But thou with joy shalt follow after those
Who now ar triumphing o're all their foes   40
It shall not then be in the pow'r, or art
Of man, to keep thee, longer from thy part
Which is laid safly up for thee, in store
When thou above the clouds, shalt sweetly soare
Have patience then a litle, litle, while   45
Foreruners, shall not thee at all beguile
But thou shalt also have as full a mese
As they, of comfort, joy, & happynese
What though before thee. they ar gone, & fled
They shall not take thine house, over thy head   50
But that shall be reserv'd, & kept for thee
Till thou from hence, remov'd, to it shall bee
A smile from Christ, when their, shall make amends
For all thy weary, restlese, longing, when's
And dayly, cryings out, how long ere I   55
Shall in the arms, of my redeemer lye

20   The soull gathering some releif from experience, though
clouded, & far from what it would have,

I see thoult not cast me off quite
because of unbeleife
But allways dost, and wilt delight
To give in some releife

Although not always in that way   5
that I do it expect
I will be thankfull for each ray   p. 188
that doth on me, reflect

The mercy is not ripe for me
or I'me not ripe for't yet   10
But I will hope, that I shall see
Thou dost not me, forget

And though I cannot get so neer
as fain I would to Christ
Yet unto me, thou makst this clear   15
that he is only pris'd

Whilst nothing else, will satisfie
or give my soull content
It tis made out, undouptedly
that on him it is bent   20

Whilst want, of satisfaction
Makes me, more restlese grow
Ther's sweetnese in't to live upon
till more, on me do flow

I find much sweetnese for to moane   25
and after thee, still pine
Untill thou fecth me, to thy throne
and cut in two, lifes line

The spirit, and the brid. say come
thou sayst, I come quikly   30
Oh let thy char'ot swiftly run
and let me, it espye

Let not these restlese breathings. cease
till swalow'd up in thee
But let them more, and more, encrease   35
continually, in me.

21   free grace the souls encouragment to seek after great things,
July 9   72

What is the reason thou shouldst not
My soull upon high projecks plot
seeing that grace is free
It may incourage thee
Still to persue   5
for somthing new

I can see nothing, in my self
Should make me cease, to seek that wealth
that's freely given to
all those that in truth doe   10
Make it. their ayme
to get the same

For if unworthynese might be   p. 189
A let, or hindrance, to the free
And boundlese, grace of god   15
I then might cease, to plod
all hopes were gone
to built apon

But blessed be, this rich, free grace
So sutable, unto my case   20
Without this I should ly
In such perplexety
as sad despair
should, be my fare

But now which way, so e're I look   25
out of my way each let is took
And answer, ther is made
To what ere can be said
by a cunning
devill. or sin   30

I may such arguments draw forth
From my own sinfullnese, as doth
Thy grace still magnifie
And lift it up on high
Whilst I run more   35
on graces score

Is sin, temptation, poverty
And want, an object fitt to try
Thine own free graces, skill
Then here oh Lord, it will   40
be throughly try'd
and magnifi'd

Here is a large feild, for, thy free
Grace, to work in always in mee
Here's work in ev'ry part   45
And corner, of my hart
to hard for me
but not for thee

I have no riches to impead
Why thou shouldst not me, take and lead   50
To graces tresurys
of free, & rich supplys
for misery
and poverty

Streangth I have none, that thou shouldst Leave   55
Me unto that, which will deceive
I meane, legs of my own
I cannot goe alone
They ar so weak
Lean'd on theyl break   60

Food I have none, to live upon   p. 190
But what doth come, from grace alone
Hunger gives right to bread
That by which thine ar fed
I shall not starve   65
whilest grace, doth carve

Drink I have none, to quench my thurst
Drink I must have or dy I must
Free grace intitles me
Unto this promise free   70
come take your fill
whoever will

But whether do I start aside
This is nott the thing, by me ey'd
But I would plead for more   75
From this abundant store
of rich, free grace
whilst in my race

The same free grace, that dos bestow
A dram, can pounds weights, to me throw   80
A drop's no easier
To give, then a greater
measure, from the
infinet sea

The weaker, is the instrument   85
On which thou workst, the more twill tend
To thy free graces, praise
When thou from it, shalt raise
glory, it will
Shew forth thy skill   90

It matters nott, what I deserve
Acordingly, thou wilt not carve
For then, I should have Just
Nothing att all but must
Lye down in greif   95
without releif

Give me then much, and take the praise
Of thine, own, influenciall rays
Give me the largest share
Of grace, and I'le not care   100
A straw for this
worlds Joy, and blise

22   Foly of ploding, and carking for the world.

It seemeth, somtimes strang to me
When I a while do stand, and see

How busily, employ'd we are
Speanding our time, our thoughts, our care

about this durty world, as if   5
Wee were, for ever here to live

Wher as our life. is but a dream   p. 191
Or rather like some hasty streame

Which swiftly runs, and sudenly
Is swalow'd in eternity   10

If reason. might but exersize
Her self, in us, or faith advize

Such fools, and Ideotts, we should not
Sure be, as thus to cark, and plot

How we may gain, a little trash   15
Which when we have. tis but a flash

That runs from us, & will not stay
Or else from it, we'r snach'd away

The world's a heap of vanitys
A book, that's stuffed full of lys   20

Ther's vanity written upon
The whole creation, all along

Since Adams fall, thus it hath been
Yet what a bustle, noyse, & din

To we make, whilst in it we live   25
For that, which it, cant to us give

We look for satisfaction
It is not here, wee place it wrong

No wonder then, we ar deceiv'd
Whilst we ar so of sence bereav'd   30

To search, and hunt, for that below
Which only from above, doth flow

Here's no contentment, to be found
On earth, if we the creture sound

Wee find it hollow, empty vain   35
Deceitfull brooks, we may soon draine

Them dry, the world it doth still reell
And turns about, upon the whell

And when we think, we have it fast
Tis gone, & then our hopes ar dasht   40

But come my soull, and learn this art
To throw this world, out of thy hart

And fill the empty, vacent, place
With Christ, with holynese, and grace

Whilst others walk, the road to hell   45
Doe thou above, in heaven dwell

And whilst unto the flesh. they sow
Upon the root, Christ Jesus grow

Whilst others seek for to grow rich
Doe thou att heavens gates, lay seige   50

Whilst others love, here to commerse
Doe thou with god still hold converse

Whilst others earthly things do mind   p. 192
Seek thou the pearll, of price to find

Whilst others feed, on vanity   55
Wind thine affections, up on high

Whilst others, for the world contend
To thou thy hart, to heaven send

Do others let time, run to wast
In heavens way, run thou with hast   60

Whilst others, they seek for renown
Do thou with speed, run to the crown

Art thou in the strength of thy head
By him thou shalt be safly led

Ther is no rest, but in thy breast   65
Oh when shall I, there make my nest

23   the worst of Christ better then the worlds best excelencys.

Christs refuse is, better by far
then this worlds hapinese
The worst of Christ, doth wholy mar
the world, in her best drese

Att the door of thy house to stand   5
is more felicity
Then earthly kingdomes, to command
or be advanc'd on high

Ther's more of heaven, in thy frown
whilst after thee, we moane   10
Then's to be found, in the renown
of kings, upon the throne

Tis better to mourn, ore thy grave
and weep, when thee we mise
Then this worlds fullnese for to have   15
with all her joy, and blise

The leavings of thy Children deer
the crums, which from them fall
Is better then the worlds, best chear
for which men tug, and hale   20

Thy glooms, the hiding of thy face
when strongly, atracting
Is better then under the rays
of this world, for to sing

A by drop, cast into the soull   25
doth yeeld more true releife
Then from this world the fullest dole
that it to us, can give

To follow thee, and bear thy crose   p. 193
brings in more true delight   30
Then this worlds gold, and sillver drose
can yeeld unto the sight

Then Lord give me, whilst I am here
still somthing of thy self
I cannot live, on this worlds chear   35
I care not for its wealth

What ever will me neerer bring
to thee, that I would crave
And that which will, make me still spring
to thee, is that I'de have   40

A litle tast of thee I prize
in duty, far beyound
All worthly spleanded, foperys
of which I cant be fond

24   The best trade.   July 10 72

Wouldst thou my soull, be very rich
A constant beger thou must be
This is the only way by which
Great riches, shall flow into thee
take up this holy trade   5
and thou'rt for ever made

Necessity it cannot blush
It knows no shame-face'd modesty
It will into gods presence rush
It cannot. will not., be put by   10
if get to speak it may
it will not, be said nay

True poverty, it doth lay claim
Unto the riches others have
Necessity will make the lame   15
to run, to cry, & loudly crave
It will not be abash'd
or out of count'nance dashs'd

A sence of want, will teach thee skill
this trade of beging, for to drive   20
Which will thy coffers, surely fill
And make thee, sudenly to thrive
This trade is ne're in vain
but brings in ceirtain gain

Begers doe often goe away   25
From rich men cause they will not give
Thy god he will not say thee nay
But still is ready to releive
from his rich store he doth
most willingly, give forth   30

Some others they ar willing to   p. 194
Give, but they have not wherwithall
But god is able for to doe
All that, for which on him wee call
our wants he can suply   35
and that abundantly

The oftener we, to others come
The sooner, weary they doe grow
Their cisterns, cannot always run
But this fountain doth ever flow   40
the more on him. we grow
the more, he will bestow

This trade of beging is an art
The which, I cant my self come by
This skill to me, doe thou impart   45
And give me wisdome from on high
Oh let thy spirit teach
that I may come to reach

Faiths, subtle, quik, dexterity
To wrastle with omnipotence   50
And pull down blessings from on high
with fervant, holy violence
Resovlving were to rest
till filled with the best

Let me, with thee, by faith so strive   55
that greater skill I may atain
And come to love, this trade to drive
From sweet experience of its gain
Such faith, on me bestow
that I may quikly grow   60

To such a vast, encrease in grace
Thriving amain, and growing high
That I may, swiftly run my race
and drop into eternity
Where I shall ever be   65
with him I long to see.

25   our mistakes for want of skill in the methouds of the spirit in
the actings of grace from whence proceeds trouble.

We fill our selfs with fear
And restlese, soull perplexety
Because we do not wisly eye
considering what is
Gods dealings here, with his   5
We look for god, & find him nott
Our ignorance doth so besott
Though he to us draw neer

We would be drawing lines   p. 195
And boldly choking out the way   10
In which he should himself display
we this way look, and pore
whilst att another door
He doth come in, & yet we flee
Away, & cry, it is not hee   15
'cept when the spirit shines

Somtimes in duty we
Do look for brokenese of hart
Litle of this he doth impart
In steed of this, he doth   20
faith, in high acts draw forth
Or else he doth desires extend
And make them strongly, to him bend
Hee's in his actings free

When we hope to find in   25
Duty, our harts with love, enflam'd
In steed of this, we ar asham'd
that we love him, no more
whom angels, do adore
And we ar brought in dust to lye   30
From sence of want, & poverty
and this from him, doth spring

Somtimes he sees it fit
To disapoint us in desire
That we his counsels, may admire   35
we look much joy, to find
and sorrow, fils our mind
In this, ther is as much of him
As when with joy, fil'd to the brim
Though we do, so slight it   40

When we doe cry, & call
And think streight to be answered
We'r only; with deniells fed
Tis fit, that thou shouldst carve
and to thy self, reserve   45
The liberty, to deall with thine
As thou seest good, who wilt refine
and do them good, by all

Doe as thou wilt, oh lord
but this one thing, I will desire   50
That I may dayly, grow up high'r
Untill I come to thee
Where I shall fully see
And veiw the products of thy love
In the Herusalem above   55
whilst I thy praise record

Oh give to me whilst here
So much, that through thy grace I may
Thy love, & bounty; still display   p. 196
that others they may be   60
drawn, to run after thee
Oh let me always run apace
Untill I end my weary race
and see my saviour deer

26   The soull courting death

When shall I bid thee welcome, death
unto this house of mine
When thou shalt take away my breath
I shall breath, more devine

I know not why, my hart should faill   5
when I shall see thy face
For why, although thou lookest pale
christs bloud, thee springled has

Thou art my freind, & canst not doe
me any reall harm   10
But break the wall, and let me through
into my saviours arm

Thou art to me, no enemy
Christ has took, out thy sting
And pousenous, malignity   15
thou art, no terours king

Though thou shouldst grip me ne're so hard
thou shalt let goe, thy hold
Thy kingdome, is now wholy mar'd
by Judays, Lion bold   20

I hope, I shall henceforth, through grace
Stand att the door, & look
To see if I can spy, thy face
to fecth me o're the brook

That thou art many ways my freind   25
oh death, will thus appear
Thou wilt to each sin, put an end
and let me to my deer

And only blessed saviour
my husband, & my head   30
My sweetest, intersesour
and constant, advocate

When thou oh death, these eyes shalt close
I then, shall see more clear
The beauty of that fairest rose   35
that grows, in heavens sphere

When I a lump of clay, shall ly
I then shall swiftly flee
To'th angelick, society
and saincts, from sin, sett free   40

when our comunion, mediate   p. 197
by death shall have, an end
to, an open and unnailed state
by itt we shall ascend,

I can out of thee, nothing cull   45
that doth me terifie
I never shall be filled full
till thou lifes knot unty

27   foly.

We foolls, to broken cisterns goe
Although the fountain still doth flow   •

To which we may, have free recourse
whilst it doth run, with a full source

What mad ons then ar we to think   5
That sweeter, is this pudled drink

And purer, then the fountain head
In which coruption, never bred

The farther from the fountain we
To goe, the dregier it will bee   10

What fools ar we, to dote upon
Thesse filthy stremes, which run along

Here through the durty veins of earth
And in our souls, will breed a dearth

Whilst we still wholsome liquor might   15
Drink, att the fountain of delight

And though thesse stremes, they run not clear
Wee doe oft times, for them pay deer

Wheras the fountain, runeth free
Whoever will, may wellcome bee   20

The stremes ar mixt with bitternese
Continually, both more, or lesse

The fountain we may still be sure
To find unmixed, sweet, & pure

At the stremes we may drink, and burst   25
But they will never quench, our thurst

The fountain that doth satisfie
And quench our thurst, when we ar dry

The sremes they will, our hopes deceive
The fountain, never doth bereave   30

Us of what we expect from it
Nor never once will intermit

To run with constant, fresh supplys
Suted, to our necessitys

The stremes drink, brackish, flatt, & dead   35
But get a tast of th fountain head

And that will put thy mouth soe out   p. 198
Of tast, thou'lt never seek about

After the stream, or cast an eye
To it, But thou wilt long to lye   40

Att fountain head, to drink thy fill
Upon the top, of Zion hill

28   The soull longing to be att home, can find no releive from the
creture, but makes its moane to the god of pitty.   July 18 72

How long shall thoughts perplex, and throng
For fear that I should here live long
and be deny'd
what is espy'd

Thesse thoughts, doe put me on the rack   5
This is the thing which I doe lack
to be posest
of heavens rest.

None knows this pain, but those that feell
Ther souls, upon the racking wheel   10
Of strong desire
whilst they aspire

And long to be posesed of
Ther hapynese which lys above
In heaven where   15
the angels are

To thee my god, to thee alone
Ile call, & cry, and make my moane
For tis but vain
once to complain   20

To man, who cannot help one whit
Or give, a plaister which may fit
the pained soul
or heall the hole

Which nothing, but a god can fill   25
Enjoyed fully, on that hill
Above, where his
residence is

Thou knowest the akeings of my hart
Only for fear, long time should part   30
And keep me here
below the spher

Of glory, where I hope to fix
When no sin, shall my Joys eclips
Or take from me   35
a sight of thee

Oh pity Lord, a restlese soull
Still reaching, out unto the goall
And cannot rest
till in thy breast   40

It nestle doth, & still shall lye
Where it shall ne're draw of its eye
from that sweet face
soe full of grace

Though yet, I cannot reach att thee   45   p. 199
I would not be, exempt, & free
From this sweet pain
which brings, in gain

For whilst thesse longings, on me grow
Though makest me, therby to know   50
that I do love
the god above

In which I read thy love, to me
By reflect beams, of love to thee
Then I am thine   55
and thou art mine

If it be thus, oh why should we
yet, Longer keept asunder bee
by this sad line
of ruged time   60

29   The soull under fears of declining.

I fear sometimes, I do decline
when I my self doe veiw
The seed, & bloom of grace is thine
Oh bid it not adeiw

I cannot hold out one short day   5
if thou lett goe, thy hold
I stumble, & fall in my way
and soon grow dead, and cold

Let not the thing, which I so fear
and always, greatly dread   10
Come on me, but let it appear
that I by thee, am led

Oh let me never, make a stand
but always climbing be
Till entre'd in the holy land   15
to take full veiws, of thee

It will be for thine honour Lord
to magnifie thy grace
When I thy praises, shall record
within thy dwelling place   20

Oh let my weaknese, be a foyl
to make thy grace, to shine
In makeing of my barren soyl
to bear, still fruit devine

In this, I would be like the sun   25
setting in a clear night
Whose glorious, rays then do run
and make the clouds, round bright

When the sun, of my life shall set
lett such a lustre be   30
That others then much good may gett   p. 200
whilst they, thy glory see

Oh let me never cease to grow
till heaven I doe reach
Lett thy grace, in me overflow   35
New lessons, to me teach

I have no strength that is my own
but it, in thee doth ly
Leave me not till unto thy throne
thou'st brought me safe, on high   40

30   Infinet power, & wisdome in bringing so much good to the
soull, out of the greatest of evills. sin.

Sometimes I cant but wonder why
Thou shouldst in us leave any sin
Seeing thou couldst, as easily
Att first full pow'r o're itt give in
Into thy counsels deep   5
we may not to far peep

But that which we doe plainly see
We may take notise of, and say
Tis for the glory, of thy free
Grace, which thou dost therby display   10
Whilst thou dost multiply
new pardons, from on high

Wee must to heaven, goe halting
Through the feilds, of thy rich, free grace
That we the praise of grace may sing   15
When we shall always, see thy face
tis fitt it should be soe
'Cause all from grace, doth flow

Hereby thou makst, thy pow'r to shine
By keeping grace, in us alive   20
Whilst sin which is so strong, in thine
Doth always for the mastery strive
Yet in this sea of sin
thou keepest our spark in

By this thy pow'r, is manefest   25
And made to shine conspicuously
In making grace, o'recome att last
And bear away, the victory
Whilst it shall triumph o're
each sin, for ever more   30

Though sin, whilst here, will not be thurst
quite out of doors, yet thou therby
Dost keep down prid, whilst in the dust
From sence of vilnese, we doe ly
Low thoughts of self, doth spring   35
From this indweling sin

From sin, which doth in us remain
Thou dost produce this sweet efect
To weane us from this world soe vain
Whilst in our thoughts, we itt reject   40
Longing as prisoners doe   p. 201
att some hole, to break through

This maketh heaven sweet, endeed
Longing to be, upon the wing
That we may get with hast, and speed   45
Out of the reach, and sight, of sin
Where we from it shall bee
eternally sett free

Oh give me leave, still to admire
That which I cannot comprehand   50
Sett thou mine hard, & love, on fire
Whilst I with great, amaizment stand
and gaze upon thine art
Which here doth shine, & dart

Upon this wonder, I would dwell   55
To think how thou shouldst make of sin
An antidote, for to expell
If self, and from it power bring
to root it out in time
out of the harts, of thine   60

Thesse Gibeonits, make att thy nod
Hewers of wood, and drawers of
Watter, for the house of my god
Till out of'th land they ar quite drove
Oh let them nere get head   65
But still be captive led

Shake of thesse fetters, from my soull
And sett thou it, att liberty
Do thou my prison state condole
Open the door & lett me fly   70
Into thy blessed arms
from the reach of itts charms

I long to be, from it set free
Say thou amen. I'me hapy then

31   The souls comfort only from free grace.

Tis well for me
thy grace is free
Or else what hope had I
When on death bed I ly
Ready from hence, to take my flight   5
Unto the awefull Judg, of right

The best duty
that ever I
Perform'd is not so free
from sin, but I may see   10
Enough in itt to make me dwell
For ever, in the Lowest hell,

Grace in high art   p. 202
is imperfect
Coruption that doth weave   15
It self with it, and leave
Such durt, and filth behind that we
Cannot by it, Justifi'd bee

Our chousest grace
In this our race   20
Hath still a tang and smell
Of that corupt vessell
In which tis poured forth wherby
We have nought wherof to glory

What cause have we   25
thankfull to be
To our deer Jesus who
makes us, with boldnese to
Come, & appear, before the throne
Cloth'd, with his righteousnese alone   30

Tis free grace which
doth us enrich
By it we ar cecure
and to the end endure
Being the strong foundation.   35
Of hoped for sallvation

When grace we veiw
we still see new
Matter of love, and praise
and whilst on it, we gaze   40
We doe with great amaizment stand
Att that we cannot comprehand

32   The soull eyeing the beauty of much grace, & deep humilyty,
breaths after such a frame.

Adde still to grace, in this my race
that I may still advance
And soe may dayly, grow apace
both in the root, and branch

And with it give humility   5
to ly under thy foot
That whilst the top, sprouts up on high
I may grow att the root

The better others, of me think
the more low let me ly   10
Ther good opinion I would wink
in'to worthlese, vanity

Oh let me be aprov'd by thee
and then it matters not
Though as to others, I should bee   15
as one dead, and forgot

Weare not thy glory, concerned   p. 203
it weare a matter small
Though I were in, mens eyes as dead
and soe forgot, by all   20

Yet tis our highest, honour Lord
to glorifie thy name
Whilst we ar here, & to record
thy glory, & thy fame

Let me shine, by devine emprese   25
of holy nese, & grace,
and let it be, my constant drese
till I shall see, thy face

The things of this life, do thou give
to those that them desire   30
Let my sins dy, my graces live
and lett me still, climb high'r

In this my day, or rather night
let holy nese in me,
Bee still a constant growing light   35
to lead many, to thee

I would be like, the violet
which casts a fragrent smell
yet downwards. always bends the head
and lowlyly, doth dwell   40

Or like unto some friutfull tree
on which mine eye, I lend
And then, its fruitfull boughs I see
by weight of fruit, to bend

The more grace, that thou dost bestow   45
the more reason have I
My self down att thy feet to throw
and in the dust, to lye

I still desire, upon the score
to run, in graces dept   50
It will encrease thy praise, the more
when I, to heaven gett

33   The souls. all, in another world July 22   72

My countrey's in another world
when shall I to it goe
Why am I soe far from it hurl'd
by unbeliefe, my foe
As that I cannot think   5
thou wilt my chain, unlink

My dear relations there doe dwell
my best freinds, are above
How can it then, with me be well
till I to them, remove   10
from this dark, irksome cell
Wher-in, whilst here I dwell

My god, and father he is there   p. 204
how can I chouse, but moane
Till I come to breath in that ayre   15
where is, his sedled throne
And where he doth remain
with all his blessed traine

In heaven lives, my dearest head
my husband, & my king   20
Who hath my soull, to himself wed
and sha'nt I long, to spring
To him, that so we may
togather, live alway

Those whom I shall be like, ar there   25
the sinlese, blessed ones
Who breath, in that imperiall ayre
and ar set on their thrones
How can I chouse, but long
in'th midst of thesse, to throng   30

The blessed angels, there remain
the winged, Cherubims
And Seraphims, with all that traine
when shall I fly, with wings
to be in company   35
with that socyety

My kingdome, and my glorious crown
is in that world above
Can I contendetly sit down?
and not long, to remove   40
To that inheritance
free, from incumberance

My hart, with my affections
ar thither pact, & gone
My highest. expectations   45
ar up, before the throne
How can I be content
to be from them here pent

My joys, my hopes, and my delight
is fled ther before-hand   50
And sha'nt I long to take my flight
into that holy land
which Whilst, I doe espy
I long to get, on high

What have I then, left here behind?   55
but this poor tent of clay
That I should yet, have any mind
Longer one day, to stay
blame me not then to long
henceforward to be gone   60

Hast thou thus taken up my all   p. 205
with an intent to keep
Me, from the beautificall
vision, that I may steep
My thoughts, in sorrow still   65
'cause, I cant have my fill

Can it with me be well
untill with thee, I dwell.

34   upon parting with a deer freind brother Gilbert,   July 26 72

What ar the comforts of this life
For which poor mortals, are att strife

Wee can enjoy them but a while
although they on us seem, to smile

They'r like unto a suden blast   5
Which flameth up, & then in hast

It goeth out, & leaves behind
sadnese, and darknese on the mind

We joy a litle in a freind
But oh how soon, this joy doth end   10

They do;nt so much refresh the hart
As gaule when we from them do part

But oh how sweet, will heaven be
Where we shall meet, & still be free

From fear of parting any more   15
From freinds, or any of that chore

That shall togather knit, in love
In the Herusalam above

Tis good to place our hapynese
In god. who leaves not comfortlese   20

We still may have recourse to him
Who only can fill, to the brim

To good to be from cretures wean'd
And have our harts, by love fast chain'd

To god, and unto him alone   25
And then be sure, thou'lt never hone

After thesse creture vanitys
If thou on him, doe fix thine eyes

His love will soe refresh, thine hart
As thou'lt be linkt by holy art   30

So fast unto the god above
Thou'lt never care from him, to move

By this affections, will be curb'd
And thou wilt never be disturb'd

By any change of providence   35
Still dwelling in omnipotence.

35   The soull under the distempers of its body releives it self, by
eyeing its future glory, and freedome.   p. 206

How doth this mouldring tent of clay
retard the soull, whilst here
In its progresive, holy way
by breaches that apear

But when to heaven, it shall get   5
It then shall freely soare
The body, then shall be a let
unto the soull no more

No pained head, or akeing hart
Shall indispose thee then   10
To sing his praise, or act thy part
among the sons of men

No malencholy, in thee there
Shall any more apear
To steall away, thy chousest fare   15
and soull delighting chear

No painfull hectic, cold, or heat
Shall when there, take ther turns
And in the body, make their seat
love only, sweetly burns   20

In heaven, the body shall be
A clog to'th soull no more
But it shall be, agile, and free
ready, with it to soare

Then cease my soull, for to complain   25
of distempers unkinnd
When thy body, returns again
each dust, shall be calcyn'd

36   Love, September 1   72

Ther is one thing, which I would crave
The which alone, if I might have
it would sufice
And be my heaven, upon earth
Keeping my soull, free from all dearth   5
Love, is the grace I prize

T'would be a heav'n in midst of hell
If love enflam'd, in me might dwell
give that to me
And then I shall not, will not care   10
For this worlds, overgiulded ware
but shall hasten to thee

Love would my soull from self unty
And teach it sweetly, to deny
it self in what   15
Er'e is most deer to it, soe that
My will, should att thy feet ly flat
Leaving to thee, my lott

Let love in me be pure, and strong   p. 207
And still encresing. all along   20
untill I see
It grow, to such a mighty flame
As may reach up, from whence it came
and terminate in thee

Oh let my love ne're ebbe, but flow   25
And more, and more, encrease and grow
Continually
Till it break through, the cretures ranks
And come to overleap, times banks
and to its centor fly   30

37   septem   3   72

thou seest itt fitt, to keep me low
That pride, may not upon me grow

Because I have not what I would
I am, by mine own thoughts befool'd

And look upon thee as my foe   5
Because att once, all doth not flow

To satisfaction, of desires
Saten, with unbeleife, conspires

To rob me of, the comfort which
Would flow unto me from the rich   10

Beginnings, of thy grace, in me
Which shall att last, perfected be

How ready, am I to take part
With Saten. who by runing art

Doth cast a mist before mine eyes   15
And cause Such darknese to arise

That what I have, I cannot see
But what I want, that's clear to me

That which I have, I doe refuse
On what I want, I lye and muse   20

Whilst I should thankfully adore
And grow in praises, more, & more

For what in mercy, thou hast done
In that thy grace, has overrun

The praise, that I to thee can give   25
Both here, and when I come to live

With thee, in an eternity
The dept will but encrease, theirby

Take thou not the advantage of
My unbeleife, oh god of love   30

But let thy grace. my strength renew
till I thy face, in glory veiw

38   I cant but pationetly long
           for that most wellcome day
           When I shall sing this blessed song
           and shall triumphing say

Oh death where is thy victory   5   p. 208
oh grave, where is thy sting
Thou hast made me, compleatly
A victor, through my king

And that not only over death
but over sin, and hell   10
Which frequently, prevaileth
O'r'e me whilst here I dwell

39   The soull under fears of hipocrisie, sees itt need of examination,
both from scripture, from the deceitfullnese of the hart, and from the
fair shews of many that have been deceived. september 4   72

What need hast thou with speed
To search about with heed
and industry
Still warily
Least thou shouldst be out in thy way   5
Twill be to late, another day

All that doth glister is
Not gold, but false varnish
thou'lt bear no weight
if counterfeight   10
The foolish may walk with the wise
Deceiving them by there disguise

How many have we seen
Like fair ships, that have been
in beauty led   15
with sayls, out-spread
That by some leak have watter drunk
And sudenly, they have been sunk

Tis written in gods word
Many shall say Lord, Lord.   20
and Christ shall say
in that great day
Depart from me, I know you not
Eternall woe, shall be your lot

Mans verdict, will not passe   25
Tis god only that has
a true insight
to Judg aright
Thosse that pase here, for a thousand
In gods acount, may ciphors stand   30

But give not way, to fear
Let still this cordiall chear
The contracts firm
what can thee harm
Tis sign'd and sealed with Christs bloud   35
And by the law, of grace stands good.

40   sep 4   The soulls Charge drawn up against intruders and compaint
to the right owner and Lord of the house.   p. 209

Cast out intruders, Lord
out of thy dwelling place
I know they ar, by thee abhor'd
and soe by me. through grace

Thesse inmates doe disturb   5
I cannot be att rest
They ar thy foes, wilt thou not curb
and of their pow'r divest

About thy house. they lurk
I cannot quiet be   10
When I'me employ'd about thy work
they ar disturbing me

Tis they that break the peace
and make stirs, and uproars
Wilt thou not make their tumults cease   15
and cast them out of doors

Thesse inmats have no right
in thy temple to dwell
Oh cast them out (dear Lord) in spight
of satten, and of hell   20

My hart it is thine own
oh cast out each vain thought
And let them not, get on thy throne
which is by purchase bought

My hart I doe design   25
to thee, as thine own part
Oh let not sin, nor Saten, wind
Into't by any art

An holy hart thou dost
of me always require   30
And that thou wouldst out of it thrust
the world, is my desire

Then why should this world break
in to my hart, tis thine
Oh gaurd it still, (for it is weak)   35
by grace, and pow r devine

Let not this vain world fill
my hart, att any time
But let it be, more holy still
and always to thee climb   40

Let not my hart be torn
by thoughts, from thee again
But let me thurst them out, with scorn
and heavenly distaine

41   The soull desiring faster growth and speedy ripnese.   p. 210

That this agrees unto thy will
I am well satisfi'd
That I should climb apace, the hill
wher glory, doth reside

Thou lovst to see thy plants to thrive.   5
which ar set by thy hand
And to maturity arive
in this thy lower land

Unto thy grace. no bound is set
this doth encourage me   10
To hope, that I, through ev'ry let
may grow up unto thee

Whatever any have atain'd
that Lord, I will desire
What ever any, might have gaind   15
to that, I would aspire

Below perfection, I would not
sit down contentedly
Oh let this be my blessed lot
A quik maturity.   20

42   The soull looking att, and longing for an eternall saboath.
sep 8   72

When shall that blessed, saboath morning dawn
That saboath of eternall rest, upon
My soull, that it might sweetly once begin
Thy love, and praise, eternally to sing
That blessed saboath which shall know no night   5
The Sun of righteousnese, shall be itts light
No sleeping, dresing, eating, in it shall
Steall out a part, away from god, but all
Of it, shall be employ'd to sing his praise
Whillst we sit under his delighting rays   10
No Luring bait of sin, and vanity
Shall from a deity, draw off our eye
In it no deviating thought shall be
Once to estrange, or steall, the hart from thee
The body shall not be. a clog again   15
Unto the soull, to keep it down, when fain
It would upon the wing, sweetly ascend
But it shall freely, to its motions bend
Our hope, into enjoyment shall be led
Our faith, into fruition swalowed   20
Our pray'rs, shall into halalujahs, turn
Our harps of praise, shall never out be. worn
The church, that we shall Joyne with, in that day
Shall have no spot, no blemish, no decay.
No Jaring discord in our musick then   25   p. 211
For want of love, but all shall say Amen
No diference in Judgment shall appear
For all things then, shall unto us, be clear
When I from this church. militent shall soar
I then shall Joyne, with that triumphant chore   30
Oh that I might but know. I quikly shall
gett to that vision, beautificall
In that eternall, sweet, saboath of rest
Where I shall in thy bosome make my nest
Looking down on this world of vanity   35
As one, that is set on a mountain high
Looks on the ship, that brought him safe to land

Liing, all broke, to shivers, on the sand
Rejoycing in this, that he is got safe
Out of the reach, of any bousterous wave   40
No depths of greif, shall swalow me again
But I shall ever with thee, live, and reign
Uninterupted communion, with thee
I shall enjoy, when I this day shall see
The world, and cretures, shall not call me off   45
From the enjoyment of him, whom I love.

43   Meditations on the glory of that day, when all the saints, that
ever were are, or shall be shall meet togather   sep 10

Oh for that glorious day, we look to see
When all the saincts shall congregated bee
That either shall be, ar, or ever where
To be fixt up, in glorys highest sphere
When earth, and sea, shall both give up their dead   5
Which in their bowells, have been buried
And shall att once, to heaven take their flight
Arayed in their robs, of glory, bright
Soe many saincts, so many shining suns
Brighter then that, which now, o're the earth runs   10
Soe many saincts, soe many crowned kings
Praising that king from whom ther honour springs
Triumphing with ther palms of victory
O're sin, and hell, & ev'ry enemy
But what's all this, unto that blessed sight   15
Which we shall have, of Christ, our harts delight
Clad in his robs, of royall majesty
How will he then, atract each hart, & eye
So that it sha'nt have time, to look about
Or gad, to find another object out   20
This day which shall rejoyce his peoples hart   p. 212
Shall upon wicked men, great terrour dart
To see him on his Judgment seat ascend
And all his gaurd of angels him attend
To execute according to what shall   25
Out of his mouth, be pronounced on all

The wicked shall by them, be thrust to hell
The saincts led to Christs palece for to dwell
Oh hapy soulls, that shall att that day stand
Aquited, & absovlv'd, att gods right hand   30
Oh hasten time, & days, out of the way
That we may see, this blessed, glorious day
Whilst we eye thosse, that are got to thy court
This may our weary, restlesse souls suport
That those that have been now long time with thee   35
Shall not without us, fully perfect bee

44   enlarged desires after the full enjoyment of god in glory,

My god, my rock. and my fortrese
my sweet salvation
The centor of my hapynese
to thee, I make my moane

Oh pity me, & fecth me hence   5
for here I live in pain
Whilst in this state, of sad absence
I am forct to remain

What can my lose campensurate
Whilst I'me absent from thee   10
And cant into imediate
embraces taken be

Ten thousand worlds, away I'de throw
if they were all my own
Provided, I might only know   15
I should be quikly gone

To have a full, & constant sight
of thee without eclips
And dwell, att the spring of delight
no more, to live on sips   20

This would me from my dullnese, rouse
and make my hart, to leap
When I think, att my fathers house
Soon, I shall full crops reap

My wine shall there, ne're no more be   25
mixt with woorwood, & gall
But I shall drink it pure, from thee
the fountain head, and shall

Lye still under thy rays devine
and influenciall beames   30
Which from thy face, shall dart, & shine
whilst I bath in loves stremes.

45   The soull clouded.   sep 12 72   p. 213

Why turnest thou thy face away
On the inshutting of the day

Whilst all things doe in darknese shourd
Thou wrapst thy self, up in a cloud

Thou knowst I cannot be content   5
Whilst I'me out of thy presence pent

Except upon my soull thou shine
I must have leave, to moane, & pine

Oh shew thy self, to me with speed
Or take mee up that I may feed   10

My eyes, to satisfaction,
Upon thy well beloved son

When it is with me att the best
I cannot here take, up my rest

Much lesse, when thou art gone, can I   15
The Least true satisfaction spy

Yet Lord, I hope, that I am thine
And though the gates of hell combine

Thy cov'nant firm, they cannot break
Or make thy promises to leak   20

Oh let my faith, break through each throng
And in the dark, make thee, her song

I must not always, live by sence
Untill thou calst me up from hence

And then I know. thou'lt clear the sky   25
On me, to all, eternity.

46   The soull by faith, triumphing over saten, & rejoycing in hopes
of future freedome. through Christ alone.

Oh what a reall comfort tis
To think, though Saten, doth here tempt
and seek to foyle
tis but a while
And I shall be, for e're exempt   5
From all thosse subtletys, of his

In duty here, he will not rest
But att mine elbow, he doth stand
my soull to vex
and it perplex   10
But when climb'd to the holy land
Hee shall me then, no more molest

He doth whilst here, still evermore
Throw in his fire brands ore the wall
for to enflame   15
and play his game
But thou shalt with him quite each score
When Christ shall set thee free, from thrall

47   Another to the same purpose   p. 214

The prience of this world is cast out
Though for a while, he makes a rout
with victory
triumphantly
Christ shall make thee, upon his head   5
With acclamations, for to tread

This ravaning, devouring, kite
To heaven, cannot take his flight
for to destroy
or thee anoy   10
Time, and this world's his boundery
He cannot soare above the sky

Wee cant be quiet here below
But he will always att us throw
his fiery darts   15
to wound our harts
In company, & when alone
Hee seeks to make our harts, his throne

His date shall shortly be expir.d
And grace shall only bee admir'd   20
for setting thee
for ever free
From all his rage, and tirany
Unto a blest eternity

48   The blessednese of a true Christian   sep 26

Oh what a blessed thing it tis to be
A Cristian in truth, and sincerity
That can look death, & danger, in the face
And trample, on the sorrows, of his race
A cristian cares not for the things of time   5
But can to heaven, in affection climb
If creture comforts doe upon him flow

His hart upon them, he will not bestow
If here hee have not where to lay his head
By faith, hee veiws his mansion prepared   10
Though cloth'd with rags, & on the dunghill laid
Hee knows that hee shall shortly, be aray'd
With robs, of glory, that shall shine more bright
Then doth the Sun, which to the world, gives light
When creture comforts, do upon him frown   15
He can with joy, look, to the glorious crown
When all the world, is in an hurly, burly
When stormes, arise, & waves mount up on high
His hope is anchor'd fast, within the vaill
And nothing can, his noble mind apale   20
His hart with joy, & comfort, doth abound   p. 215
When trouble, doth encompase, & suround
If in a prison, he confined be
Hee knows, how ther to walk att liberty
He can mount up, on contemplations wing   25
And unto heaven, in a moment spring
The Christians trade, is always heavenly
His marchandise, is for eternity
He drives an hiden, cecreet, unknown trade
With heaven, and comes home, still richly lade   30
The vanity, & cheating glory of
This world, doth not att all, his hart once move
This durty world, bears no weight, in his scales
Each providence, is as wind, to his sayls
To make him, move more swiftly, to that port   35
Of glory, where his god, doth keep this court
The Christians feett, stand, where other mens heads
Whilst he on all things, sublunary, treads
And if this durty world, doe on him smile
He trusts it not, it cannot him beguile   40
A Christian can rejoyce, when men defame
Hee knows that in the book of life, his name
Is written down, and shall att last appear
When god shall make itt, shine, both bright and clear
Ther is no streit, a Christian can be in   45
But he knows where to run, unto a spring
Of sutable subply, and neer att hand

Wher he by faith, may as itt were comand
It is the Christian only, can outbrave
The devill, to his face, and make him rave   50
And when he comes runing with open mouth
For to devour, he can from Christ, draw forth
Such strength, as makes him run away with shame
Whilst riches of free grace, he doth proclaime
When god himself, doth seem to frown, the true   55
Beleiver, can by faith, run with the new
Cov'nant of grace, establis'd in the hand
Of a mediator, which doth firmly, stand
And is made good, in gods new cov nant court
From whence he doth receive, a safe pasport   60
For why, he knows god cant himself deny
The sinner in Christ, for to Justifie
When sin, the law, and saten, doth accuse
Tis he hath skill, the promises to use
Hee knows against all these, how to opose   65
A redeemer. & vanquish all his foes
When death the king of terrours maks att him   p. 216
With looks, and countenance both stern, & grim
Hee fears him not. but goes, with joy to meet
Him. knowing he. shall tread, him under feet   70
He knows the worst that death can to him doe
Is but to break the wall, and let him through
Out of this world, of sin, and misery
In his redeemers, sacred, arms to ly
He can bequeth his body, to the dust   75
In hope of'th resurection of the Just
He knows, it is to Christ so united
As't shall be rays'd, by vertue of its head
Who would not then, a reall Christian be
That doth his priveledges, veiw, and see   80
yet all is from free grace, through Christ alone
By which we doe climb up unto the throne

49   Satens malice, and the saincts victory

The livly Christian, doth alarm hell
And bring the devill, mad out of his cell
Hee's forct to come, out of his den to see
What is the news, be cannot quiet bee
Let him but see, a Christian march apace   5
And he'l opose him, to his very face
And call about him, all the pow'rs of hell
To see if he, the pow'r of grace can quell
But god will hear us, when we cry, and crave
And has laid help on one, mighty to save   10
A legion of these devils, cant withstand
His word, when he from us doth them comand
This serpents rage, and malice, is restrain'd
By him that has this roaring Lion, chain'd
On foot beyound his chain, he can not step   15
His bounderys he cannot overleap
This serpents head, itt is allready crusht
And into heaven, he can never thurst
How may we here, admire the pow'r of god
Whilst Saten, doth design, combine, & plod   20
Which way, he may, us surely overthrow
He overshoots him, still in his own bow
He dogs us att our heels, continually
But god doth gaurd us, with his wacthfull eye
Were we not kept, by thine almighty pow'r   25
This greedy Lion, would us soon devour
This murderor, of soulls doth hunt for bloud
And sendeth still, out of his mouth a floud
Of new temptations, & perplexetys
Which makes us run, to god with ernest crys   30
Who will not faill, to succour us when we   p. 217
Through Christ, by faith, away to him do flee
How may we here, break forth in holy praise
And long our halalujahs, for to raise
Among the sinlese, sweet, redeemed ones   35
Who ar out of his reach, upon their thrones
Giving, blessing, praise, honour, and renown.
To him that doth their heads, with victory crown

50   Concerning the precyousnese of time.

Oh time, oh time, that precyous thing
How doe we wast
thee. though with hast
Thou fly'st away, upon the wing
To eternity vast   5

Wee cannot call thee, back again
yet down we sitt
and intermitt
Our work, by Childish toys, most vain
which cannot benefitt   10

What ever tis wee ar about
time will not stay
But posts away
And our short sandglase, runeth out
whether we work, or play   15

Our day is short, our work is great
what need have we
active to bee
That sin, and saten, doe not cheat
of time, which still doth flee   20

Whilst we ar sleeping, time runs on
and hastyly
away doth fly
And in itt, wee, doe glide along
into eternity   25

Shall we by recreation
and foolish play
Throw time away
Whilst we neclect salvation
the great work, of the day   30

Whilst we ar eating, drinking, we
with time pase on
and run along
Into eternity, we flee
thither, we must be gone   35

What would the damned spirits give
For one moment
of time, that's speant
If back they might but come to live
sure, they'd be diligent   40

What brainsick fools, ar we to throw   p. 218
our time aside
which will not bide
Or wait whilst we our work shall doe
but slyly on doth glide   45

How doe men hoord, and lay up gold
with heed, and care
But time most rare
(A Jewell which should, not be sold
but tresur'd up with care)   50

Away we doe, att our heels throw
and cast it by
regardlesly
Till by the want, its worth we know
when entring, on eternity   55

Could we but get, a right, insight
and come to veiw
into the true
Nature of time, upon the flight
all sloth, we would eschew   60

Help me, by grace, so to improve
my time, whilst here
in holy fear
That when I dy, I may remove
with joy, to heavens spher   65

That an abundant entrance may
then unto me
ministred bee
Into thy kingdome, att that day
where I, thy face, shall see,   70

51   The sweet benefitts, that flow from union with Christ. sep 22 72

From union, with our deerest head, & king
Most sweet comunion doth unto us, spring
By union tis, we doe atain to this
Still to pertake with Christ, of what is his
The soull, and body, of a true, sincere   5
Beleiver, now is Christs, by indenture
And tearms, of firm, agreement which we make
When we do him, as Lord, and Saviour, take
And ar by pow'r, and vertue of the godhead
Unto his humane nature united   10
This blessed union, it is misticall
Tis constant, firm, & alsoe mutuall
Christ gives himself, wholy unto the soull
The soull again, gives ittself, to him whole
It is an union neer, and intimate   15   p. 219
An union, which hels, rage, cant separate
By this it is we do pertake of grace
And glory, also, when we have run our race
By this our dust, doth to him, firmly cleave
Whilst in the grave, we doe the body leave   20
By this, we shall att last be quikened
And raysed up, & Joyn'd, unto our head
This is so great, & deep, a mistery
As cant be fathomed, by carnell eye
Tis like to the new name, and the white stone   25
Which can be read, & understood by none
By he that has it, given unto him
And reads it, by the spirits light, not dim
The saints themselfs, they cannot come to spell
This blessed mistery, fully till they dwell   30
By pow'r, & vertue, of it, up above

Where all their ignorance, shall quite remove
Oh who can chouse, but long to look, & pry
Into this blessed, glor'ous, mistery
This mistery, so full of love, & grace   35
Shown, unto Adams, lost, and sinfull race
That thou shoudst cull out, such a worthlese bride
For ever with thee, to live, & abide
And fix thy tender love, thine hart, & eye
Upon such blacknese, & deformity.   40
What praises then, can we render to thee
Unto, the ages, of eternity.

52   September 25   72

          Why sittst thou musing thus
          my soull a-way
          All cretures, ar not worth a rush
          compared with one ray
          Which from the sun of righteousnese   5
          Doth dart, upon the comfortlese

Arise, my soull, arise.
here's not thy rest
Tread under foot, earths vanitys
and hasten to thy nest   10
Of sweetnese, where, thou hapst to ly
Secure, to all eternity

Why standst thou Idle here
Arise, be gone
The day in which thou must apear   15
draws nigh, therfore goe on
Goe on apace, till in the land
Of glory, thy feett firmly stand

See what hangs o're thy head   p. 220
A glorious crown   20
And wilt thou here, upon the bed
of sloth, and ease, ly down
And not gett up for to possese
This glorious crown of hapinese

Make hast unto the goall   25
tis for a prize
Why sitst thou in this durty hold
as listlese to arise
For shame, my soull, make hast, & run
Apace, untill the prize be won   30

That glorious diadem,
and heavens crown
Tis Christ, in that Jerusalem
That sweet plant, of renown
Come then, my soull now bid adeiw   35
To this vain word, and him persue

53   The souls complaint   sep 27 72

Thou'lt scarsly let me look
but clapst the door too
And leavest not a hole, or nook
at which I may, look through
Thou givest me a tast   5
and drawst away, in hast

I cannot have my fill
of what, I somtimes see
That is reserv'd for Zion hill
then thou wilt satiete me   10
Oh let me, swiftly fly
Unto that mountain, high

This is our sowing time
we may not reap, as yet
Tis well if we, before we climb   15
a sheaf of glory gett
And may have leave to top
an ear, of the full crop

Sometimes I cant but cry
from small experience   20
Is this soe sweet, oh what shall I
enjoy, when I goe hence
And quikly I, would be
Transplanted, unto thee

I cannot but complain   25
How short thy visitts are
Thou wilt not with me, long remain
but goest e're I'me aware
A full, clear, sight of thee
Would be hev'n unto me   30

If this I must not have   p. 221
yet still encrease, my love
I know thou wilt nott always stave
me off, but wilt remove
Mee, to that place where I   35
Shall drink, eternally

54   dedication,

My hart dear Lord, itt is thine own
thou disdst itt make
Tis thine I say, and thine alone
Oh let it of thy grace pertake
and beautifie   5
it from on high

Thou calst for it, & here, I give
it up to thee
Oh let thy spirit, in it live
And purg out sin, that it may be   10
the dwelling place
of love, and grace

Acept the dedication
of this my hart
And lett it be to me made known   15
by glorys filling ev'ry part
thy love display
on it alway

55   febru: 11   72/3

Oh blessed day, when I shall still
Have my heart suted to my work
And my work, suted to thy will
Noe backwardnese, shall in me lurk
This will not be whilst I am here   5
Untill I move, in glorys spher

What ar the comforts here below
I cannot Lord, upon them live
Nothing, but what from thee doth flow
Can satisfaction, to me give   10
Poure of thy fullnese, upon me
Or call me hence, to live with thee

I am tormented, with desire
For that, which heaven only brings
Enjoyment, att which I aspire   15
let me unto it flee with wings
Oh manefest thy self to me
Or fecth me up in hast. to thee

Christ is my food, my only meat   p. 222
Ther's nothing else, will me content   20
Hunger, and want, makes greif so great
Words to exprese't I cant invent
Thy self, in thine allfulnese, give
Or take me up, with thee to live

56   mr H

My soull doth pine, and long, to be
Transplanted, Lord, up unto thee

Tis litle here, that I can get
And that doth but, my hunger whet

My sins, doe cause thee frequently   5
To hide thy face, and from me fly

But faith, would venture unto thee
Knowing in heaven I shall see

Thy face, and have my fill of love
Which makes me long, for my remove   10

Sin as a clog, whilst here, I bear
And as an Iron chain, I wear

Oh that thou wouldst lifes knot unty
That I from it, away might fly

Created comforts, ar to me   15
But drose, and dung, compar'd with thee

In thee, in thee, I would expire
The only object I admire

Oh pity Lord, a love-sick soull
Doe thou my state, sweetly condole   20

And take mee up, with thee to dwell
Out of this dark, and durty, cell

But stay a while, what's this I hear
Thers one that would put me in fear

As if in longing, to be gone   25
I were, most grosly, in the wrong

Now though my hart, doth sink, and ake
This frame, I am loth to forsake

I cant but crave, to make defence
For this, my chousest evedence   30

Of love to Christ, which first must flow
From his own love, and out on't grow

Pray let me reason, yet a while
Ere you of this, doe me beguile

Must saincts, with this world, fall in love   35
And be unwilling to remove

From hence, to that celestiall Spher   p. 223
'Cause they ar capeble whilst here

Of doing that, for god which they
Cannot, when hence, they ar cald away   40

Can sinfull praise, more honour bring
Then sinlese praise, unto our king

Cause faith is good, unto that state
of love, and of imediate

Enjoyment, may we not aspire   45
And bend to it, with strong desire

Can we a person, love endeed
And not make out, with hast, and speed

To meet the only object of,
Our deerest, and intirest, love   50

Can any thing, we have acquir'd
Make our. imperfect stat desir'd

Then worthy sir, why do you say
Tis good to live, here many a day

Ar ther soe many, in the throng   55
Of this world, that, doe truly long

In their redeemers arms to lye
That you should thus, att them let fly

Discouraging them in ther race
To the fruition, of his face   60

The most I think, soe much desire
Long life, you had more need to fire

Them, out of ther poluted nest
That they may seek, a better rest

But as for those, that have a sight   65
And tast, of Christ, there harts delight

All your perswasions ar in vain
To make them wilingly, remain

In this sad, distant, absent, state
Your arguments ar come to late   70

Ther harts they ar already gone
To'th object, they would live upon

And tis beyound your skill, to tole
Ther harts back, to this durty hole

You may perhaps, doe good on those   75
That never smelt, sweet Sharons Rose

Experience of the best of saincts   p. 224
Which on the earth, have had their haunts

You seem by this, for to condemne
Whilst you such durt, to throw on them   80

As if they were, grown weary of,
Ther work, and therfore, would remove

To Judg the hart, you should beware
To god alone, is this made bare

And those whom you, condemne, he will   85
Shortly, acquit, on Zion hill

And call that love, which you call Laze
Making, ther troubled souls, amaize

Hath not st paull. (now Lodg'd above)
Pronounc'd them bles'd, who truly love.   90

The sweet apearing, of the Lord
Is it not down, upon record,

That truly, blessed, ar the dead
Which in Christs, arms, have laid ther head

Doth not the whole creation, cry   95
And groan, and wait, for liberty

Ar we not said, in tents of clay
To long for that most glorious day

When absent from the body we
Shall present, with Christ Jesus be   100

May not the church, ernestly cry
Why stays his char'ot whells, oh why

Do they not run amain. Ag'en
Come quikly, Lord Jesus amen

By gods own word, I will abide   105
And by that, shall my cause be try'd

If that acquits, I will not care
Though men condemne, they shall not scare

The church crys out, Lord Jesus come
Amen, say I, & fecth me home   110

That I may fully, thee, enjoy
And no sin, may my soull anoy

Tis Christ alone, that I desire
To be with him, I will aspire

And will not care, what man can say   115
But hast, to an eternall day.

57   The souls strength only in god,   p. 225

Lord I have none, but thee on earth
Thou art my hope, my strength, my stay
Whilst I am in, this land of dearth
Leave me not, one step of my way

My gasping soull, doth reach, and pant   5
That itt of thee, might have its fill
Waiting, untill thou doe transplant
It up unto, thy holy hill

Tis sweet on thee, to hang, and cry
As on the mother, doth the Child   10
Oh let me on thy strength rely
And then, I know, I sha'nt be foyl'd

Lett me not from thee, start aside
Or once of thee, let goe my hold
But doe thou by me, still abide   15
And in thyne arms, my soull enfold

58   The soull complaint, being greatly perplexed. May 6:73

What cloudynese, hath me possest
What dis-mall fears, do fill my breast

What Jealousies, doth me surround
And cause my greif, for to abound

Love unto Christ, is cal'd self love   5
And that which came not, from above

Sence of sloth, and, cecurity
Augments, my fears, and Jealousies

Saten, doth Joyne, his force, with fear
No Joy, or comfort, doth apear   10

I think that alls, hipocrisie
Soe fair, and spleanded, to the eye

Fears doe arise, to such a height
As quite, to overtop, my faith

My hart doth sink, and dy away   15
For want, of an enlightning ray

Somtimes, I think, that thou wilt take
Each talent, & me quite forsake

My mouth is stopt, and all that I   p. 226
Can doe, is for to Justifie   20

Thy dealings with me, though I dwell
For ever, in the lowest hell

Wishing that there, I might but love
And praise, the god, that dwels above

But fears of hell. doe not molest   25
Although, my soull be sore oprest

Nay comfort, will not me content
Desire is not, upon it bent

I cant upon a litle live
Abundance of thy self then give   30

It tis perfection, I desire
att full enjoyment, I aspire

Till fully thou, thy self impart
I feell a restlese, dying, hart

Except from sin, I could be free   35
And keep a constant sight of thee

I look not to find comfort here
Whilst in, this lower hemispher

Charge me not with unthankfullnese
I know, I cannot, cry, guiltlese   40

But pity Lord, a gasping soull
Oh come thy self, and fill that hole

Which thou hast made, and thou alone,
What thou hast done, do not disown

59   may 7 73 Faiths triumph, over temptation.

Whilst by temptation, I am tri'd
I shall from drose, be purifi d'

When, thou shalt bring, me forth as gold
Thy meaning I shall then unfold

Ther's no afliction, that doth seem   5
Joyous, att present, nay we deem

It griveous, although therby
Thou dost refine, and purifie

Tis Sattens busy time, and hee
Will not, one moment, Idle bee   10

The neerer his time's att an end   p. 227
The thicker he his darts will send

To keep from heaven hel endevour
Or else he'l send us weeping, thither

Hee is from heaven quite cast down   15
And envies us the glorious crown

And though he cant us, of it rob
Hee'l make our harts to ake, and throp

He'l represent that to our sight
That may amaize us, and afright   20

Hee'l raise a mist, before our eyes
And throw such fears, and Jealousys

Of god, and of his love designs
As shall distract, our harts, and minds

Whilst malice he on us doth shoure   25
God doth make use, of it, to scoure

The saincts, and make them shine more bright
Ere they, to heaven, take their flight

Then from his rage, for ever they
Shall be set free, and still display   30

The riches of, that grace wherby
They have atain'd, the victory

Oh hasten Lord, that blessed time
When I thy holy hill shall climb

Hee shall not then again molest   35
But I from him, shall be att rest

I shall be for his reach, too high
No dart of his can thither fly

60   May 12   73

My soull, art heaven-born then be sublime
And up unto itt, in affection climb

Thou wert not made, in dunghills for to rake
But of the devine nature, to pertake

The world shall shortly, in whit ashes lye   5
With all its beauty, and its braviry

Oh wilt thou fix thine. hart, and eye upon
That which shall soe soon, wear out, & be gone.

And not with care, and diligence make sure   p. 228
Of'a crown, and kingdome. which shall still endure   10

This world att best, is but a durty hole
Unsutable, to an immortall soull

Whose Larg capacytys, can only be
Satisfi'd and fil'd with a deity

This world was ne're, intended for thy rest   15
And wilt thou here erect, & build, thy nest

It is thine inne, to Lodg in for a night
Oh use itt soe, and disappountments slight

As knowing itt is not thy home, only
A baiting place, towards eternity   20

Pack up with hast, & speed, for thy remove
Unto thy house, & countrey, up above

Thou art impris'ned in a tent of clay
Yet mayst thou look, & long, for that sweet day

When death shall ope the door, & let thee fly   25
Unto a sinlese, immortalyty.

Take heed of sleeping, when the bridgroom shall
Come, thee, unto the marraige feast, to call

Gett oyl, to make thy lamp burn clear, & bright
That when he comes, thou mayst to him, take flight   30

And enter with him, for to solemnize
The marraige feast, among the truly wise

Stand therfore, with thy loyns, fast girt about
Still att the door wacthing, and crying out

Oh when, oh when, will my sweet bridgroom come   35
To consumate the macth, and fecth me home

And in the meane time, as heir to a crown
Scorn once, to any base work, to stoop down

Oh live as one, thats truly heaven-born
Who doth all sublunary, glorys, scorn   40

As knowing they, cannot compared be
With that which is reserv'd, in heaven for thee

61   Wonders & misterys of devine love   p. 229

Oh strang, oh wonderfull
Ther is no reason given why
Thou shouldst not let, thy creture lye
Among the sons, of Adams race
Who did fall, from thy love, and grace   5
From them, thou givst a pull

It makes me stand amaysd
When I somtimes, doe lett thoughts run
Upon the work, that thou hast done
Whilst with amaizment, I doe see   10
Thy love, and grace. which flows soe free
Therby my wonder's rays'd

Oh separating love
Oh rich, free, distinguishing grace
Whilst others, ar in the same case   15
Plunged, as deep in misery
Yet they ar left, in it to ly
Whilest love, thy bonds, remove

On deep, cals to another
Whilst we electing love, do veiw   20
Unto thy litle flock, and few
Oh mistery, deep, and profound
Oh depths of love, which none can sound
Why me, & not the other

How greatly this doth fill   25
The hart, with love, when seriously
We on thesse wonders, look, & pry
This makes us long, for to begin
Our hymes. of love, and praise, to sing
on Zions cacred hill.   30

62   Experience. may 23 73

What mistery,
is this I spy
My hart was in me, sunk, and dead
Because of sin, which captive led
And when temptation, did surround   5
Thy love, and grace, did superabound

I was afraid   p. 230
And in hart, said
Now look for nothing, but displeasure
And anger, in a fivefold measure   10
Because temptations, they did storm
And deviations, they did swarm

But whilst that I
For victory
Was att a strife, thou didst reveill   15
The truth of grace, and to it seall
It was not comfort, that did flow
Or high joys, that thou didst bestow

It gave releife,
In midst of greife   20
Whilst sin, more bitter, was then hell
Longing out of this durty cell
Of misery, for to be gone
Fainting, for thy salvation

Whilst love did flow   25
encrease, and grow
Whilst hapynese, and heavens blise
Was nothing to me, without this
A liknese unto him, I love
Which made me, restlese, to remove   30

Unto the praise
Of grace alwais
Efections, answerable wear
So strong, I hardly them, could bear
My hart, was brok, for fear that I   35
Should'be long under, sins tiranny

I never should
Nor never would
Forget this token of thy grace
Which may support me, in my race   40
When Saten shall, as frequently
He doth charge, with hipocrisie

Its strang to me
When I do see
That'th more that sin, in me bare sway   45
The more, thou didst thy grace display
outshooting Saten, in his bow
Breaking the darts, that he did throw

th' Glory of all   p. 231
now surely shall   50
Be given unto thee, alone
My sweet, and blessed, only one
Compleat thy work, now speedyly
And fitt me, for, eternity

63   may 28   73   The soull wondring itt can get no more. seeing
ther is such a fullnese in god and grace is free.

What is the reason, I can gett no more
Seeing ther is, such an, abundant store
Of grace, to be, extended free
To thosse, that for it, come to thee
From thy rich tresurys   5
Of sutable subplys
Oh why doe I
with hunger dye

Somtimes I think, if thou shouldst give me much
That sure, for prid, I should be, a non-such   10
But then I know, that thou canst take
Away pride, and me humble make
This then can be no let
When thou thy grace, shalt set
On work, for mee   15
to set me free

Sometimes I think, itt is for want of faith
That I cannot attain unto that height
Of love, and grace, at which I ayme
Oh glorifie, thy holy name   20
And give such faith wherby
I with activity
And strength of grace
may run, my race

Sometimes I think, tis spirituall sloth   25
Because I d'ont my uttmost strength, put forth
Thou wilt not me, with victory crown
Whilst I, thus lasily, sit down
The slothfull mans desire
Do kill, and soe expire   30
Oh draw thou me
I'de run, to thee

Oh that thou wouldst, be pleas'd to shew thy skill   p. 232
And not thy pow'r, only, but alsoe will
I know that thou canst for me doe   35
Great things, and ev'ry lett, break through
be pleas'd on me, to shine
And by thy rays, devine
make grace, to spring
and cast out sin   40

64   The souls, longings to be gone. with the reasons of itt.

Oh when shall I
to heaven fly
And mount above, the starry sky

I'de run apace
to see that face   5
Soe full of beauty, and of grace

I'me sick of love
For a remove
Unto thy self, who dwelst above

Oh come away   10
make no delay
Hasten my much, desired day

Sin haunteth mee
I cant be free
When shall I, from this tirant flee   15

This enemy
I cannot fly
Untill thou doe, lifes knot. unty

I moane, and pine
For fear the time   20
Should yet be long, e're I doe climb

Up unto thee
That I may see
Thy face, and be from sin, set free

I'me sore opprest   25
and find no rest
To be with thee, I know tis best

Give me my fill   p. 233
On Sion hill
Thy long delays, doe even kill   30

Thy worthlesse bride
would fain abide
Where her deer bridgroom, doth reside

Temptation.
doth on me throng   35
Which makes me think, thine absence long

Coruption, doth
whilst here bud forth
And grace, is att, imperfect growth

Sin, that doth clip   40
my wing, and nip
My joys, att best, ar but a sip

Desertions be
frequent, with me
An unveil'd face, I'de always see   45

For'a perfect state
I long, and waitt.
As pris'ners that look through the grate

65   may 30 73 The soull in overwhelming perplexety

T'was sweet with me, when I
could think, that I should ly
quikly, in my redeemers, arms
Out of the reach, of sinfull harms
But those blest days, ar gone, and past   5
Thy sky is black, and overcast

Tis now far otherwise
my hart within me dys
I am more fitt each day for hell
Then with a holy god, to dwell   10
Though righteousnese, I look for none
To Justifie, but Christs alone

Thou canst no sin, evence   p. 234
Who art thy self soe pure
If thou for mee, hast any love   15
This frame of hart thou wilt remove
From this vile drose thou'lt separate
And ripen, for a sinlese state

I'me dayly worse, & worse
I think, neer to some curse   20
Find out a way, to kill each sin
Though in the room, thou should send in
The heaviest affliction
Hell, would be heav'n in comparation

My hart doth gad, and stray   25
From thee, each hour and day
A holy hart, I doe desire
Oh give me this, and I'le admire
Thy love, and grace, continually
Both here, and to eternity   30

Thy grace which runs soe free
Oh poure it out, on me
Where ar thy earning bowels, Lord
Thy faithfullnese, is on record
Have I out sin'd whats infinet   35
Thy love, and grace, is boundlese yet

How long, shall saten foyle
And sin polute, & soyle
No wonder thou, thy self dost hide
Can holynese, it self abide   40
On such a dung hill, for to shine
By influencyall rays, devine.

66   No rest below perfection, June 3 73

I could complain
but yet I hardly dare
Of unthankfullnese, I would beware
I dont deserve the least
Yett ev'ry day, I fain would feast   5

My wants encrease
and hunger that doth grow
What e're thou dost on me bestow
No comfort I espye
In what I Joy'd in formerly   10

Oh weary life   p. 235
Thou holdest to my veiw
Somthing that is unto me new
and lovly to the eye
Which makes me reach out restlesly   15

It to attain.
And if thou dost bestow
It upon me, desires to grow
and whilst on want, I pore
I am as restlese, as before   20

However Lord.
I would not be deny'd
This frame, whilst to the body ty'd
Tis all my comfort here
Till, I get my fill, of heavens chear   25

67   The souls desire, June 6   73

A burning beacon, of pure love
Still strongly, flaming up to thee
I'de be, untill thou doe remove
Mee up, where love. shall perfect be

This grace of love, is mine eye   5
The thing, I greatly doe desire
For itt the richest pearls, should lye
Under my feett, as durt, and mire

I will desire no greater pleasure
Then in thesse flames, of love to ly   10
I will seek for, noe richer tresure
Then. wings of love, wheron to fly

If thou'lt not fill me to the brim
Whilst here, oh hasten my remove,
Unto that place, where I shall swim   15
In seas, of pure, unmixed, love

68   An occationall addition June 16   73

Oh let my flames, of love burn pure
Unmixed, from self love, that when
The triell comes, it may endure
Thy own work, thou wilt not condemne

It is a comfort to apeall.   5   p. 236
To thee, the searcher of all harts
who wilt att that great day reveall
thosse inward, hiden, cecreet parts

That I esteem pure love, to thee
A heaven, in the midst of hell   10
Though thou shouldst never smile on me
Or take me up, with thee to dwell

To thee, tis sweet, to make my moane
When overwhelm'd in depths of greife
In'th throng of cretures, I find none   15
That yeeld me any, true releife

Thou never art, so sweet to me
As when thesse sumer brooks ar dry
Whilst thou therby, art teaching me
That'th best of men, are vanity   20

Ther's nothing then to interpose
And keep me, from, a full, clear, sight
Of'th beauty of that fairest Rose
That is both heaven, and earths delight

Yett with high joys, thou feedst me not   25
Thosse daintys, ar to good for me
And thosse that think, they ar my lot
They doe mistake me, utterly

For hunger, is my only feast
And pationet desires, for more   30
Which by denialls, ar encreast
Whilst on my wants, I dayly pore

Break thou mine Idols, then that I
May dote no more, on them henceforth
But wind my soull, still up on high   35
And ripen, to a perfect growth

69   Grace better then peace   June 22 73

Oh what is peace, compar'd with grace
Though I ne're see good day
Whilst runing, in, my weary race
thy grace, in me display

I'de rather have, much holynese   5   p. 237
That like thee, I might grow
Then for to have the fullest mese
of comfort, on me flow

I would have both, Lord, if I might
that I thy praise, may sound   10
But if thou shalt deny, the light
of joy, lett grace abound

If thou seest fitt, for to refuse
both, on me to bestow
Grace is the thing, that I doe chouse   15
though I in sorrow sow

I'de rather have, but litle peace
and grace, in a full measure
Desiring it may still encrease
unto a richer tresure   20

Then to have joy, fill full my cup
and have but litle grace
The lese I have, the more s laid up
'gainst I have run my race

Lett me soe thrive, in holynese   25
I may'nt be leane, & lank,
I'de trust thee, with my hapynese
to store itt up, in bank

70   June 23   73   Satens spight.

Oh why am I
Soe frequently
Foyld, by temptation small
wilt thou stand by
and yet deny   5
To help, me when I call

No cause, to boast
when I have most
For then be sure, I meet
with Satens spight   10
to's unmost might
for to ensnare, my feett

I will aspire   p. 238
and doe desire
Much of thee, to enjoy   15
But still I find
when thou'rt most kind
That saten will anoy

When grace is clear
and doth apear   20
In brightest, evedence
That to be sure
he cant endure
But with all diligence

He'l make us blot   25
and soe, bespot
Our evedence, that we
May'nt have a sight
Of what.s our right
through grace, and mercy, free   30

Oh now step in
my god, and king
And bind up saten, in thy chaine
that he no more, / may rob the store
That thou shalt give to me again   35

The god of peace
shall make to cease
His rage. when he sees meet
remember Lord
thy faithfull word   40
And tread him, under feet

His rage though great
doe thou defeat
And bring much good to me
that I, always   45
may sing, the praise
of grace, and love soe free

71   perticular meditations. June 24   73

Why ask you me, what tis that I would have
What would content, what is the thing I'de crave

I have, soe frequently found it in vain
To moane to man, I think I sha'nt again

Why should I when I may, have free accese   5
To him who only, can my wants, redrese

Yet let not Satten, think hereby to gain   p. 239
For if he doe, through grace, he'l lose his aym

This, resolution, shall not make me keep
His counsell, least he bring to sorrows deep   10

But to begin, where first I left, tis not
Earths hapynese, I can take as my lott

Of grace, & holynese, I'de have as much
As ever any had, and still keep touch

As to atainments, with the best of thine   15
Who in the world, as lights did ever shine

The excelencys, of each sev'rall sainct
(which has, or ever once here, had ther haunt)

Compris'd in one, is that I would obtain
And what was wanting in them, that I'de gain   20

And if to this, I might atain, itt will
Not doe. I know I shall be empty still

Whilst sweet perfection, hovers in mine eye
And full enjoyment, that behind doth lye

Yett Lord. I know I am unworthy of   25
The Least by dropings, of thy grace, & love

That which thine own, deer Children leave behind
I dont deserve, either to take, or find

But why should this put cheak, to my desire
Where not grace free, I durst not thus aspire   30

But now I cant contentedly sitt down
Untill I come, to reach. the glorious crown

The crown, of blessed, sweet perfection
When with my house, from my he'ven Ime cloth'd upon

I cant here hit the mark, oh let me fly   35
With hast to'a sinlese immortalyty.

72   lett your light so shine, before men that they may see, your
good works and glorifie your father which is in heaven. June 24   73

I know when I   p. 240
to heaven fly
I shall be like thee then
Oh let, me heare
thine image bear   5
Among, the sons of men

Thy holy name
I'de praise the same
Whilest lasts my short lifes lease
When in the grave   10
a place, I have
This work, shall wholy cease

I cannot speak
untill I break
Through sinfull modesty   15
Tis 'to hard for mee
But not for thee
Do thou, my tounge unty

Find out some way
wherby I may   20
Be of some use, whilst here
Till thou shalt call
mee hence, and shall
Fix me in heavens sphere

By rays devine   25
let me soe shine
That I may glorifie
Thy love, and grace
throughout my race
And to eternity.   30

73   The devills picture, June 25

Why lookst thou, with a grudging eye
On those, that have atainments high
This weed, impure
god wont endure

Shall worthlese clay, att him repine   5
Who seeth fitt for to refine
thosse, hee intends
for higher ends

Why wouldst thou have, none better then
Thy self, among the sons, of men   10
Sure this doth smell
too strong of hell.

p. 241

What wouldst thou shine, thy self alone
And in the world, wouldst thou have none
with thee to vie   15
for sanctity

Why fearest thou, others should be
More holy, then thy self, and see
more of the love
of god, above   20

Oh what art thou, thus to aspire
Who art far worse, then durt, and mire
unworthy of
a look of love

Oh Saten, I doe somtimes see   25
My self, by this, soe like to thee
that I doe hate.
my self, and state

And if I knew, which way to run,
From itt, away, I would be gone,   30
This dismall sight,
itt doth, soe fright.

74   June 25   73

For what thou givst, I'le thankfull be
And what thou dost, deny to mee
sence of the want of itt
shall make me, att thy feet

To ly low, in humility   5
Plunging, in self abhorrancy
as unworthy, to be
once, looked att by thee

Those that doe nothing, (Lord) deserve
Should humbly take, what thou dost carve   10
always adoring thy
free, soveraignity

Nought, I can chaleng att thy hand   p. 242
Or in the least, of thee demand
what e're thou givest me   15
alls from thy bounty, free

Oh lett not poor, and worthlese clay
Contend with him, who doth display
his grace, as he sees fitt.
And none, may question itt.   20

Let not proud dust, contest again
with him, who doth, & still, will reign
and deall out unto men
what he sees good, and when.

I should despair, of much from thee   25
But that thy grace, is purely free
and thou somtimes dost take
The vilest, for to make

Thy glory shine. conspicuously
Unto the eyes, of standers-by   30
I will not then despair,
To feed on nobler fare.

Thy promise, thou wilt not forget.
To thosse whose apitites, ar whet,
Whosse hungry souls, cant rest,   35
Till filled, with the best.

The hungry, thou wilt surely fill,
And if not heare, on Zion hill,
Thou hast laid up in store,
For thosse, that long for more.   40

75   June 26   73

To man, att first. thou didst dispence
A law, of pure, obedience

T'was personall, and perfect too
And universall, runing through

Each precept of, thy blessed will   5
Which thou requirst, we should fullfill

Yett leaving man to liberty
The devill, with malicious eye

Did by his subtle, wiles creep in   p. 243
And our first parents, quikly bring   10

With all ther sad posterity
Into all kinnd, of misery

Yet love, & grace, made no delay
But lookt about, to find a way

Our liberty, for to restore   15
And fix it faster, then before

By putting itt, into the hand
Of Christ, we now more firmly stand

Hee came into the world, to doe
Thy will, and alsoe suffer to   20

Hee fully answer'd thy demands
And now by thee, acquited stands

T'was he the dept, did fully pay
And Justise, hath no more to say

But from a foe, is turn'd our freind   25
Our cause to plead, and to defend

And god is Just, in pardoning sin
To his, as well, as punishing.

And pouring wrath, down upon those
That this remi'ding law oppose   30

Doth Saten, fresh inditments bring
From new, out breakings of thy sin

This cant make void, or nulifie
That cov'nant, which to Christ doth tye

His bloud is of the same force still   35
As when att first, he did it spill

He upon whom, our sins ar lain
A sacrifice, doth still remain

How happy then ar thosse, who be
Secure, by cov'nant right to thee   40

Tis easy in notions to fly
But hard, oh hard, for to aply

From unbeleife, do thou repreive
And make me, savingly, beleive

76   June 26 73   two foes.   p. 244

This world, and I, can nere agree
I wonder what's the matter
I frown on it, and itt on me
Wee dont, each other flatter
Wee ne're can cotten long togather   5
Oh when wilt thou, two foes disever

I'me far more fearfull of its smiles
then of its lowring looks
Oh keep me, from its subtle wiles
and its deceitfull hooks   10
Not by its smile, nor by itts frown
Lett me, e're to itt once bow down

I think, I care, as litle for itt
as itt can doe for me
Could I but once, out of it get   15
I'de gladly. from it, flee
And hope with joy, from itt to goe
When thou its gates, shalt open throw

Tis still to me, an enemy,
and slyly seeks to kill   20
Yea from my tender infancy
It still, did thawrt, my will
T'was well, I found, from itt, such measure
Which fixt my love, upon durable tresure

It hates because the god above   25
(I hope) hath out on't chose
If soe, a fig, a straw, for its love
What care I, though it oppose
lett it with sorrow, fill my cup
Thou wilt outt of itt call me up   30

Ther's none that have, more cause then I
to 'be thankfull unto thee
For writing on it vanity
and imbitt'ring it to me
I care not what from itt, I find   35
If up my hart, to thee thou'lt wind.

77   Death no respecter of p'ersons   p. 245

Death, he doth make. no diferance
Between the pesant, and the prince

Vain beauty he doth not respect
The crys of youth, he doth reject

It overtakes the young, and swift   5
And from the rich, receives no gift

It makes, the strongest hart, to yeeld
And where itt comes, still wins. the feild

His arows first, or last, they shall
Reach unto all, both great, and small   10

He shrinks not from the statly crown
But in the dust, he throws itt down

No sort, no quality, or age
But must come forth, for to engage

And graple with this enemy   15
Who will att last, lifes knot unty

But yet this. foe, hath lost his sting
And unto thine no harm, doth bring

Whilst hee o'recomes them in the strife
Hee lets them into endlese life   20

And to the fill enjoyment of
The object of ther deerest love

I will stile thee, (if it be soe)
No more, a tirant, and a foe

But thou shalt be, my welcome guest   25
A freind, most greatly in request

78   A chearfull countenance, the duty of gods, people, June 28   73

Why walkst thou droupingly
Dost thou not know each carnall eye
Will take ofence, and vainly think
Ther brutish swill is better drink
Then what thou hast to live upon   5
if thou walk sadly on

p. 246

They cannot see thy hart
Or come to pry, into that part
None knows what's there, but god, and thee
Wilt thou lett others in to see 10
And give to them free enterance
by thy sad countenance

Besides all this itt will
Thy gracious god, dishonour still
Whilst thou dost make, the world to take 15
Up prejudice, & soe forsake
God, and his plesent ways
Robing him, of his praise

My soull henceforth be shy
And still avoid most carefully 20
Whatever may occation give
To make the world think that do live
And lead a life of holinese
is vain, and comfortlese

Look with a plesant face 25
What e're thou meetst with in thy race
Least others in their harts doe say
That they shall never see good day
If they their vanitys forsake
And to a holy life betake 30

Oh shew thy love in this
In rendering thosse ways of his
So sweet & lovly to the eye
Of those that ar but standers by
That they from sin may be drawn off 35
And on him fix their love,

79   June 29: 73 - worlds deceitfullness

Oh pitifull empty world, & vain
unworthy thou'rt of
The least of our love
By loving of thee, oh what doe we gain
But great pain, & smart   5
Which reaches, the hart

Who can thy trechery, (world) endure   p. 247
It is still thy way
to kise, and betray
Thou'lt leave us then, in the lurch to be sure   10
when we, unto thee
for succour, doe flee

What doe thy flaterers get att the last
when conscience doth nip
thou'lt give them, the slip   15
When they doe most need thee, then thou wilt cast
them off, and look shy,
with distainfull eye

Thou wilt forsake, even those that doe thee
as their god avouch   20
and bow down, and cructh
How then should they, from thy malice be free
who still to defame
thy beauty, and name

Thou art but a meer, base Jugle att best   25
deceiving the eye
by varnish, & dye
Ther's nothing but falsnese, hid in thy breast
for when thou dost smile
tis but, to beguile   30

If this bee thy triks, then world farwell
I'le trust thee, no more
but get up, and soare
Thou art att best, but a durty cell
a prison to me   35
from which, I'de be free

80   July 1   73

Oh why wilt thou, leave sin in thine
who couldst soe easily.
Att first, make grace, in them to shine
and from those bonds, unty
The methouds of thy grace, ar high   5
Above the reach of our weak eye

Tis this will keep us, humble here.   p. 248
and nip pride, att the root
These wintor blasts, our sins breeds fear
and lays us, att thy foot   10
Wee cant whilst here, reach thy design
But up above, thy grace shall shine

By this thou wilt encrease, the dept
of thankfullnese, and praise
When we through grace, to heaven gett   15
and on these wonders gaze
Thou wilt then wipe sin, off the score
And wilt remember itt, no more

81   gods promise put the soull into a firmer better state, then any
thing of merit could doe, July 2

Though by desert, we nothing claime
Yet promise free, makes itt the same

And what by merit, we cant reach
Thy faithfullnese, to plead will teach

Thy promise, is a surer ground   5
Then any meritt, can be found

By promise stablish'd in the hand
Of Christ, we now more, firmly stand

In our converses mediate
Then Adam, in his sinlese state   10

A promise we may feast upon
When outward comforts, we have none

The heirs of promise, happy are
And feed upon, delicious fare

The heirs of promise, they cannot   15
(Though all the world against them plot)

Be brought to totall misery
For why, ther comforts ar so high

And in the promise, lokt so fast
They cant out from their right be cast   20

Tis better have a promise gaurd   p. 249
Then all the world, keep wacth, and ward

Thosse that know how, for to improve
By faith, a promise, may remove

With ease, all anxtious thoughts that may   25
Molest, or trouble, in their way

May I but in the bosome, lye
Of a promise, I shall then defie

The base, and subtle, enterprise
Of my most cruell enemies   30

In this sweet priviledg invest
And give to me an interest

In promises, through Christ alone
And I've enough to live upon

A promise, that will cary through   35
This world, untill we reach unto

The port of glory, where we shall
The crop, & harvest, reap of all

That which in them, has been laid up
Shall then, be wrung into our cup.   40

82   An addition of wonder.

But why shouldst thou such grace bestow
And bind thy self by promise soe

That wee may now our right demand
(Though not from meritt) att thy hand

By promise thou a deptor then   5
Art now become to sinfull men

Who were in dept, soe far before
And can soe greatly, on the score

That ages of eternity
Could nere hav clear'd us thorowly   10

If thou hadst only sett us free
From dept t'had been great grace in thee

But that thou shouldst become to us   p. 250
A deptor, this should make us blush

How doth thy grace, and love, shine forth   15
In giving both, thy word, & oath

That those that unto thee belong
Might have strong consolation

From each ofence, thou dost discharge
And unto us givst bonds, of large   20

Donations, which thou wilt bestow
Both here, and when from hence we goe

Each of our depts, thou dost remove
Wee owe thee, nothing now, but love

And filliall obedience   25
Which thou hast promis'd to dispence

And give to us, that we may bring
It unto thee, our sacred king

And here we shall, run on in dept
If we, through grace, to heaven get   30

Whilst we the fruit of love, shall reap
And thou new favours, still shalt heap

Our depts shall grow, & multiply
To'th ages of eternity

83   Infinet love, & grace.   July 2 73

If thou from hell, hadst only set
Us free. twere mercy. infinete
to those, who did rebell
But love, and grace, breaks through each let
and o're the banks did swell.   5

Thy love that rose exceeding high
In sending down, thy son to dye
our depts, for to discharg
And set, our soulls, att liberty
to walk in postures larg   10

If thou hadst only to the race
of sinfull Adam, shew'd this grace
To Let them still live here
Though they should n'e're have seen thy face
or in thy sight, apear   15

This had been sure, a mercy great   p. 251
But oh loves vigour, strength, & heat
to these who from thee fell
That thou shouldst them, in heaven seat
that they, with thee, might dwell   20

If thou for many yeers hadst let
us ly in hell, t'were infinet
mercy in thee, if then
Thou shouldst att last, forgive the dept
unto the sons, of men   25

But that thou shouldst now nulifie
And quite make void, the penallty
and that just law, recinde
Wherby we were condemn'd, to dy
when we in Adam sin'd   30

Is such a mercy, that should wee
In nothing else, employed be
then in't to search, and pry
It would be work enough, to see
into, this mistery   35

This condescending love of thine
Which thou hast made, in us to shine
we cannot but admire
And dayly long, in praise, to Joyne
with the unsuiing quire.   40

84   severity in love, better than prosperity in anger July 3 73

How often dost thou strik our fingers off
From thosse delights, on which we set much love
Somtimes thou takst them quite away from us
And dost att once our I'dols, kill, and crush
Somtimes, thou dost to us imbitter it   5
And that way makst us, losser from it sitt
By that time we ar wean'd from them a while
Soon after, somthing else, doth us, beguile
And slyly steall away, from thee our hart
And of our love, itt takes away thy part   10
So that thy love, is forced to begin
Again, with us, and put a smartter sting
Into the thing, wee dote upon that we   p. 252
May off from it, be drawn again to thee
Thus wee doe cut out, sad work for our selfs   15
Whilst we like weak, and silly, foolish elves
Do still against, thy love, & wisedome strive
As if we better knew, how to contrive
Whilst we might live, both free, from toyle & care
By leaving all, att gods dispose, we are   20
And doe our selfs, disquiet, & molest
For that which is but vanity, att best
I rather chouse, in love, to be deni'd
And stript of all. then to be soe fast ty'd
To any thing, that itt should hinder me   25
In the outgoings of my soull to thee
Tis better thou out of our hands shouldst strick
What e're is deer, then keep't with thy dislike
I'de rather upon bread, & watter live
Then thou in anger, shouldst unto me give   30
Any enjoyment, that may separate
My soull from thee, in this my present state
Or in the least, should clog, or hinder me
In my swift motion, to eternity

85   Oh bring my will soe, fully ore to thine
        That I no more may know a will of mine
     If mine in competition, with thee stand
Oh tread itt down, and gett the uper hand
And never give, me, my desires but when   5
They'r suted to thy holy will, and then
Though my desires, they, may not granted be
I know, I shall have, what is best for me
Do thou my will, soe fully bow, & bend
That I may ne're for itt, with thee, contend   10
And then if what thou dost, I do not vill
I know I cant, but come, to have my will
Ther shall be no appearance, then of strife
(Whose will shall stand) throughout the course of life
For when my will, in thine is swalowed   15
To all felicyty, I shall be led
Till unto this, I come, I ne're shall know
The sweetnese, which from such a life shall flow
Or practically, Learn what doth belong   p. 253
To that sweet art, of contentation   20

86   July 4   73

A stranger: in a sorry inne
will sooner Lodg, & rest
Then venture, to a forain king
being an unknown guest
His princely, liberality   5
He dares not trust, unto, or try

But unto one, he dos know well
att any time, he'l goe
Yett never will he care to dwell
with one, he dos not know   10
Those that from thee, estranged bee
They cant desire, to live with thee

Oh let me soe, familiarly
be, acquanted with thee here
That I into eternity   15
may venture, without fear
As knowing him, to my freind
To whom I shall, through grace, ascend

Let no day passe, wherin I may
not see new tokens of   20
Thy grace, & love, that in that day
when I shall hence remove
I may not be afraid to leave
This world which doth me still deceive

Give in such new discoverys   25
to me that dayly I
May long to soare, above, the skys
in thy sweet arms, to ly
Breaking through all, with speed to be
Ingulph'd & swalow'd, up in thee   30

87   What thou, through riches of free grace
Hast thrown to me, in this my race

Oh take itt not, away again
Till I, to my, desires attain

I think the mercy, now to rare   5
And sitting down, of it despair

I am both hartlese, & dismaid
Because the mercy, is delay'd

Which I did once most restlesly   p. 254
Long for to see, and to espy   10

And like to one, whose hopes ar gone
I think tis vain, to hope, and long

For that which seems, farther to get
Whilst my desires, ar on itt set

Somtimes, I think, that Saten hath   15
An hand in itt, to weaken faith

And also slaken diligence
That when thou callest me, from hence

I may be unprepar'd to dye
And unfitt, for eternity   20

What's his design, I do not know
But thou who knowst, wilt over throw

What he against me, doth devize
And bring to nought, his enterprize

Thou'lt surely for me, undermine   25
Each stratagem, and each design

He shall be troden down att last
Thy promise free, has bound thee fast

To give to me, the victory
O're him, and ev'ry enemy.   30

88   Romans 8 28 v   July 4

All things, togather, work for good
To them, that doe unfeinedly
Love god, and are redeem'd by bloud
And called from eternity
in'th cecreet purpose of   5
his rich, free grace, and love

Oh what a well of water's hear
A well of life, I may stile itt
The spring it is, both pure, and clear
And we att it, may freely sitt   10
tis full unto the brink
yet only faith can drink

All things shall work. if all then sin
The worst of evills, worse then hell
An antidote from it, thou'lt bring   15
It self, in time, for to expell
And work out, by degrees
Its cursed dregs, and lees

All things shall work for good, if soe   p. 255
then triells, and afliction   20
Shall make our graces, thrive, and grow
Though here, they may, make us look wan
Thou'lt by them purifie
And then, thou'lt throw them by

All things shall work for good, to thine   25
Temptations, and Satens rage
Whilst he against them, doth combine
Thou wilt for them, thy power engage
to keep them from a fall
and doe them good, by all   30

Desertions, and thy very frown
Shall bring much good, to thine elect
Whilst they doe humble, and cast down
Thou wilt therby in them erect
a greater value of   35
thy favour, face, and love

Thosse evills, that cant be withstood
And providences, most adverse
Shall unto thine, work out much good
Whilst in the world, they doe commerse   40
by thesse, thoult throughly weane
ther harts, from things, terene

Each disapountment, that they meet
With in their weary, pilgrimage
Shall make their Joyrneys end more sweet   45
And their affections disengage
from earthly. vanitys
and all sublunarys.

That soull, that has itts interest clear
In this one promise, and can plead   50
It out with god, what need he fear
His unbeleife, that may impead
But can be break, through that
each foe shall fall down flatt

89   Gods fullnese, common bounty, and specyall love, the souls
chouse, July 5   73

When we our minds, and thoughts, doe set
Upon thy fullnese infinet

We ar soon driven to a stand
At that, we cannot comprehand

Though, from thee all our mercys flow   5   p. 256
Thou'st ne're the lese, for to bestow.

When we thy providence doe eye
And see thy liberallity

We run our selfs, into a maize
att all thy providencyall waies   10

Thou spreadst a table, out for all
Both young, & old, both great, and small

Thou dost extend, thy bounty wide
And dost for this vast world, provide

Thou dost provide sutable fare   15
Both for the beasts, and birds, of'th ayr

Thou hearst, the ravens, when they cry
And sendest in, to them suply

Thy bounty, yt itt self, extends
Both to thy foes, and to thy freinds   20

Thy foes, they, have the largest share
Somtimes, of that the world counts rare

And yett thou makest, vast difirence
To thine, for why the spring from whence

Ther mercys flow, is fountain love   25
And cove'nant right to, th god above

So that ther little hath much more
In it then all the wickeds store

Tis only they that truly feast
Though in the world, they may have least   30

the curss from itt thou dost remove
& with ther litle, they have Love:

I never would my portion gett
with them, on whom thy love's not sett

As litle, as thou wilt give me   35
Soe mingled with thy love itt be

Thy grace, & love, is that I chouse
All other things, I doe refuse

When from this, they ar separate
As that with me, will bear no weight   40

If I have thee, I need not care
For this worlds, overguilded ware

I'me sure I cannot want if I
share in thine allsuficiency

oh give this world, to whom thou wilt   45   p. 257
It is not here, that I have built

My nest, or plac'd my hapynese
Ther's nothing will, content me lese

Then to enjoy a deity,
And live, with thee, eternally   50

90   July 6 73 Loth to part

When we doe get, so neer to thee
As glimpses, of thy face to see
Oh how it pains, the hart
to think that time, doth part
And as a skreen   5
yett stands between

When thou to us hast so apeer'd
As our affections, ar endeer'd
And drawn up unto thee
tis hard to think, that wee   10
must down again
to this world, vain

When from the mount, we do come down
Upon the world, we cant but frown
As on an enemy   15
And with distainfull eye
we hate soe much
as it to touch

When we doe of thy sweetnese tast
How doth it make us long, with hast   20
To get upon, the wing
and up to heaven spring
To drink our fill on Zion hill

When we on heavens, daintys feed
This doth imbitter sin endeed   25
And makes us long to dy
that from captivity
we may be free
att rest with thee

When thou thy self, dost so impart   30
As to draw up to thee, our hart
In duty, we do find
our selfs, with love entwin'd
And where we ly
there, we could dy   35

Though for a time, part here we must
yet let each sip, encrease our thurst
And make us grow more dry
that we may gredily
Gasp for, to be   40
filled with thee

91   experience of satens malice   July 7   p. 258

The devill will withstand
Us most, in whats of grand
Importance unto us, therby
Filling us, with perplexety

Hee slyly, lys in wait   5
to cacth us, by his bait
Eather before, or at the time
We should, to some, great mercy climb

Thus weakens he our faith
When cald for, in itt height   10
Entangling of us, in his net
When we the greatest good, might get

It may be he hath seen
That our designs have been
To get new strength, to throw him out   15
No wonder, then hee lays about,

Hee will fly in our face,
whilst we do seek for grace,
And strength, to thrust him out of doors
Making new tumults, and uproors   20

Hee has no place by right,
But what he gets by slight,
My all, belongs to thee alone,
And wilt thou nott, safegaurd thine own

Oh wilt thou not engage   25
thy pow'r against the rage
Of thy professed enemy,
Whom thou hast, in, captivity,

Oh blame me not to long
from this foe, to be gone   30
How can I chouse, but greive, and pine
To see, him thus, intrude, on thine,

Oh when wilt thou unty,
life's knot. that I may fly,
From this my enemy, who still   35
Doth lead, me captive, att his will

92   1 John 3 2 July 8

We cannot tell whilst here
what we shall one day be
But when thou shalt again apear
we shall be like to thee

Thy glory, then shall dart   5   p. 259
On us, iradiently
When we shall see thee, as thou art
and be, transform'd therby

Wee see now in our race
thy glory, somtimes beame   10
But then we shall see face, to face
and no cloud, intervene

A soull transforming sight
of thee whilst here below
I would desire, that soe I might   15
into, thy liknese grow

Still dayly, more, & more
in this imperfect state
Untill I come, through grace, to soare
to sights, imediate   20

93   July 9

What is itt, that thou dost require
whilst thou art smartly, knocking off
Our fingers, from what we admire
by it, thou calst for all, our love
What cause have we, if itt be soe   5
To wonder, thou shouldst stoop so low

What is our love (deer Lord,) to thee
Thou'rt in thy self, to great, to high
To, gain by it, tis only wee
That ar advantaged, therby   10
Yet art thou pleas'd thus low to bend
As for soe meane, a thing to send

All we can have, for to bestow
It will fall short, infinetly
Of that which we, to thee, doe owe   15
When ages of eternity
Shall still be speant in pouring forth
Our love, on thee, when att full growth

Oh then what madnese, desparate
Is it to set our love upon   20
Thosse things, of no moment, or weight
Which also, will be quikly gone
When alls to litle, we can give
Unto the god, on whom we live

Do thou by some soull scorching beam   25
From thee, cause love, on fire to be
Lett the whole to-rent, and the stream
Of my affections, run to thee
That when the creture, calls to share
I may, find none, for them, to spare.   30

94   The day of Judgment   July 9   p. 260

Oh how doth it amaise, to think of thy
Tribunall seat, and awfull majesty
When thou shalt on thy regall throne ascend
And all thy glorious angels thee attend
When those, great trumpetors of heaven, shall   5
Summon before thee, all, both great, & small
Both high, and low, both rich, and poor which here
Have acted, in this lower hemisphere
Though to the rocks, & mountains, we should cry
We cannot, be hid, from a deity   10
But all must give, a strict account what they
Have thought, or spock, or done, in this their day
Thou wilt each hidden, cecreet thought descry
By thy severe, hartsearching, scrutiny
Each hiden work, shall then be brought to light   15
And shall appear to men, & angells sight
No place shall then be found, wherin to hide
But each this fiery triell, must abide
And from thy sentence, ther is no apeall
Acordingly, must be, our woe, or weall   20
The practicall, beleife of this, would make
Us to a strickt, and holy life, betake
And strive to get the Judg now beforhand
To be our freind, & on our side, to stand
That we may'nt be condemned with the world   25
Which shall out of his presence, then be hurld
But may with his, march up triumphantly
To live with him, to all eternity.

95   Coveteousnese. 10 July 73

Oh what is this, that steals our harts away
This white, & yelow drose, refined clay
Litle of itt, will cary through
To that world, we ar going to
Yet doe we grasp, and crave   5
Still more, of itt, to have
this vanity
we deifie,

Ther's few contented with their own confines
But would break through, to win the golden mines   10
The stake, the sceptor, & the crown
Do all, to this Idoll bow down
Oh foolish, & unwise
Thus for, to Idolise
That which cant stead   15
When we have need

Though this be strang, tis not so strang, as true   p. 261
When neer to death, this world, we most persue
A thing we could not well, beleive
Did not experience. undeceive   20
Whilst we doe dayly see
Those ready hence, to flee
most strongly grasp
and hold, it fast

Oh let my soull, to greater things aspire   25
Then that which grows, & springs, from durt, & mire
More coveteous. I still would grow
But not for thesse things, here below
But for the things above
to which, I shall remove   30
Within, the space
of a short race,

96   July 11   73

The nations, of the world do reell
What work is now, upon the whell

Though great storms, yet, we may endure
Thine interest, thou wilt cecure

The sky is black, & overcast   5
But thus, it shall not always last

Thou wilt cause itt, again to clear
And in thy glory, wilt appear

When all the world's in an uproar
Thy people, they may find a door   10

Att which they may, by faith goe in
And shroud themselfs, under thy wing

The Canopy, of thy great pow'r
Will keep them dry, in'th greatest shoure

Ther is a faithfull, word wherby   15
Wee may abide, confidently

Thy word asures us, that thou wilt
Avenge the bloud, that has been spilt

By that sad generation
Which doe delight, to feed upon   20

The flesh of thine, and drink ther bloud
Thou wilt upon them, pour the floud

Of pure unmixt, vengeance wherby
Thy great name, thou wilt glorifie

That shall be read, in history   25
Which is now write, in prophecy

That babilon, that city great
Is thrown from her emperyall seat

And is quite fallen down, & sunk   p. 262
Who make her self, soe often drunk   30

With larg draughts, of the bloud of thine
As with most sweet, delicious, wine

The nations, blinded, by this whore
Shall be deceiv'd by her no more

Thy gospell then must needs shine clear   35
When her delusions, shall apear

And be made manifest, to all
The nations, both great, and small

Oh hasten (Lord), this blessed day
And throw this block, out of the way   40

This mistery, of inniquity
Which always, in the way doth ly

For to apose, thine interest
And of thy glory, thee devest

Then shall those halalujahs, be   45
For that, sung out, by thine, to thee

97   An expostulation of the soull with it self. July 11

What unbeleife is this
thus hastily
to long to dy
And all because of this
Black cloud, that now, thus overspreads   5
And threatens, to poure on our heads

Wher is thy faith, wherby
with confidence
beyound thy sence
Thou shouldst on god rely   10
His interest he will cecure
His word, to thee, doth this ensure

Thou wouldst to heaven get
and on the shore
wouldst land, before   15
Thy time, whose periods set
Till that be come, tis vain to strive
Sooner unto it, to a-rive

Why art thou soe afraid
of this black day   20
and wouldst a-way
No more to be dismai'd
with dayly fears of what may be
Or what thine eyes, may live to see

If thine immortall soull   25
be but cecur'd
what eres endur'd
Thoult get safe to the goall
And shalt through grace, atain the crown
In peace, therfore, my soull, ly down   30

Under the canopy   p. 263
of devine love
which from above
Is spread out over thee
Gods pow'r and alsufficiency   35
Shall be thy sweet cecurity

98   the soull having examined the world, sum'd her up, & found, her, empty, vain, & deceitfull, take its solemn farwell beforehand. July 12

Oh world, what is in thee, to be desir'd
What great things, have those, that love thee acquir'd
What reall good doe those receive from thee
That give them selfs, thy druges for to bee
Letts veiw thee round, & stricktly now enquire   5
Didst ever fill, or satisfie desire
Those that have had, the most of thee, have found
Ther vesals empty when they them, doe sound
What canst thou do, when we to thee do call
Canst thou, from wrath, deliver us att all   10
When we into a-nother world do goe
No comfort can from thee, unto us flow
If lean'd upon, thou wilt deceive our hopes
Our confidence, shall prove, but sandy ropes
When we doe, count, and sum up all thy tresure   15

All we can find, is honour, profit, plesure
And of thesse three, thou hast but the bare name
But nothing, in deed, or truth, of the same
Thy honour's but a windy puff which will
Not once, att all, satisfie us, or fill   20
Thy plesure, that is altogather vain
An after-sting, is all by itt we gain
Thy profitt, riches, thats but vanity
Which will take wing, and soon from us will fly
Then world, before thou shalt me thus deceive   25
I will of thee now take, my solemn leave
I'le thrust thee now, out of this hart of mine
Before thou shut on me thosse doors of thine
Least I should have my Lodging for to look
When thou shalt utterly, have me forsook   30
Ile now make sure on't in that world above
transporting all in order to remove
And only use thee, as a passenger
His inne, that's going to a countrey far   p. 264
Where is his only home, & wher he knows   35
He shall be truly welcome made by those
Which doe expect his coming, ther to dwell
Once more vain world, I bid thee now farwell

99   Somthing – soull would know the meaning of but cant yet
resovlvs, through grace, to go on July 21   73

What is the reason (Lord) that I
In duty, cant, that comfort spy
That doth me fill, or satisfie

Though thou somtimes, my evedence
for glory, when I goe from hence   5
Dost clear, no comfort, springs from thence

When I unto those, dutys goe
In which to others, comforts flow
My fears, and sorrows, they doe grow

And great disatisfaction   10
Because I cannot feast upon
A clear sight, of my only one

I'me full of reslesnese, & pain
Because I cant, to that atain
Att which desires, doe strongly, aym   15

Somthing I'de have, I cant tell what
But till unto itt, I am got
Sorrow, and greife, must, be my lot

I think if thesse desires, did spring
Purely from thee, that then the thing   20
I long for, should be given in

If Saten may be Judg he saith
It is for want of saving faith
and crys out, hipocrite in'th height

But hee's a lier, that I know   25
For if t'were so, he would not throw
His darts, and soe enraged grow

I am resovlv'd, through grace, I will
Ne're leave thee, till thou shalt me fill
And if not here, on Sion hill   30

100   The souls fixt desire,

I would frequently, from thee hear
Untill thou doe, thy self apear.

And fecth me, from this sinfull state   p. 265
To enjoyment. immediate

oh give me leave, to speak out plain   5
I would not flatter, lye, or fein

Love letters, will not serve the turn
Come thou thy self, or else I burn

It is thy self, thy self, alone
My sweet, and blessed, only one   10

Tis with thy self, that I would live
And that would satisfaction give

Oh deerest Jesus, come away
My soull doth faint, with thy delay

Oh take thy steps, both larg, and wide   15
And quikly, fecth away thy bride

Who would from hence, faign be releas'd
To solemnize the mariage feast

And ever take repose, and rest
In her deer bridgrooms, sacred breast   20

Till in his arms, shee be, intwin'd
What comfort, can shee, take, or find

Where should the brid, be nourished
But with her husband, and her head

Lord, thou art mine, and I am thine   25
Do thou me, in thine arms entwine

Oh hasten that sweet day, when I
Shall live, with thee, eternally

And in the meane time, take my hart
As, a pledg, we sha'nt be long apart.   30

Come, Lord Jesus, come quikly.

The First Century

The title 'The First Century' is not used in the manuscript

2

(p. 1) l.14: *& fitt me for the Joys above,* inserted, replacing *That I may soare, to thee above* deleted

(p. 2) l.15: *And* deleted at beginning of line; *dear* inserted (abbreviated *dr*)

3

(p. 2) l.6: *z* in *Gaze* superimposed on illegible letter

(p. 3) l.24: *f* deleted before *an*

4

(p. 3) l.8: *fullfill* deleted before *fulfill*

(p. 3) l.13: *ro* in *through* superimposed on illegible letters

(p. 3) l.14: *quickly cooll again,* inserted, replacing *soon grow cold, again* deleted

(p. 4) l.23: *We're* abbreviated *We* ʳ

5

(p. 5) l.14: *wast* deleted before *speand*

6

Poem in two columns: ll.1-28 in left hand column, ll.29-56 in right hand column. The final couplet (ll.57-58) is at the top of the next page in the manuscript.

(p. 6) ll.15-16: inserted, replacing *Which makes me that / I cannot move* deleted

(p. 6) ll.17-20: *unbelieving ... thee* (written as six lines) inserted, replacing *unbeleif, / is very strong / I know not how / To god along* deleted

(p. 6) l.18: *heart* abbreviated *ht*

(p. 6) ll.25-28: written as two lines, inserted, replacing *Nothing I see / But sin within / Which makes an / Outcry, & a din* deleted

7

(p. 7) l.2: *Ther angels see thy face* deleted; written again at line 3

(p. 7) l.26: final *e* in *there* deleted; tilde over *er* in *ther* has been expanded to *their*

8

(p. 8) l.4: *e* in *the* deleted

9

(p. 9) l.13: *e* in *taste* deleted

10

(p. 10) l.1: *how* deleted at end of line

(p. 10) l.6: *tk* deleted before *take*; *a* inserted

(p. 11) l.47: *saints* abbreviated *sˢᵗ*

11

(p. 12) l.11: smudge after *lay* may be an *e* deleted

(p. 12) l.24: *god* (abbreviated *g:*) *from* and *them* inserted; replacing *whom god* deleted, following *them*

(p. 12) l.25: *when thou* deleted at end of line

(p. 12) stanza between ll.36 and 37 deleted: *Humilyty's the way to honour / Its spoken by the Lord / And he will set the garlend on her / Acording to his word*

(p. 13) l.51: *a* inserted

(p. 13) l.66: *V* in *Vew* superimposed on *S*

12

(p. 14) l.2: *e* in *goe* superimposed on illegible letter

(p. 14) l.6: *to* inserted

13

(p. 15) l.32: inserted, replacing *Lord, it is even soe* deleted

(p. 16) l.41: *The cutting* inserted, replacing *And alsoe,* deleted

(p. 16) l.42: *From th* inserted, replacing *The* deleted

(p. 16) l.43: *soe* superimposed on *a*; *a* inserted. Line formerly read *in a great measure*; now reads *in soe great a measure.*

(p. 16) l.60: *ing* inserted

(p. 16) l.63: *alo* deleted before *in*

(p. 17) l.85: *for* deleted before *can*

(p. 17) horizontal line (which Palmer uses at the end of each poem) after l.92 suggests that she is making a new start in the poem, evidenced also by the different meter and stanzaic structure

14

(p. 18) title followed by seven shorthand symbols

(p. 18) l.6: *to* inscrtcd

(p. 18) l.7; *rock* superimposed on illegible word

(p. 18) l.21: *knitt* deleted before *knitt*

(p. 19) l.40: first *c* in *According* inserted; *l* at end of *According* deleted

(p. 19) l.49: *faith and* deleted before *truth*; *t* deleted before *oath*

(p. 20) l.65: *y* in *thy* superimposed on illegible letter before two deleted letters

15

(p. 20) l.11: *s* in *promise* superimposed on illegible letter

(p. 21) l.21: *he* deleted before *his*; *guid* inserted, replacing *Lead thee,* deleted

(p. 21) l.22: *thou in glory do reside* inserted, replacing *he bring thee, safe to glory* deleted. *Thou* and *glory* superimposed on *to glory.*

16

(p. 22) l.17: *W* in *When* superimposed on *T*

17

(p. 23) l.10: *To* deleted at beginning of line

(p. 24) l.21: *d* in *behind* superimposed on *g*

18

(p. 24) l.14: *love* deleted before *bloud*

(p. 25) stanza between ll.24 and 25 deleted: *And seeing Lord, it thy hart / Let it now highly scorn / With sin, or saten, to take part / Being, more nobly born*

(p. 25) l.25: *now* inserted, replacing *Oh* deleted

(p. 25) stanza between ll.32 and 33 deleted: *Thou didst itt purchase, for a place / To 'habit in thy self / Oh let itt be adorn'd with grace / Cast out, all rubish pelf*

(p. 25) l.34: *oh* and *it* inserted; *&* inserted after *oh* then deleted; *it well* deleted before *apace*

(p. 25) l.39: *Oh* and *lett* inserted, replacing *That* deleted; *may* deleted before *still*

(p. 26) l.53: *black* deleted before *black*

19

(p. 26) l.8: *And* deleted at beginning of line

(p. 26) l.18: inserted, replacing *Christ is the only true prophet* deleted

(p. 26) l.20: inserted, replacing *He will thee, in the right way set* deleted

(p. 27) l.29: *th* inserted, replacing *the* deleted; *thy* inserted

(p. 27) l.31: *godhead t'was that* inserted, replacing *devine nature,* deleted

(p. 27) stanza between ll.36 and 37 deleted: *And thou afraid least he should touch / Who is the avenger of bloud / Christ is the city of refuge / Where defence is both strong, and good*

(p. 27) l.37: *d* in *pack'd* superimposed on *t*

(p. 27) l.38: illegible word starting with *A* deleted at beginning of line

(p. 27) l.40: *must* inserted, replacing *But* deleted

(p. 27) l.42: *deny* deleted before *self*; *deny* inserted after *self*

(p. 27) l.44: *vain* and *vai* deleted before *worlds*; *vain felicity* inserted, replacing *vain, & foolish pelf* deleted

(p. 27) l.47: *u* in *wourld* deleted

(p. 27) line deleted between ll.49 and 50 *Sweetened with speciall love*

(p. 28) l.66: *a* in *saten* superimposed on *t*

(p. 28) l.70: *s* in *froms* deleted

(p. 28) l.78: *am* deleted before *still*; *am* inserted after *still*

20

(p. 29) l.24: *let* deleted before *lent*

(p. 30) l.48: *re* in *foregoe* superimposed on illegible letter

21

(p. 31) l.4: *Or vex us any* deleted at beginning of line

(p. 31) l.7: *is* deleted after *is*

(p. 31) l.15: three-letter word ending in *e* deleted before *be*; *be* deleted before *afraid*

(p. 31) l.17: *NOe* deleted before *Noe*

(p. 32) l.45: *ayle* inserted, replacing *meane* deleted

(p. 32) l.48: *tastting* deleted before *teach*

(p. 32) l.57: *not* inserted

(p. 33) l.66: *(* deleted at end of line

(p. 33) l.74: *saints* abbreviated *s'ts*

(p. 33) l.95: *e* in *The* deleted; *in* inserted; *in* deleted before *shall*

(p. 34) l.101: *that groweth* inserted, replacing *alsoe grows* deleted

(p. 34) l.110: illegible letter deleted after *pearl*

(p. 34) l.111: *to us foretold* inserted, replacing *this to us* (before *hath*) and *told* (after *hath*) deleted

(p. 34) l.112: inserted, replacing *Therfore, it is no Cheat* deleted

(p. 34) l.117: *e* in *reveill* superimposed on *a*

22

(p. 35) stanza between ll.12 and 13 deleted: *The world shall then no longer Jostle / With sin, I shall no more wrastle / But in Christs bosome, I shall nestle*

(p. 35) l.33: *low* deleted before *ly*

(p. 35) l.35: *I take* deleted at beginning of line; *true* and *is* inserted

(p. 36) l.53: *Have* deleted at beginning of line

(p. 36) l.59: *so* deleted before *though*

23

(p. 39) ll.50-52: inserted, replacing *Vain then shall find the same / It yeelds thee noe whitt better measure / Its comforts, ar but lame* deleted

24

(p. 40) l.11: *con* deleted before *chousen*

(p. 40) l.14: *so* deleted before *overcome*

(p. 40) l.17: *s* deleted before *struck*

(p. 40) l.27: *onlly* deleted before *only*

(p. 40) l.38: *indeed* inserted after *then*; *endeed* deleted at end of line

(p. 40) l.40: *muse on the same* inserted; replacing *on grief doe feed* deleted

25

(p. 41) l.5: *write* deleted before *after*

(p. 41) ll.6-8: inserted, replacing *Tis he must hold thy lord steady / Or else, thou'lt blare / And also share* deleted

(p. 41) l.14: *did* inserted; *ed* in *committed* deleted

(p. 41) stanza between ll.16 and 17 deleted: *His life was blamlese, & holy / He lived unto god soly / Holynese is, the angels blise*

(p. 43) ll.75-76: inserted, replacing *A hart of stone / Twill make to* [illegible word] deleted

26

(p. 44) l.21: *no grace* inserted; *nothing* deleted before *see*

(p. 45) l.42: *grace* deleted before *pride*

(p. 46) l.81: *th* deleted before *in*

(p. 46) l.88: second *t* in *contentedly* superimposed on *d* or *e*

(p. 47) l.108: *despond* deleted before *extoll*

(p. 47) ll.109-112: inserted, replacing *If soe my soull, then thou hast need / For to look still about / And with all s*[two illegible letters]*full carefull, heed / Still to send out thy scout* deleted

(p. 47) l.115: *continually* inserted, replacing *Therfore;* deleted; *always* deleted before *goes*

27

(p. 48) l.13: *g* in *Thoug* deleted

(p. 48) l.20: *sp* deleted before *stoop*

(p. 49) l.43: *grace* deleted before *love*

(p. 49) l.45: *wilt* inserted, replacing *would* deleted

28

(p. 50) stanza between ll.12 and 13 deleted: *I cannot understand / This word seems strange to* [two illegible letters]*e / Concerning the work of* [three illegible letters]*hand / Saith god,* [seven illegible letters]*d you* [two illegible letters]*e*

(p. 50) l.22: *great* inserted

(p. 51) l.44: *striving* deleted before *thriving*

29

(p. 51) p.46 mislabelled p.45 by Palmer

(p. 52) l.28: *d* deleted before *tread*

(p. 53) l.51: *It a*[illegible letter] deleted at beginning of line; *pous'nous* inserted, replacing *fierce* deleted

(p. 53) l.52: inserted, replacing *Shall be for aye laid fast* deleted. *Christ* abbreviated *+t*

30

(p. 53) l.3: *t'* inserted, replacing *It* deleted; *chearfully* inserted, replacing *fore to* deleted

(p. 53) l.12: *The blessing,* deleted at beginning of line

(p. 54) l.28: *p* in *Trampling* superimposed on *l*

(p. 54) l.29: *active* deleted after *active*

(p. 54) l.40: *rack* deleted before *rake*; *durt g* deleted before *dung*

(p. 55) l.58: letter after *U* in *Upon* deleted

(p. 55) l.71: *mi* deleted before *is*

(p. 56) l.94: three illegible letters deleted before *itt*

31

(p. 56) l.10: *p* in *spotlese* superimposed on *t*

32

(p. 59) l.55: *to* deleted before *bee*

33

(p. 59) l.5: *the* inserted

(p. 60) l.23: *d* in *Thoughd* deleted

34

(p. 61) l.16: *oh* inserted, replacing *Then* deleted

(p. 61) l.20: *ou will* superimposed on *ey can*; *br* in *break* superimposed on *l*

(p. 61) l.29: *can* deleted before *now*; *can* inserted after *now*

35

(p. 62) l.4: *i* in *greist* superimposed on *e*

(p. 62) l.16: *('* and *')* inserted

(p. 62) l.19: *to thee* inserted; *to thee* deleted after *me*

(p. 63) l.24: *f* in *fill* superimposed on *w*

36

(p. 63) l.1: *thers none* inserted twice, replacing *Nothing* and *nothing* deleted

(p. 63) l.6: inserted, replacing *compared with thy self* deleted

(p. 63) l.8: inserted, replacing *in this love let me delve* deleted

(p. 63) l.13: *e* in *shade* superimposed on *,*

(p. 64) l.18: *(* and *.)* inserted

(p. 65) l.67: *he* deleted before *sit*

(p. 65) l.75: *it* deleted before *mee*

37

(p. 66) l.3: *heart* abbreviated *ht*

(p. 67) l.30: *Impresed, do* deleted before *hope*

38

(p. 67) l.17: *weary of* inserted, replacing *of* deleted; *weary* superimposed on illegible word

(p. 68) l.29: *doth* inserted; *th* deleted at end of line

(p. 68) l.37: *The soull* deleted at beginning of line

40

(p. 71) l.16: *h* in *strectht* superimposed on *t*

(p. 71) l.23: *such* deleted after *such*

(p. 71) l.25: *have* deleted after *have*

41

(p. 72) l.5: *I* deleted before *could*

(p. 73) l.37: two illegible letters deleted before *best*

(p. 73) l.58: *s* in *longs* deleted

42

(p. 75) l.22: *laid* deleted before *open*; *laid* inserted after *open*

(p. 75) l.24: inserted, replacing *untill we reach heaven* deleted

(p. 75) stanza between ll.32 and 33 deleted: *The angell of the covenant / Doth move within this pooll / By faith step in we may warent / that thou shalt be made whole*

(p. 75) l.37: *praise* inserted, replacing *hearing* deleted

43

(p. 78) l.39: *the* deleted before *by*

44

(p. 80) l.26: *un* in *unquiet* superimposed on *in*

(p. 80) l.37: *42* deleted at beginning of line

45

(p. 81) l.36: *s* in *earthss* deleted

46

(p. 83) l.31: *do* inserted; *an* deleted before *eternity*

(p. 83) l.32: *b* in *imbraces* superimposed on another letter

(p. 83) l.34: *for* inserted; *us* deleted before *imbrace*

(p. 83) p.77 mislabelled p.78 by Palmer

(p. 83) l.53: *be* deleted before *subject*; *be* inserted after *subject*

47

(p. 84) l.3: *father,* inserted, replacing *god* deleted; *my god* inserted, replacing *dear fathers,* deleted

(p. 84) l.6: *earthy* deleted before *earthly*

(p. 84) p.78 mislabelled p.79 by Palmer

(p. 84) l.10: *Scorning* deleted at beginning of line

(p. 84) l.22: *wher is* deleted at beginning of line

(p. 84) l.25: *n* added to *an*; *lawfull,* deleted after *an*; *adopt:* inserted

(p. 85) l.42: *of vanity,* inserted, replacing *into nothing* deleted

(p. 85) ll.43-44: inserted, replacing *When faith my soull, to god, doth link /
mounting itt on the wing,* deleted

48

(p. 86) l.21: *ther* deleted before *this*

(p. 86) l.35: *Aod* deleted at beginning of line

(p. 87) l.60: *d* deleted before *still*

49

(p. 88) l.20: *this* deleted before *this*

(p. 89) l.45: *(* and *)* inserted

50

(p. 89) title *4* deleted before *50*

(p. 89) stanza at beginning of poem deleted: *Sin is the grand evill, of evills /
to god it is bot foull / It makes us like unto the devils / whilst in us it doth role*

(p. 89) l.1: *Sin* inserted, replacing *It* deleted

(p. 89) l.5: *who* deleted before *will*

(p. 89) l.17: *its* deleted before *in*

(p. 89) l.22: *ot* deleted before *on*

(p. 90) l.40: *e* in *worke* deleted

(p. 90) l.48: *soulls* deleted before *souls*

(p. 90) l.53: *Sin* MS has "Sis"

(p. 90) l.58: *for a'nother to come* deleted at beginning of line

(p. 90) l.59: *thus* inserted, replacing *Till* deleted

(p. 90) l.60: inserted, replacing *itt doth* [followed by illegible words] deleted

51

(p. 92) l.30: *still* deleted before *shall*

53

(p. 93) l.11: *shalt* deleted before *speedyly*; *shalt* inserted after *speedyly*

(p. 94) two pencil scribblings in left margin at top of p.88

54

(p. 95) l.11: *hid.* deleted before *heed*

(p. 95) l.23: *s* deleted before *move*

55

(p. 97) 1.27: *If were* deleted before *if*

(p. 97) 1.43: *ld* in *fivefold* superimposed on *ild*

(p. 97) 1.50: *desire* deleted before *this*; *desire* inserted after *this*

(p. 97) 1.52: *'to* inserted; *I aspire,* inserted, replacing *is my blise* deleted

(p. 98) 1.53: *e* in *apeall* superimposed on illegible deleted letter

56

(p. 98) ll.5-8: inserted, replacing *Litle time, with her casualltys / has speedyly worn out / The name, and fame, of great worthys / which here have made a rout* deleted

(p. 98) 1.6: *the* deleted at beginning of line

(p. 98) 1.23: space between *thy* and *horn*

(p. 98) 1.25: *the* deleted before *wicked*; *men* inserted after *wicked*

57

(p. 99) title: *The freenese of grace in its actings* deleted at beginning of line. *Christ* abbreviated +*ᵗ*

58

(p. 101) 1.33: *grace* inserted, replacing *joy* deleted

59

(p. 102) 1.13: *for* deleted at end of line

(p. 102) 1.19: *cable* MS has "rable"

(p. 102) 1.22: inserted, replacing *tis but for a moment* deleted

60

(p. 104) title: *5* deleted before *60*

(p. 104) 1.4: *th* deleted before *depths*

(p. 104) 1.20: *shall* deleted before *from*

(p. 104) 1.30: text reads *atttending* (copyist error); *ing* deleted after *att* in *atttending*; *n* in *on* superimposed on illegible deleted letter

(p. 105) 1.33: *h* in *thy* superimposed on *i*

61

(p. 105) title: *51* deleted before *61*

(p. 105) 1.2: *itt dont* inserted, replacing *that* deleted; the *s* in *belongs* deleted, followed by *not* deleted

(p. 105) 1.3: *Least* and *itt dont* deleted at beginning of line

(p. 105) 1.16: *hast* abbreviated *hst*

There is no poem 62 in the 'First Century'.

63

(p. 106) title: *53* deleted before *63*; *7* deleted before *71/2*

(p. 107) 1.17: *w* and *h* in *Unworthynese* superimposed on illegible deleted letters

64

(p. 107) title: *6:* in *64:* superimposed on *5*; *ge* deleted after *prive* in *priveledges*

(p. 107) 4: stanzas between ll.20 and 21 deleted: [1] *Each sainct, is alsoe a Joynt heir / with Christ ofer what is his / In heaven they shall largly share / of hapinese, and blisse*

[2] *Heauen is theirs* [three illegible letters] *in reversion / they are the lawfull heires / Which shortly shall goe take possession / of what by right is theirs*

[3] *Christ, is to each sainct his lovly a bridgroom / each sainct, his lovly brid / Hee hath prepar'd of them a room / with him they shall abide*

[4] *The earth is theirs, with all its good / all else ar usurpers / Ther title's good its bought with bloud / theyr only the true heers*

(p. 108) l.39: *doth* deleted before *lyes*; *s* in *lyes* inserted

(p. 108) l.42: inserted, replacing *who is the confortor.* deleted

(p. 108) l.44: inserted, replacing *enriching, each corner* deleted; *swell* actually *(,swell,* probably because *swell* written as subscript

65

(p. 109) title: *6* in *65:* superimposed on *5*; *M* in *Mansion* superimposed on *m*

(p. 110) l.7: *w* deleted before *is*

(p. 110) l.15: *I* and *In* deleted at beginning of line

67

(p. 113) l.3: inserted, replacing *I'le seeke for to bee macthlese* deleted

69

(p. 117) l.15: *glori* deleted before *god*

(p. 118) l.28: *acts* MS has "arts"

(p. 118) l.33: *that* deleted before *makes*

(p. 118) l.45: *fain* deleted before *then*

(p. 118) l.48: indented because lower left corner of page torn out

70

(p. 119) l.1: *upon* deleted at end of line

(p. 122) l.109: *lik* deleted before *live*; *d* in *do* superimposed on *t*

(p. 122) l.111: *name* deleted before *name*

72

(p. 125) l.27: *with briers* inserted, replacing *disapointment,* deleted; *still* inserted

(p. 125) l.28: inserted, replacing *and dost defile our horn* deleted

(p. 125) l.31: *with* deleted before *in*; *unkind* inserted, replacing *vai* deleted

73

(p. 126) l.12: *t* deleted before *eye*

(p. 126) stanza between ll.28 and 29 deleted: *I earnestly desire to scale / the*

walls of that cyty / But cant untill thou rend the vaill / of flesh, and lay it by
(p. 127) l.59: *love* deleted before *life*

74
(p. 129) l.56: *g* in *thoug* deleted

75
(p. 130) l.12: *k* in *thinking* superimposed on *g*
(p. 130) l.19: *needts* deleted before *needst*
(p. 130) l.23: *do thou* inserted, replacing *Only* deleted

76
(p. 132) l.41: *sottish,* deleted before *mad*; *& sottish* inserted after *mad*; *then* deleted before *ar*
(p. 132) l.43: *th* deleted before *time*
(p. 133) l.55: *then* inserted, replacing *Therfore* deleted; *e* in *while* and *itt* inserted
(p. 133) l.59: *else* deleted before *that*

78
(p. 135) l.19: illegible letter deleted before *we*
(p. 136) line between ll.46 and 47 deleted: *Of th wicked, and profane*

79
(p. 137) l.23: *somthing* inserted; *somthing* deleted before *that*
(p. 137) l.36: text reads *thy thy* (copyist error)

80
(p. 138) l.9: *stand* inserted, replacing *ar* deleted
(p. 138) l.37: *thou shalt* inserted, replacing *my soull* deleted

81
(p. 139) l.5: *r* deleted before *walls*

82
(p. 141) l.1: *dost* deleted before *why*
(p. 141) l.8: *th'* inserted, replacing *the* deleted
(p. 141) line between ll.18 and 19 deleted: *Then thy deviner nobler drink*

84
(p. 144) l.17: *here* inserted, replacing *ther,* deleted
(p. 144) l.25: *as* deleted at end of line
(p. 144) l.36: *warth* deleted before *warmth*
(p. 145) l.47: text reads *let let* (copyist error)
(p. 145) l.64: *e* deleted before *in*
(p. 145) l.72: *S* deleted before *till*

85
(p. 146) l.10: *sweet* deleted before *pleasing*
(p. 147) l.34: *of God* deleted before *from*

86
(p. 148) title: above *86 The soull* are seven shorthand symbols
(p. 148) l.1: *behold thy king* inserted, replacing *& tocch veiw thy king* deleted
(p. 148) l.2: *glory* deleted before *low*
(p. 148) l.7: *its* inserted, replacing *the* deleted
(p. 148) l.16: inserted, replacing *and bow down at his feet* deleted
(p. 149) l.36: *all* deleted before *by*
(p. 149) l.50: *rai* deleted before *Judg*

89
(p. 152) l.16: *life,* deleted before *to*

90
(p. 152) l.12: space between *left.* and *when*

91
(p. 154) l.23: *m* deleted at beginning of line

92
(p. 155) l.17: *ee* in *thee* superimposed on illegible letter
(p. 155) l.18: *satisfie* deleted before *fill*
(p. 155) l.31: *And* deleted at beginning of line
(p. 155) l.43: *quiet* deleted before *think*

93
(p. 156) l.3: *w* deleted before *how*
(p. 156) l.9: *art thou* deleted before *art thou*
(p. 156) l.23: *day t* deleted before *to day*

95
(p. 159) l.14: three illegible letters deleted before *from*

96
(p. 160) l.13: *that* deleted before *the*
(p. 161) l.44: *spri* deleted before *spring*
(p. 161) l.53: *by* deleted at end of line
(p. 161) l.56: *l* deleted before *use*
(p. 162) l.82: *rich* inserted; *rich* deleted before *through*

97
(p. 163) l.16: *y* in *deny'd* superimposed on *i*

98

(p. 164) l.20: *aym* deleted before *ayme*

(p. 165) l.28: illegible letter deleted after *d* in *dung*

100

(p. 169) l.17: *gh* in *though* deleted

(p. 169) l.23: *Fare s e* deleted at beginning of line

(p. 169) l.33: *g* deleted before *quikly*

The Second Century

The title 'The Second Century' is not used in the manuscript

The first poem in the second century is not titled

(p. 171) l.5: *me* inserted

2

(p. 171) l.4: *Th* deleted at beginning of line

(p. 171) l.5: *still* inserted before *doth*; *still* deleted after *doth*

(p. 171) five couplets between ll.14 and 15 deleted:

[1] *If wee, in p*[four illegible letters] *doe begin / To e*[six illegible letters] *with him, he'l creep in*

[2] *And if to him, the ear be lent / Hee by his subtle argument*

[3] *Will never cleane persuading ly / To* [three illegible letters]*ge, till we with him comply*

[4] *And if his head, he can thrust in / His body after, he will bring*

[5] *And never will he*[three illegible letters] *nestling still / Untill the chort, he came to refill*

(p. 172) l.30: *c*[three illegible letters]*nl* deleted before *cuningly*

(p. 173) l.60: *t* in *that* superimposed on *y*

(p. 173) l.61: *keep us off from that which will* inserted, replacing *c*[two illegible letters]*e his cursed will, to have* deleted

(p. 173) three lines between ll.61 and 62 deleted: *Which is comonly off to stave / from that which might advantage more / And bring to us, a greater store*

(p. 173) three couplets between ll.62 and 63 deleted:

[1] *Of solid comfort, joy, and peace / And rich, and plentifull encrease*

[2] *If Saten can, but wind his tayle / Into the hart, we shall bewaill*

[3] *Our misery, because his sting / He will be sure, to leave therin*

3

(p. 174) l.7: *in its* deleted at end of line

(p. 174) l.10: *for on* deleted at beginning of line

4

(p. 176) l.36: *Lord,* deleted before *to*

5
(p. 178) l.48: *higher* deleted before *fuller*

6
(p. 179) l.21: *n* in *drawn* deleted
(p. 179) l.26: *Wihle* deleted at beginning of line
(p. 179) l.43: *p* in *poluted* superimposed on *b*

7
(p. 180) l.12: *t* in *fecth* superimposed on *h*

9
(p. 182) l.4: *listles* deleted before *listlesnese*
(p. 183) l.10: *We* deleted at beginning of line
(p. 183) l.18: *ʒ* in *laʒe* superimposed on illegible letter
(p. 183) l.22: *e* in *taste* deleted
(p. 183) l.25: *atait* deleted before *atain*

10
(p. 185) l.31: *pelf* deleted before *worldly*
(p. 185) l.45: *s* in *set* superimposed on *L*

11
(p. 186) l.5: *war* deleted before *worse*
(p. 186) l.12: *d* in *unkindd* deleted

12
(p. 188) l.28: text reads *I'le I'le* (copyist error) with first *I'le* in margin and *and* deleted before second *I'le*

14
(p. 189) title: - probably a shorthand symbol (its edges curve upwards)
(p. 190) l.30: *ull,* deleted before *all*

15
(p. 191) l.22: *tis* deleted before *tis*
(p. 192) l.52: *be* deleted before *below*
(p. 192) l.53: *flows to* deleted before *shall*

16
(p. 193) l.11: *Coul* deleted at beginning of line; second *ll* in *dwellll* deleted, first *ll* superimposed on illegible letters
(p. 194) l.26: *sones* deleted before *sons*
(p. 195) l.72: *r* deleted before *nor*
(p. 196) l.95: *bak* deleted before *backward*
(p. 198) l.143: *And* deleted at beginning of line

17

(p. 198) l.2: *th* deleted before *high*

(p. 198) l.5: *For* deleted at beginning of line

(p. 198) p.184 mislabelled p.183 by Palmer

(p. 199) l.40: *th* deleted before *his*

(p. 200) l.49: *thee* inserted

(p. 200) l.74: *de* deleted before *I*

(p. 200) l.76: *l* deleted before *might*

18

(p. 201) l.4: *g* in *acording* superimposed on illegible letter

(p. 201) l.13: *true* deleted before *true*

(p. 201) l.18: *sweet* deleted before *sweet*

(p. 201) l.20: *seems* deleted before *seems*

19

(p. 202) l.4: *Wh* deleted at beginning of line

(p. 202) l.13: *er* in *Wher* superimposed on *y*

(p. 203) l.47: text reads *as a full a mese* (copyist error)

(p. 203) l.51: *rv* in *reserv'd* superimposed on illegible letters

20

(p. 204) l.5: vertical line with a hook at the bottom left (shorthand symbol?) between *not* and *always*

(p. 204) l.14: *faign* deleted before *fain*

21

(p. 205) l.26: *Each let it* deleted at beginning of line; *each let is took* inserted, replacing *took* deleted

(p. 207) l.94: *but* inserted

22

(p. 208) l.5: *Abought* deleted at beginning of line; *as* [with long 's'] deleted before *as*

(p. 208) l.25: *make* deleted after *make*

(p. 209) l.37: *T* in *Them* superimposed on *Y*

(p. 209) l.40: *d* in *dashtd* deleted

23

(p. 211) l.40: *rac* deleted before *have*

24

(p. 212) l.31: *doe* deleted before *to*

(p. 213) l.37: *n* in *oftener* superimposed on illegible letter

25

(p. 214) title: *s* in *spirits* deleted
(p. 214) l.1: *s* in *selfss* deleted; *elfs* in *selfs* superimposed on illegible letters
(p. 214) l.8: *d* in *tod* deleted
(p. 214) l.16: *s* in *spirits* deleted
(p. 215) l.50: *but* inserted, replacing *Only* deleted; *one* inserted

26

(p. 217) l.37: *lump* deleted before *lump*
(p. 217) l.39: *'th* inserted, replacing *the* deleted
(p. 217) l.41: *when our* inserted, replacing *When mediatᵉ*. deleted; *mediate* inserted
(p. 217) ll.42-44: inserted, replacing *of death shall by ther cease / Immediate. revelation / Shall then on me encrease* deleted
(p. 217) l.42: *(* before *an end*, probably because *an end* written as superscript
(p. 217) l.47: *fild* deleted before *filled*

27

(p. 218) l.16: *of* deleted before *of*

28

(p. 219) l.7: *possed* deleted before *posest*
(p. 220) l.53: *thee* deleted before *me*
(p. 220) l.55: illegible letter deleted before *I*

29

(p. 221) l.25: *n* in *In* inserted

32

(p. 225) l.6: *y* in *thy* superimposed on *e*
(p. 226) l.17: *Wea* deleted at beginning of line
(p. 226) l.27: text reads *be,,* (copyist error)
(p. 227) l.47: *to throw* deleted before *down*
(p. 227) l.49: *desire* deleted before *still*

33

(p. 227) l.3: *s* deleted before *I*
(p. 228) stanza between ll.36 and 37 deleted: *My patrimony, goods, and store / are are there laid up far above mee / How can I chouse but long to soare / that I may look and see / the goods, that I have got / in my prepared lot*

34

(p. 229) l.3: *litle* deleted before *while*

35

(p. 231) l.17: final *c* in *hectic* superimposed on *to*

36
(p. 232) l.28: *k* in *ranks* superimposed on *g*
37
(p. 234) l.32: *set* deleted at beginning of line
39
(p. 235) l.22: *thatt* deleted before *that*
41
(p. 237) l.5: *thrive* inserted, replacing *grow* deleted
(p. 237) l.8: *this* deleted before *this*
42
(p. 238) l.25: *then* deleted before *then*
(p. 238) l.32: *vits* deleted before *vision*
43
(p. 239) l.26: *b* deleted before *on*
(p. 240) l.29: *s* in *days* deleted
(p. 240) l.35: *time* inserted
44
(p. 241) l.26: *woorwood* deleted before *woorwood*
48
(p. 244) l.20: *can* deleted before *nothing*
(p. 245) l.81: *is* deleted before *all*; *Christ* abbreviated +*t*
50
(p. 247) l.24: *away* deleted before *along*
(p. 248) l.36: *woud* deleted before *would*
51
(p. 249) l.12: second *u* in *mutuall* superimposed on *i*
(p. 249) p.219 mislabelled p.220 by Palmer
(p. 249) l.23: *ar* deleted before *a*
(p. 249) l.27: *given* deleted before *given*
(p. 249) l.29: *saints* abbreviated *s^{ts}*
53
(p. 251) l.16: *shefe of* deleted before *sheaf of*
54
(p. 252) l.2: *tis thine* deleted at beginning of line
55
(p. 253) l.2: *heart* abbreviated *h^t*

56
(p. 254) title followed by sixteen shorthand symbols
(p. 254) l.2: *Th* deleted at beginning of line
(p. 254) line between ll.19 and 20 deleted: *When fainting on thee I do roll*
(p. 255) l.34: *doe* deleted before *of*
(p. 257) l.106: *sh* deleted before *by*

57
(p. 258) title: *only* deleted before *strength*
(p. 258) l.13: *e* in *starte* deleted

58
(p. 258) l.2: *fears* deleted before *fill*

59
(p. 260) title: *Sep* deleted before *73*
(p. 260) l.13: *heaven* deleted after *heaven*

60
(p. 262) l.13: second *a* in *capacytys* superimposed on *y*

61
(p. 263) l.9: text reads *Uupon* (copyist error)
(p. 264) l.14: *lov* deleted before *grace*

64
(p. 267) title: *soll* deleted before *souls*

66
(p. 271) l.25: *I* is superscripted, suggesting it should not be emphasized metrically

68
(p. 271) title followed by seven shorthand symbols

69
(p. 273) l.13: *u* in *thou* superimposed on *se*
(p. 273) l.25: *me* deleted before *me*

70
(pp. 274-275) leaf torn at fore edge of pp.238-239

71
(p. 275) l.2: *thing* inserted
(p. 276) l.21: *w* deleted before *will*
(p. 276) l.31: *w* in *now* superimposed on *t*
(p. 276) l.36: *Whi* deleted at beginning of line

75

(p. 281) l.30: *law* inserted

(p. 281) l.39: *p* deleted before *happy*

76

(p. 281) l.6: *v* in *disever* superimposed on illegible letter

(p. 282) l.26: *chouse* deleted before *chose*

77

(p. 283) l.18: *ine* in *thine* superimposed on *ee*

(p. 283) l.22: *d* deleted before *object*

78

(p. 283) l.1: *u* in *droupingly* superimposed on illegible letter

(p. 284) l.22: *d* in *do* superimposed on *t*

79

(p. 285) title: - probably a shorthand symbol (its right edge curves upwards)

(p. 285) l.4: *oh* deleted before and after *of*; *oh* inserted before *what*

(p. 286) l.31: first *e* in *bee* superimposed on *y* deleted

80

(p. 286) title: *love* deleted before *July*

(p. 286) l.8: *d* deleted before *pride*

82

(p. 289) l.27: *brink* deleted before *bring*

(p. 289) l.34: *e* in *the* deleted

83

(p. 289) l.2: *s* in *Uss* deleted

(p. 289) l.3: *to* inserted, replacing *Do* deleted

(p. 290) l.23: *then g* deleted before *then*

84

(p. 291) l.17: *D* in *Do* superimposed on *T*

87

(p. 294) l.27: *att last* deleted before *down att last*

Palmer has skipped number 88, but has two poems numbered 96, therefore there are 100 poems in the second century

88

(p. 294) poem 88 mislabelled 89 by Palmer

89

(p. 296) poem 89 mislabelled 90 by Palmer

(p. 296) line between ll.6 and 7 deleted: *Whilst we receive*[six illegible letters]*h fo*[two illegible letters] *coth*
(p. 296) l.10: inserted, replacing *Att which we only stand, and gaze* deleted
(p. 297) l.26: *e* in *the* deleted
(p. 297) ll.31-32: inserted, replacing *For why thy love yeelds daintys rare / Beyound the choisest bils of fare* deleted

90
(p. 298) poem 90 mislabelled 91 by Palmer

91
(p. 299) poem 91 mislabelled 92 by Palmer
(p. 299) l.11: *ing* in *Entangling* superimposed on *ed*
(p. 299) l.16: *makes no rout* deleted before *lays about*
(p. 300) l.26: *r* in *ther* deleted
(p. 300) l.35: *my* inserted, replacing *thine*

92
(p. 300) poem 92 mislabelled 93 by Palmer
(p. 300) l.12: *intervene* deleted before *intervene*

93
(p. 301) poem 93 mislabelled 94 by Palmer
(p. 301) l.12: *think* deleted before *thing*
(p. 301) l.22: *c* in *Which* superimposed on illegible letter

94
(p. 302) poem 94 mislabelled 95 by Palmer
(p. 302) l.6: illegible letter deleted before *&*

95
(p. 302) poem 95 mislabelled 96 by Palmer
(p. 302) l.1: *are* deleted before *our*
(p. 303) l.11: *k* in *stake* superimposed on *f*
(p. 303) l.20: *x* in *experience* superimposed on illegible letter

96
(p. 303) title followed by six shorthand symbols
(p. 304) l.23: *f* and two illegible letters deleted before *wherby*

97
(p. 306) l.28: *o* in *goall* superimposed on *a*
(p. 306) l.35: *y* in *alsufficiency* superimposed on *e*

98
(p. 306) title: *th* deleted before *take*

(p. 307) l.31: *that world above* inserted, replacing *an other hand* deleted

(p. 307) l.32: inserted, replacing *And send away my goods, now beforehand* deleted

99

(p. 307) title: - probably a shorthand symbol (its edges curve upwards)

(p. 307) l.5: first word of line originally *of*: *o* in *of* deleted; *or* in *for* inserted

(p. 308) l.17: *I am* deleted before *I am*

(p. 308) l.24: inserted, replacing *And hipocrisies in the heigth* deleted

100

(p. 309) l.9: *sefe* deleted before *self*

(p. 309) l.10: *swe* deleted before *sweet*

(p. 309) l.18: *i* in *mariage* superimposed on illegible letter

(p. 309) Palmer's convention of drawing a horizontal line after each poem is used here after l.30, indicating that the final line of the manuscript is a type of epigraph

The First Century

(p. 1) [Dedication]
This is an invocation of the Holy Spirit, very common at the beginning of a collection of religious poetry in the seventeenth century. In asking for the aid of the Holy Spirit, it implicitly attributes responsibility for the poetry to God: see Dedication to George Herbert's *The Temple* (1633), and the Dedication, 'To my Sisters', in *Eliza's Babes* (1652).

3
(p. 2) l.15 Revelation 19.15.

4
(p. 3) Title: *ordinances*: a word particularly used by Presbyterians to describe services, especially the Sacrament, ordained by authority.
(p. 3) l.8 *To*: probably 'do'.
(pp. 3-4) ll.18, 25, 29, 34 *duty, duty, Dutys*: religious duties such as the Sacrament.
(p. 4) l.23 *rod*: the punishment of God.
(p. 4) l.42 *incomes*: 'The coming in of divine influence into the soul: spiritual influx or communication.' (OED, sense 1b: 'common in 17th c, now Obs. or rare').

6
(p. 6) This bare verse form is reminiscent of Herbert in 'Discipline' and conveys a similar sense of anguish.
(p. 6) ll.29-30 Psalm 38.2.

7
(p. 7) l.8 *rowll*: Nonconformist jargon for 'depend'.

8
(p. 8) l.9 *circumsised hart*: see Romans 2.29.
(p. 8) l.17 Proverbs 4.18.

9
A poem which resolves itself in an extraordinarily strong Calvinist celebration of God's sovereignty.

10
This poem is in the metre characteristic of the Nonconformist hymn. It is rather a good and very early example of the emotional piety (the term used is 'affectionate') that became more common in the 18th century.
(p. 10) l.7 Song of Songs 1.3.
(p. 10) l.24 *Oh sweet fruits, of thy merits*: she is referring to the joy of being in heaven which has been won as a result of the merits of Christ rather than any deserving of hers.

(p. 11) l.39 *roull*: Nonconformist jargon for 'depend'.

11

(p. 11) ll.1-4 II Peter 2.4.

(p. 11) l.3 *How*: probably 'who'.

(p. 12) ll.13-16 Luke 14.11.

(p. 12) l.18, 41 *cecreets, cecreet*: secrets, secret.

(p. 13) ll.49-50 Psalm 34.18.

(p. 13) l.51 *give in*: Nonconformist sense of 'give in' not recorded in OED: it seems to mean the immediate supernatural giving of God. See Katherine Sutton, *A Christian Womans Experiences of the Glorious Workings of Gods Free Grace* (Rotterdam, 1663), 44, where she says of her poems 'I assure you Courteous Reader these are not studed [sic] things, but are given in immediately'. *many a dole*: many gifts.

(p. 13) ll.53-54 Matthew 5.3.

(p. 14) l.81 'cov'nant grace': a virtue that is given as part of the covenant made by God with the believer.

12

In this little poem faith and love are compared to the two sisters-in-law, Ruth and Orpah, who follow their mother-in-law to the borders of a foreign country. Thereafter, Orpah goes home, but Ruth cleaves to her mother-in-law Naomi as love stays with the believer at death. See Ruth 1.11-18.

13

(p. 17) l.89 Isaiah 64.8.

(p. 17) l.96 *give in*: see note on the 'First Century', 11, l.51. She means 'might my prayers be directly answered by God'.

14

(p. 18) Title: *struclings*: strugglings.

(p. 18) l.4 *of*: off.

(p. 18) l.7 *rock of ages*: the translation of the original Hebrew of Isaiah 26.4. Julia Palmer has several phrases like this: see *house of wine* for the AV 'banqueting house'. It is unlikely that she knew Hebrew herself, but she probably heard these translations in a sermon. Her pastor at the Presbyterian church in Westminster was Thomas Cawton, son of the famous Orientalist Thomas Cawton.

(p. 18) ll.9-10 Mark 7.27.

(p. 18) l.14 *resolve*: resolve.

(p. 18) l.15 *roull*: Nonconformist jargon for 'depend'.

(p. 18) l.16 *absovle*: absolve.

(p. 19) ll.29-30 Isaiah 54.10.

(p. 19) ll.45-6 Isaiah 49.15.

(p. 19) l.50 *within the vaill*: a favourite phrase of Palmer's, referring to the veil of the Temple, behind which only priests could go, which was torn from top to bottom at the moment Jesus died. The significance of this for New Testament Christians was that they were all admitted to the Holy of Holies, and there was no need any longer for a priesthood. See Hebrews 6.19.

(p. 19) l.55 Isaiah 55.1.

(p. 20) ll.61-2 Psalm 42.5.

(p. 20) l.63 *roll*: Nonconformist jargon for 'depend'.

15

(p. 20) l.12 Romans 8.28.

(p. 21) l.15 *rod*: the punishment of God.

(p. 21) ll.24-25 This idea may be from Herbert, 'Faith':

> What though my bodie runne to dust?
> Faith cleaves unto it, counting every grain
> With an exact and most particular trust,
> Reserving all for flesh again.

The idea is also present in Henry King's 'The Exequy' ll.65-6, and Hester Pulter's manuscript poem (probably from about the same period as Julia Palmer), Leeds University, Brotherton Library MS Lt q. 32, f. 86:

> Tho' I to Atoms am dispers'd,
> I in their dances am unvers'd
> yett shall no Dust
> of my old Carcase e're be lost
> 'tho in a thousand Figures tost
> for thou art Just.

(p. 22) l.44 *doupts*: doubts.

16

(p. 22) ll.13-14 Psalm 116.7.

(p. 22) l.15 *g'in*: given.

(p. 22) l.18 *quit*: quite.

(p. 23) l.28 *within the vaill*: see note on 'First Century', 14, l.50.

17

(p. 23) l.3 Jonah's gourd was the one comfort he had—he was able to shelter from the sun under it—and God made it wither up. Jonah 4.4-11.

(p. 23) l.5 *Lothsome smoke*: possibly that from the sacrifices of the rebellious people of Isaiah 65.2-5, which were not acceptable to God.

(p. 23) l.11 *propense*: inclined or disposed.

18

(p. 24) l.14 *told down*: paid.

(p. 24) ll.15-16 *the precious golden fleece*: an allusion to the mythical story of Jason and the Argonauts who captured the golden ram from King Aeëtes with the help of the king's daughter.

(p. 25) l.20 *sanctification*: the process whereby the believer becomes holy. In this poem she begins with the idea of 'justification by faith' whereby the believer is deemed to be righteous because of Christ's sacrifice, but at this point she asks for 'real' holiness. The image she goes on to use is of a coin being stamped with its value: she asks in line 24 for that imprint to go really deep, so that she becomes authentically holy.

(p. 25) l.31 *seace on*: probably 'seize one'.

(p. 25) l.41 *enflam't*: a request to God.

19

(p. 26) l.16 *fecth*: fetch.

(p. 27) ll.21-24 Hebrews 7.25-6.

(p. 28) ll.57-60 Nonconformist spirituality expects an experience of 'sealing', when the Holy Spirit gives the believer a tangible assurance of salvation.

(p. 28) l.60 See note on 'First Century', 10, l.24.

(p. 28) l.66 *malious*: probably a mispelling of malicious. The extra syllable is needed for the metre.

(p. 28) l.72 *trambled*: trampled.

(p. 28) l.73 *Catholicon*: universal remedy or prophylactic: a panacea..

20

(p. 29) l.27 *hast*: probably 'hasten'.

(p. 30) l.59 *Christs imputed righteousnese*: a doctrine central to Reformed theology, and precious to Nonconformists. On salvation, the believer is 'imputed' righteous because Christ's holiness is 'imputed' to him: he is therefore holy in God's sight whatever his actual behaviour. This transfer is explained in Romans chapter 5.

21

(p. 31) Title: *A dark glance*. This perhaps refers to the difficulty of envisaging the heavenly state, as in I Corinthians 13.12: 'For now we see in a glass, darkly; but then, face to face'.

(p. 31) l.1 Psalm 16.11.

(p. 31) l.13 *cecreet*: secret.

(p. 33) ll.81-82 II Corinthians 3.18.

(p. 33) ll.93-6 Revelation 21.23.
(p. 34) ll.97-100 Revelation 21.22.
(p. 34) ll.101-104 Revelation 22.2.
(p. 34) ll.109-10 Revelation 21.21.

22

(p. 34) l.6 *pelf*: 'filthy lucre'.
(p. 35) l.11 *emanuells land*: 'Emmanuel' means 'God present with us'. See Isaiah 7.14.
(p. 36) l.43 *endenture*: a reference to the 'indentures' of apprenticeship, a system with which Palmer would have been very familiar in seventeenth-century Westminster.
(p. 36) l.48 *roll*: Nonconformist jargon for 'depend'.
(p. 36) l.60 *cark*: be anxious.

23

(p. 39) l.59 *pelf*: 'filthy lucre'.

24

(p. 40) l.2 *A most unkinnd step dame*. The 'cruel stepmother' stereotype was common in this period: see Anne Southwell describing England which 'hath layd on mee an envious stepdames hand': Jean Klene, ed., *The Southwell-Sibthorpe Commonplace Book* (Tempe, Arizona, 1997), 137.
(p. 40) l.12 *hats*: hates.
(p. 40) l.17 God is knocking earthly things out of the believer's grasp in order that they should concentrate their love on Him. See 'Second Century', 84.
(p. 40) l.32 *rod*: the punishment of God.
(p. 40) l.35 *reflections*: criticisms.

25

(p. 42) ll.41-2 John 4.34.
(p. 42) l.43 *pelf*: 'filthy lucre'.

26

(p. 44) l.14 *security*: a word with negative connotations in Nonconformist spirituality, equivalent to 'complacency'. See also l.70, *cecure*.
(p. 44) ll.18-20 'Satan will spur us on to perform duties so that there will be no point in depending on our Saviour in the way that we should'.
(p. 44) ll.25-28 these lines are in Satan's voice.
(p. 45) l.55 *roll*: Nonconformist jargon for 'depend'.
(p. 46) l.65 *rod*: the punishment of God.
(p. 46) l.84 *leaven*: yeast. Used as a metaphor for subtle evil as in Matthew 16.6: 'Beware the leaven of the Pharisees'.

(p. 47) ll.101-2 *emenent/ Saincts*: Perhaps Palmer is thinking of Samuel Clarke's 1662 volume, *A Collection of the Lives of Ten Eminent Divines, Famous in their Generations for Learning, Prudence, Piety, and painfulness in the work of the Ministry. Whereunto is added, the Life of Gustavus Ericson, King of Sweden, who first Reformed Religion in that Kingdome, and of some other Eminent Christians*: her depression, expressed here, would be an interesting psychological response to the exemplary lives in this volume, clearly not intended by the author.

(p. 47) ll.115-6 I Peter 5.8.

(p. 47) l.125 *six thousand years*: Palmer is using Archbishop Ussher's dating for the beginning of the world. In 1660 he published *Chronologia Sacra*, which traced all the generations of humankind beginning with Adam from the Bible, and produced a figure for the age of the earth.

27

(p. 48) l.7 *doe*: probably 'to'.

(p. 48) l.15 *carver*: someone who helps herself.

(p. 48) l.20 *kise thy rod*: See Germaine Greer et al., *Kissing the Rod* (London, 1987): 'To kiss the rod, in the words of Torriano's *Proverbial Phrases* (1666), 575, means "not only to have patience, but also to thank those by whom one hath been chastis'd, and as it were to seem to be beholding to them for their correction; taken from Children, who when they do amiss, and are punish'd, they are made to vent their vexation no otherwise than by kissing that rod with which they were punish'd"' (Editors' Note, xvi).

(p. 48) l.24 *seall*: confirm with a particular experience of God's grace.

(p. 48) l.27 *smart*: painful.

28

This poem is reminiscent of George Herbert's poems in several ways. Prayer is Herbert's 'Church-lock and key' (stanza 3): his poem 'Decay' also refers to Exodus. 32.9-10 (ll.13-14): and the final stanza (beginning 'Give me, this holy art') recalls Herbert's style and vocabulary.

29

There are two direct echoes of Herbert's poem 'Death' in this poem by Palmer. Stanza 2 recalls Herbert's lines:

> But since our Saviours death did put some bloud
> > Into thy face;
> > Thou art grown fair and full of grace.

The idea of the grave as a comfortable bed which is dwelt on in the last part of Palmer's poem is encapsulated in Herbert's final stanza:

> Therefore we can go die as sleep, and trust
> > Half that we have

> Unto an honest faithfull grave;
> Making our pillows either down, or dust.

There is an intriguing mixture of Christian and pagan imagery in stanza 4.

(p. 51) l.16 *paid the shot*: made payment.

(p. 52) ll.45-8 I Corinthians 15.55.

30

(p. 53) ll.5-6 Hebrews 11.1. *evedence*: technical term describing the experiences that convince the believer she is saved as in the phrase 'evidences for heaven', current in this period among Nonconformists. Edmund Calamy published Mrs. Moore's 'Evidences for Heaven' in his *The Godly Mans Ark* of 1658.

(p. 55) l.56 *free graces*: i.e., free grace's. Free grace is a phrase beloved of Nonconformists describing Christ's unmerited grace, which operates to save and justify believers without any effort of their own.

(p. 55) l.75 *falases*: fallacies.

(p. 55) l.79 *roll*: Nonconformist jargon for 'depend'.

(p. 56) ll.85-6 Habbakuk 3.17.

32

(p. 58) ll.25-6 Proverbs 3.17.

(p. 59) ll.53-4 Numbers 13.23 describes spies being sent by Joshua into the Promised Land of Canaan. They brought back some grapes that they found there as an example of how fruitful the land was.

(p. 59) l.59 *Zion hill*: the city of God: Palmer uses it to mean 'heaven'.

33

(p. 59) l.4 *rod*: the punishment of God.

(p. 59) l.12 *prole*: prowl.

(p. 60) ll.14-16 Jeremiah 2.13.

(p. 60) l.15 *cirterns*: cisterns.

(p. 60) l.32 *ty'd to three*: probably a reference to Ecclesiastes 4.12. The 'three-fold cord' is often used as a metaphor for the Trinity.

34

(p. 61) l.29 *mortifie*: 'put to death' as in Romans 8.13.

(p. 61) l.31 Genesis 32.26.

(p. 62) l.53 *earnest*: guarantee, down payment, as in Ephesians 1.14 *improve*: Nonconformist jargon meaning 'make the most of'. Among things which could be 'improved' were time, and providences.

35

(p. 62) ll.9-10: II Samuel, chapter 11. David should have gone to war, but was spending most of the day in bed when he first caught sight of

Bathsheba washing herself. The subsequent adultery led to David's murder of her husband, the 'mercylese' act referred to in l.11.

(p. 63) ll.25-26 Ephesians 5.16.

(p. 63) ll.29-30 John 9.14.

36

(p. 63) l.13 Isaiah 32.2.

(p. 63) l.15 *strock*: stroke.

(p. 64) l.48 *pelf*: 'filthy lucre'.

(p. 64) ll.67-8: Presumably means something like 'Thou knowest I can't submit quietly to lack of enjoyment of what I desire'.

(p. 65) ll.73-74 She enjoys the pun on the two senses of 'comprehend', to understand and to seize, suggested by Philippians 3.12.

38

(p. 67) l.8 *lett*: hindrance.

39

The doctrine of perseverance was a Calvinist refinement of the idea of election: if God had elected the believer to eternal life, he could never fall away. However, the corollary of this doctrine, which caused much anguish, was that if a believer apostasised it was a sign that he was not elect in the first place. Stanza 2 expresses this belief.

(p. 70) l.17 *to*: do.

(p. 70) ll.17-22 Isaiah 40.31.

(p. 70) ll.33-4 Revelation 3.11.

40

The ideal deathbed scene envisioned here may be the result of reading Samuel Clarke's *A Collection of the Lives of Ten Eminent Divines*, in which it featured strongly.

(p. 71) ll.31-2 II Peter 1.11.

41

(p. 72) l.2 *thou needst not fear excese*: Nonconformists were encouraged towards ecstatic love for Christ. See Thomas Watson, *Christs Loveliness* (London, 1657), 367: 'Excesse here makes us sober!'

(p. 72) l.10 Song of Songs 5.10.

(p. 72) l.20 Song of Songs 2.1. Jesus Christ, as the Bridegroom as the Song of Songs, is equated with the Rose of Sharon.

(p. 73) l.25 Song of Songs 1.2.

(p. 73) l.28 Song of Songs 1.3.

(p. 73) ll.49-51 Song of Songs 2.17.

(p. 73) ll.53-54 Song of Songs 2.11.

(p. 74) l.59 *book*: enter in a list.

(p. 74) l.70 *handfasted*: contracted or engaged by joining of hands; betrothed.

(p. 74) l.71 *prole*: prowl.

42

(p. 75) ll.31, 35 *Dutys*: religious duties: here, communal prayer, praise and the Sacrament.

(p. 76) l.49 She is talking about the Day of Pentecost: see Acts 2.1-4.

(p. 76) l.61 *earnest*: guarantee, down payment, as in Ephesians 1.14.

(p. 76) l.73 *incomes*: 'The coming in of divine influence into the soul: spiritual influx or communication.'(OED, sense 1b: 'common in 17th c, now Obs. or rare').

(p. 77) l.77 *improve*: Nonconformist jargon meaning 'make the most of'.

43

(p. 77) l.16 *in ward*: in prison.

(p. 78) l.28 *prole*: prowl.

(p. 78) l.36 *Zion hill*: heaven.

(p. 78) l.43 *riding post*: at express speed, in haste.

45

(p. 80) l.1 cf. the opening lines of Herbert's 'The Flower':
> How fresh, O Lord, how sweet and clean
> Are thy returns!

(p. 81) ll.41-2 Psalm 115.1.

(p. 82) l.49 *give in*: see note on 'First Century', 11, l.51.

46

(p. 82) ll.1-4 II Peter 3.11.

(p. 82) l.11 *horn*: often used figuratively in the Bible for strength, or pride.

(p. 82) l.15 *Zion hill*: heaven.

47

(p. 84) Title: 'Experience' as a name for the perception of God's presence and work in the believer is the stuff of the spiritual journal as recommended by Richard Rogers in his *Seven Treatises* (1603) onwards: it had mutated into the title of autobiographies, as in the Baptist Jane Turner's *Choice Experiences of the kind dealings of God before, in, and after Conversion* (1653).

(p. 84) ll.25-6 Romans 8.17.

(p. 85) ll.41-3 *wink ... to*: the OED gives 'bring into a specified state by a glance or nod' citing Herbert's 'Home', 39-40:
> What is this woman-kinde, which I can wink
> Into a blacknesse and distaste?

(p. 85) l.43 *faih*: faith.

48

(p. 85) l.7 From the Sermon on the Mount: Matthew 5.8.
(p. 85) l.8 *soull, delighting*: 'soul-delighting'.
(p. 86) ll.27-30 Revelation 2.17.
(p. 86) l.40 *cecreets*: secrets.
(p. 86) l.45 *ken*: know.
(p. 87) l.55 *house of wine*: Song of Songs 2.4: 'banqueting house' in Authorised Version. See note on the 'First Century', 14, l.7.

49

(p. 88) l.13: *a tendred Christ*: she means that she will once again receive Christ, offered by God in her place, as she did when she first became a Christian.
(p. 88) ll.32, 47 *roll*: Nonconformist jargon for 'depend'.

50

(p. 89) l.15 *makbate*: makebate, something which creates contention or discord, a breeder of strife.
(p. 90) l.40 *to*: do.
(p. 91) l.68 *thurst*: thrust.

51

(p. 91) l.7 *cecreet*: secret.
(p. 92) l.31 *Chore*: choir.

52

(p. 92) Title: see note on 'First Century', 47.
(p. 92) l.4 *though:* thou.
(p. 92) l.5 *duty*: religious duty, such as the Sacrament.

53

(p. 94) l.13 *d'e*: probably 'do you'.
(p. 94) l.16 *hag*: personification of evil, usually gendered female, which l.39 tends to confirm.

54

(p. 95) Title, l.3 *lets* hindrances; l.1 *let*: hindrance.
(p. 95) l.2 *doe*: probably 'to'.
(p. 95) l.16 *list*: desire.

55

(p. 96) l.5 *goe-by:* goodbye.
(p. 96) l.15 *let:* hindrance.
(p. 97) ll.21-22 Psalm 55.6.

(p. 97) l.41 see note on the 'First Century', 41 l.2.

(p. 97) l.43 *a fivefold mese*: refers to the story of Joseph and his brother Benjamin. Joseph had been sold by his brothers into Egypt as a slave, where he rose to power and prominence. His brothers, oppressed by famine, came to Egypt seeking food from Joseph, whom they did not recognise. He sent them all portions of food—'messes'—but to Benjamin, the youngest, he gave five times as much as a mark of particular love. Genesis 43.34.

(p. 97) l.46 *free grace*: see note on 'First Century', 30, l.56.

(p. 97) l.51 *ken*: kin.

56

(p. 98) l.10 See Revelation 20.12,15 for the Lamb's 'book of life' in which the names of the righteous are written.

(p. 98) l.23 Psalm 92.10. *horn*: often used figuratively in the Bible for strength, or pride.

57

(p. 99) l.14 *streightly*: narrowly.

(p. 99) l.23 *Sharons Rose*: Song of Songs 2.1. Jesus Christ, as the Bridegroom as the Song of Songs, is equated with the Rose of Sharon.

(p. 99) ll.25-6 Genesis 8.8-12.

58

A poem in praise of double predestination, involving a complex treatment of the concept of 'free grace' in the title.

(p. 101) l.24 *a fivefold mese*: see note on 'First Century', 55, l.43.

(p. 102) l.51 *free grace*: see note on 'First Century', 30, l.56.

59

(p. 102) ll.1-4 II Timothy 1.12.

(p. 102) ll.6-8 Matthew 16.18.

(p. 102) ll.9-10 Deuteronomy 33.27.

(p. 103) l.33 She is looking for reasons to be hopeful of God's love to her. One of them is that she is showing signs of holiness, but she is afraid to use that as a claim on God, since that is all due to His working within her.

(p. 103) ll.37-40 Psalm 30.5.

(p. 103) ll.45-6 Revelation 21.4.

(p. 103) l.59 *Chore*: choir.

60

(p. 104) l.32 *lelft*: left.

61

(p. 105) l.14 *ther*: probably 'there's'.

(p. 105) l.17 Titus 3.2.

(p. 106) l.28 *dram*: a weight; in Apothecaries' measure, 60 grains.

(p. 106) l.31 *clip*: a reference to the practice of adulterating coinage by clipping the edges of gold and silver coins.

63

(p. 106) l.12 *house of wine*: Song of Songs 2.4: 'banqueting-house' in the Authorised Version. See note on the 'First Century', 14, l.7.

(p. 107) l.22 *ane*: probably 'one'.

64

(p. 107) ll.13-16 Ephesians 4.15-16.

(p. 107) l.17 Revelation 1.6.

(p. 107) ll.21-2 Corinthians 3.22-23.

(p. 108) ll.25-28 Malachi 3.17. See Thomas Watson, *Religion Our True Interest* (London, 1682), pp. 176-77.

(p. 108) l.36 *peculiall*: probably 'peculiar'.

(p. 108) l.37 Deuteronomy 32.10.

(p. 108) l.41 I Corinthians 3.16.

(p. 109) ll.78-9 Romans 16.20.

65

Based on John 14.2: 'In my father's house are many mansions ... I go to prepare a place for you'. Informed by ideals of the 17th century superior dwelling (OED says the phrase is current by mid-century).

(p. 110) l.10 *down told*: paid.

(p. 110) l.17 This mansion is a fortified manor house with defences.

(p. 111) ll.55 *give in*: see note on the 'First Century', 11, l.51.

66

Yet another poem that offers Christ as the source of all requirements.

(p. 112) l 8 *carve*: to help or serve oneself.

(p. 112) ll.25-32 reminiscent of Herbert's poem 'The Quip' when the believer is accused by personifications of the World: Beautie, Money, Glorie, Wit and Conversation and answers them all with the refrain: '*But thou shalt answer, Lord, for me*'.

67

(p. 113) Title: l.2 *let*: hindrance.

(p. 113) l.3 *mess*: see note on 'First Century', 55, l.43.

(p. 113) l.15 *free grace*, l.22 *free graces* (i.e. free grace's): see note on 'First Century', 30, l.56.

(p. 114) l.27 *carve (unto)*: to serve up.

(p. 114) l.36 Promised, for example, in Matt. 7.7.

(p. 114) l.39 *that*, l.40 *it* both refer to *sin* in l.37.

68

(p. 115) l.19 *Earths-cumber-ground*: A cumber-ground, according to the OED citing Luke 13.7, is 'a person that uselessly cumbers the ground'—in this case, herself.

(p. 116) ll.28-34 a rather tortuous way of describing the pain of the body of Christ which is the church dismembered by death: of Christ, the head, and of other members.

(p. 116) ll.35-6 It is possible that Palmer is referring to her own father and husband as being dead, and therefore in heaven: she describes herself as 'fatherlese' ('First Century', 70, l.12) and we know that her husband was dead by 1680 (see introduction). However, she is just as likely to be spiritualising the family metaphor, to mean God and Christ.

(p. 116) l.39 *bowels yearn*: deep instinctive love as in I Kings 3.26, the love of the true mother for her baby son.

69

This poem, about the 'holy art' of contentment, celebrates the cheerful submission to God's will that is compulsory for Nonconformists: see Thomas Watson, *Autarkeia, or The Art of Contentment*, first published 1653 and reprinted frequently throughout the rest of the century. The first part of the poem uses the pronoun 'it' to refer to the individual will.

(p. 117) Title: *contentation*: contentment.

(p. 117) l.12 *sterne*: stern. The metaphor is of steering a ship.

(p. 118) l.31 *prole*: prowl.

(p. 118) l.47 *weaned hart*: i.e. a heart 'weaned off' the things it desires like a child weaned from milk.

70

A spiritual autobiography. As is usual, she says nothing about her circumstances (although it appears from the early stanzas that she may have been an orphan). She has an early childhood experience of God's grace but this is consistently attacked by Satan. God however laid 'a cecreet [secret] traine' to lure her back to himself (20-1). Complacency was shaken with a 'storm' presumably of doubt that she was saved (37-40) as no 'fruit' appeared (presumably the 'fruit of the Spirit' as in Galatians 55.22). She seeks 'inherant grace' (45), a source of grace permanently within her. However, she follows the path of hard duty until Christ finally makes her give herself to him in covenant (61-2). This did not, however, result in unalloyed happiness: the most she got from God was a strong desire for holiness (76-78). She has had experiences of God's presence, and absence. Recently she has been assured that her devotion to God will pay off (85-88). She accepts that she is blessed to have been elected for salvation and aspires to more holiness and a fuller experience of God. Her last prayer is that she will glorify God (109-110).

This narrative is typical of Nonconformist salvation histories: the gradual wooing of the elect soul by God, the soul's persistence in sin, the futility of unloving religious duty, doubts about salvation: this stage ending with a climactic experience of covenant (sometimes expressed as 'betrothal') after which the soul is unambiguously God's possession but not necessarily continuously in God's presence. The subsequent narrative is one of turbulent mixed emotion, corresponding to senses of God's presence or absence. All is assumed to be in the cause of the personal holiness of the believer.

(p. 119) l.20 *traine*: sense 7 in OED (obs.): pieces of carrion laid to lure a beast into a trap.

(p. 119) l.24 *pelf*: 'fifthy lucre'.

(p. 121) ll.69, 103 *cecreet*: secret.

(p. 121) l.73 *gavest in*: see note on 'First Century', 11, l.51.

(p. 121) l.80 Psalm 126.5-6.

(p. 122) l.97 *free grace*: see note on 'First Century', 30, l.56.

71

(p. 123) l.9 *futurietys*: futurities, future events.

(p. 123) l.30 *Zion hill*: heaven.

(p. 124) ll.49-51 Hebrews 6.19.

(p. 124) l.51 *within the vaill*: see note on 'First Century', 14, l.50.

(p. 124) ll.55-57 I Corinthians 15.19.

(p. 124) ll.60-61 *they, them*: refers to faith and hope in l.58.

72

(p. 124) l.10 *The world's an outside painted fire*: the 'painted fire' is a familiar metaphor for 'falseness' in the seventeenth century.

(p. 125) l.35 *pelf*: 'filthy lucre'.

73

(p. 126) ll.21-24 Alludes to the story of the capture of Jericho (Joshua, chapters 2 and 6).

(p. 128) ll.73-76 Since the prayers in the poem were inspired directly by God she is expecting God to answer them.

74

A poem with an unusual metre: uneasy and breathless reflecting the anguish of the poem. She may have read Herbert and imitated poems like 'Affliction (iv)'.

(p. 129) l.31 Carries the same idea as Isaiah 42.3: 'the smoking flax he will not quench'.

(p. 129) l.45 *pelf*: 'filthy lucre'.

75

(p. 130) ll.1-4 I Samuel 27.1.

76

(p. 131) l.11 *tiwll*: probably ''twill', an abbreviation for 'it will'.

(p. 132) l.42 *to minde that by, the by*: to take notice of irrelevant things.

(p. 133) l.55 *work while, itt tis cal'd today*: John 9.4.

(p. 133) l.70 *improve*: Nonconformist jargon meaning 'make the most of'.

77

(p. 134) l.16 *iregularly move*: express itself inappropriately.

(p. 134) l.25 *my apounted Change*: the day God has appointed for her death.

78

Palmer lists the disasters of the 1660s, widely seen as judgements of God (and not just by Nonconformists). Stanza 4 refers to the great plague of 1665: stanza 5 refers to the catastrophe of the Dutch War in which Dutch ships sailed up the Thames and sank the cream of the English navy: stanza 6 refers to the Great Fire of London, 1666.

(p. 135) l.11 *horn*: often used figuratively in the Bible for strength, or pride.

(p. 136) l.40 *rod*: the punishment of God.

(p. 136) l.41 The same idea as the famous lines from Herbert, 'The Church Militant', 235-6:

> Religion stands on tip-toe in our land,
> Readie to passe to the *American* strand.

A common prayer in this period was that God would not take his gospel—the Reformed version of Christianity—from England in punishment for the nation's sin, as in ll.52-56 of this poem.

80

In this poem Palmer seems to confront the possibility of martyrdom. Nonconformist diaries in the 1660s and early 1670s, such as Elizabeth Turner's (Kent Archives Office, MS F. 27) show anxiety about a French invasion and subsequent possible prosecution of Protestants.

(p. 138) ll.9-12 a celebration of predestination that is at the same time positive and fatalistic.

(p. 138) l.13 *rack*: probably 'rock'.

(p. 138) l.25 *by them*: by foes.

(p. 139) l.43 Luke 12.4-5.

81

(p. 139) l.13 *rafer*: probably 'racer'.

(p. 140) l.31 *Zion hill*: heaven.

(p. 140) l.35 *prole*: prowl.

(p. 140) l.43 *whens*: all the questions beginning with 'when'.

82

(p. 141) l.17 *purblind*: totally blind.

(p. 141) l.28 *cecurity*: see note on the 'First Century', 26, l.14.

(p. 142) l.31 *rang*: range.

(p. 142) l.33 *cecreet*: secret.

84

(p. 143) Title: *inntabilyty*: probably 'instability'.

(p. 144) l.27 *trambled*: trampled.

(p. 145) l.49 *enlargment*: Nonconformist term describing a sense of freedom in prayer or spiritual experience.

(p. 145) l.60 *vill*: possibly 'vilify'.

(p. 145) l.65 *moat*: mote, as in the speck in the eye of Luke 6.41.

85

(p. 147) l.34 *drosinese*: 'drowsiness'.

86

(p. 148) The structure of this poem is of a meditation on Christ's life and death.

(p. 148) l.13 Isaiah 52.14.

(p. 148) ll.21-2 Luke 22.44.

(p. 148) l.29 *pilats*: Pilate, the Roman governor who judged Jesus.

(p. 149) l.46 *Zion hill*: for once, not a metaphor for heaven, but the Mount of Olives, on which it was thought Jesus would descend at His Second Coming, since it was the place from which he ascended into heaven (Acts 1.12).

88

(p. 151) ll.5-6 Psalm 90.4.

89

(p. 151) ll.9-11 She enjoys the pun on the two senses of 'comprehend', to understand and to seize, suggested by Philippians 3.12.

(p. 152) l.22 *Sion hill*: heaven.
(p. 152) l.27 *my times ar in thy hand*: Psalm 31.15.

90

(p. 153) l.21 *tose*: probably 'toss'.
(p. 153) l.27 *Sion hill*: heaven.

92

Note the date sequence here. The last dated poem, number 63, was dated March 3rd: apparently nearly 30 poems were written in the intervening period.
(p. 156) l.47 *disanull*: to cancel.

93

(p. 157) l.35 *cecreet*: secret.

95

(p. 159) l.15 *quikning*: a word common in Nonconformist spirituality: 'making alive'.

96

(p. 160) l.19 refers to those whose names are written in God's Book of Life, and are therefore saved.
(p. 160) l.36 *free grace*: see note on 'First Century', 30, l.56.

97

(p. 162) l.1 Exodus 33.23. God showed Moses his back because 'there shall no man see me, and live'. By extrapolation this is all believers are allowed to see on this earth.
(p. 163) l.23 *give in*: see note on 'First Century', 11, l.51.

98

(p. 164) l.13 *port*: behaviour, conduct.
(p. 165) l.28 Philippians 3.8.
(p. 165) ll.29-30 I Corinthians 2.2.
(p. 165) l.38 *Stephen*: the first Christian martyr. See Acts chapters 6 and 7.
(p. 165) l.50 *sion hill*: heaven.

99

(p. 166) l.10 *ken*: knowledge.
(p 166) l.25 *thee*: she means herself. Since no man can accompany her to the judgement seat of God and make excuses for her she will not listen to their opinions now.
(p. 166) l.26 *excusive*: probably 'excusing'.

Second Century

2

(p. 171) see 1 Peter 5.8.

(p. 171) l.14 *ell*: a measure of length, 45 inches in England.

(p. 172) l.18 *Lees*: dregs.

(p. 172) l.22 *thurst*: thrust.

(p. 172) l.29 This means something like 'In religious duty (such as prayer or Communion) he will not keep away but will cunningly lurk about to see whether he can steal the heart away from God. Then he will try to rob us of the comfort which might flow to us from rich spiritual gifts of grace'.

(p. 172) l.35 *incomes*: 'The coming in of divine influence into the soul: spiritual influx or communication'. (OED, sense 1b: 'common in 17th c, now Obs. or rare').

3

(p. 174) l.1 *ernest*: guarantee, down payment, as in Ephesians 1.14.

(p. 174) l.8 *craky*: probably 'creaky'.

4

(p. 175) Title: *free grace*: see note on 'First Century', 30 l.56.

(p. 176) ll.36-7 Means something like: 'By this [thine absence] thou art pleased to keep mankind from temptations to the sin of pride'.

(p. 176) l.49 II Corinthians 12.10.

(p. 176) l.50 *my head*: my Head, i.e., Jesus Christ.

(p. 176) l.57 *quikning*: a word common in Nonconformist spirituality: 'making alive'.

5

(p. 177) l.5 *porst*: pourest.

(p. 177) l.12 *t'shall*: 't shall.

(p. 177) l.13 *hard thought*: critical thought.

(p. 178) l.34 *because not dead*: because sin within the believer is not mortified, or 'dead'.

(p. 178) l.39 *roll*: Nonconformist jargon for 'depend'.

(p. 178) ll.45-8 I Corinthians 10.13.

6

This poem appears to refer to political developments in June 1672. There had been bloody engagements at sea between the English, with their French allies, and the Dutch. Meanwhile news from Holland was of French advances on land, with many Dutch refugees fleeing before them. This poem shows that the Declaration of Indulgence had not quelled misgivings amongst Nonconformists about a war which involved a Catholic ally and a Protestant enemy, and was therefore profoundly disturbing. The twenty lines following ' Oh wilt thou on, the wicked shine' (l.25) seem to apply to Catholicism, with its feared aim of stamping out Protestantism: the 'former victorys' Palmer claims in l.47 must be the Protestant triumphs of the Armada, and the Gunpowder Plot (and possibly the Parliamentarian victories of the Civil War).

(p. 178) Title: *cloudy providences* it seems difficult to qualify 'providences', which are events ordained by God, by negative adjectives such as 'cloudy': but Nonconformists were able to conceptualise circumstances as being at the same time unpleasant and divinely ordered.

(p. 178) l.4 *rod*: the punishment of God.

(p. 179) ll.17-18 Revelation 16.1.

(p. 179) l.27: *eterprise* enterprise.

(p. 179) ll.29-35: This appears to refer to the alliance of the Catholic French and persecuting English government, whose military endeavours are prospering at the moment. Palmer is fearful that 'true religion' will be wiped out.

(p. 180) l.59 Psalm 141.10.

7

This poem beings with a meditation on 'walking', a familiar Biblical word for spiritual living. It then turns into a catalogue of those who 'walked by faith' (Romans 8.1).

(p. 180) ll.2-5 *creep*: here and in poem 9 of the 'Second Century', seems to be a favourite word of Julia Palmer, as it was of George Herbert.

(p. 181) ll.23-30 *Abraham*: Hebrews 11.8-10 celebrates the faith of Abraham in following the calling of God to an unknown country. 27-30 closely paraphrase Romans 4.20 which specifically refers to the begetting of his son Isaac when he and his wife were both aged.

(p. 181) l.31 The patience of Job was and is legendary.

(p. 181) l.32 *Moses*: 'the man Moses was very meek, above all the men who were upon the face of the earth', Numbers 12.3.

(p. 181) l.34 *Jehosophat*: a good and successful king of Judah. See II Chronicles, chapter 17.

(p. 181) ll.35-6 *John*: John 13.23 describes the disciple John, 'whom Jesus loved', 'leaning on Jesus' bosom' at the Last Supper.

(p. 181) l.37 *David*: here celebrated for his status of divine poet, assumed to be the author of the Psalms.

(p. 181) l.39 *Paul*: here Palmer uses Ananias' words to describe the apostle. Acts 9.15.

(p. 181) ll.41-44 The metaphor of Christ as copy-text for the believer is commonplace in seventeenth-century sermons.

8

(p. 182) ll.9-10: This seems to be referring to the incident recounted in Jude 9 where the archangel Michael was rebuked by God for telling Satan he lied. By contrast, Palmer is implying, the believer is encouraged to call Satan a liar.

(p. 182) ll.13-15 Psalm 125.1.

(p. 182) ll.17-18 Romans 16.20.

9

(p. 182) l.5 *fivefold mese*: see note on 'First Century', 55, l.43.

(p. 183) l.18 *sick, of the laze*: presumably 'sick of laziness' although the unusual form may be meant to suggest the disease of leprosy ('lazar' means 'leper').

(p. 183) l.19 *cecreet*: secret.

(p. 183) l.27 *let*: hindrance.

10

(p. 184) l.23 *free grace*: see note on 'First Century', 30, l.56.

(p. 185) l.31 *pelf*: 'filthy lucre'.

(p. 186) l.62 *Zion hill*: heaven.

12

An 'occasional' poem on the greeting 'How do you do?' It is typical of Palmer that she has to investigate the serious implications of a common convention.

(p. 187) l.4 *stilling*: to become still.

(p. 188) l.39 *a stand*: a state of checked or arrested movement.

13

(p. 188) ll.1-2 Proverbs 3.17.

14

(p. 189) l.7 *sore amus'd*: put into a muse, distracted.

(p. 190) l.25 *cecreetly*: secretly.

(p. 190) l.35 *ernest*: guarantee, down payment, as in Ephesians 1.14.

(p. 190) ll.45-6 a conventional prayer by seventeenth-century evangelists, rather startling to the modern ear, that they should act as a kind of introduction agency for Christ and the believer. See Thomas Vincent, *Christ the Best Husband* (London, 1672), 23.

15

(p. 191) l.13 *sublunary* mundane, material, gross. OED quotes Bishop Hall's

Breathings of a Devout Soul (1648), p. 3: 'Can ye hope to find rest in any of these sublunary contentments?'

(p. 191) ll.25-7 Isaiah 9.6.

(p. 192) ll.32-4 Isaiah 32.2.

(p. 192) l.40 *cheak*: check.

(p. 192) ll.49-50 John 15.1.

(p. 192) l.55 John 14.6.

16

A poem on the life of Christ.

(p. 193) l.1 *bouled*: boiled.

(p. 193) l.11 *alfullnese*: all fullness.

(p. 193) l.15 *The:* probably 'Thou'.

(p. 194) ll.36-40 Luke 2.46-50.

(p. 196) ll.77-9 Luke 22.19-46.

(p. 196) l.89 *To ken*: The token, or 'sign' of the Sacrament.

(p. 196) l.95 John 18.6.

(p. 196) ll.99-101 Mark 14.53-65.

(p. 197) l.112 Ephesians 4.8.

(p. 197) l.130 *nick*: point, stage, degree (OED sense 10c, obs.).

(p. 198) l.138 *sound*: swoon.

17

(p. 198) ll.9-10 referring to the parable in Matthew 15.27.

(p. 199) l.20 *full mese*: presumably a large portion, such as Benjamin's fivefold mess mentioned in 'First Century', 55, l.43.

(p. 199) l.24 *house of wine:* Song of Songs 2.4: 'banqueting house' in Authorised Version. See note on 'First Century', 14, l.7.

(p. 199) l.30 *dram*: a weight: in Apothecaries' measure, 60 grains.

(p. 200) l.58 echoing Paul's words at the end of I Timothy 1.15.

(p. 200) l.62 *free grace*: see note on 'First Century', 30, l.56.

18

(p. 201) ll.1-4 Explores a common New Testament architectural metaphor, here used of God's construction of the holy soul. The 'topmost stone' is the 'corner stone' of Ephesians 2.20 and I Peter 2.6.

(p. 201) ll.5-6 Romans 11.29.

19

(p. 202) l.2 *within the vaill*: see note on 'First Century', 14, l.50.

(p. 202) l.22 *and*: an.

(p. 203) l.47 *full a mese*: presumably a large portion, such as Benjamin's fivefold mess mentioned in 'First Century', 55, l.43.

(p. 203) l.54 *when's*: see note on 'First Century', 81, l.43.

20

(p. 203) l.4 *give in*: see note on 'First Century', 11, l.51.
(p. 204) l.29 Revelation 22.17, 20.

21

(p. 205) Title, 19, 39, 43-4, 69, 77, 79, 87 *free grace*: see note on 'First Century', 30, l.56.
(p. 205) l.26 *let*: hindrance.
(p. 206) l.66 *carve*: serve up.
(p. 207) ll.71-2 Revelation 22.17.
(p. 207) l.80 *dram*: a weight: in Apothecaries' measure, 60 grains.
(p. 207) l.92 *Acordingly, thou wilt not carve*: 'Thou wilt not give grace to me according to my desert'.

22

(p. 208) Title: *carking*: being anxious.
(p. 208) l.25 *To*: probably 'do'.
(p. 209) l.54 *pearll, of price*: Matthew 13.46.
(p. 210) l.58 *To*: probably 'do'.
(p. 210) l.63 *thy head*: thy Head, i.e., Christ.

23

(p. 210) ll.5-6 Psalm 84.10.
(p. 211) l.20 *hale*: drag or tug.
(p. 211) l.25 *A by-drop*: a leftover crumb as opposed to the *fullest dole* of l.27.

24

(p. 212) Title: *The best trade* is ironic, as she is describing a relationship with God in which conventional 'trade' is inappropriate: with God, the poem decides, begging is the best and only kind of trade in which to take part.
(p. 213) l.39 Jeremiah 2.13.
(p. 213) l.43 an echo of Herbert's 'Gratefulnesse': 'See how thy beggar works on thee/By art?'.

25

(p. 214) l.10 *choking*: probably 'chalking'.
(p. 215) l.44 *carve*: serve up.

26

(p. 216) ll.7-8 See note on 'First Century', 29, stanza 2.
(p. 216) l.14 I Corinthians 15.55.
(p. 216) l.20 *Judays, Lion*: the lion of Judah, as in Jacob's blessing on his son Judah in Genesis 49.9. Used typologically of Christ, as in Revelation 5.5.
(p. 216) l.31 *intersesour*: intercessor.

27
(p. 217) l.1 Jeremiah 2.13.
(p. 217) l.5 *ons*: probably 'ones'.
(p. 217) l.10 *To*: probably 'do'.
(p. 218) l.29 *sremes*: streams.
(p. 219) l.42 *Zion hill*: heaven.

28
(p. 220) l.50 *Though*: thou.

29
(p. 221) l.13 *make a stand*: be in a state of checked or arrested movement.
(p. 221) ll.19-20 Revelation 22.17.

30
(p. 222) l.4: *give in*: see note on 'First Century', 11, l.51. 'You could, as easily, bestow full power over sin on us as soon as we become Christians'.
(p. 222) ll.9, 14 *free grace*: see note on 'First Century', 30, l.56.
(p. 222) l.13 *Wee must to heaven, goe halting*: reference to Mark 9.45.
(p. 223) l.31 *thurst*: thrust.
(p. 223) l.51 *hard*: heart.
(p. 224) ll.61-66 *Gibeonits*: see Joshua 9.3-27. God ordered Joshua to kill all native tribes as he entered the promised land. However, the Gibeonites deceived Joshua into thinking they had travelled a long way to serve him, and Joshua made a treaty with them. When he realised the truth he condemned them to servitude, providing firewood and water for the Hebrews. Typologically, the native tribes of Canaan are interpreted as the sins of the flesh: Palmer is suggesting that until certain sins are completely stamped out, presumably at her death, they should be made to serve God in some way, like the Gibeonites. Thus their presence can become an antidote to pride (l.33).

31
(p. 224) Title, l.31 *free grace*: see note on 'First Century', 30, l.56.
(p. 225) l.20 *choucest*: choicest.

32
(p. 226) l.11 *wink ... in'to*: see note on 'First Century', 47.

33
(p. 227) l.16 *sedled*: probably 'settled'.
(p. 228) ll.43-4 See Herbert's 'Home', l.69: 'My thoughts and joys are all pact up and gone'.

34

(p. 230) l.16 *chore*: choir.

(p. 230) l.23 *To good*: probably ''tis good'.

(p. 230) l.26 *hone*: to whine or pine for, to hanker after (OED sense b).

35

(p. 231) l.7 *let*: hindrance.

(p. 231) l.17 *hectic*: fever.

(p. 231) l.22 *clog*: 'a block attached to the leg or neck of a man or beast, to prevent escape or impede motion'(OED).

(p. 231) l.28 *calcyn'd*: reduced to ash. Palmer seems to have misunderstood a phrase used by Herbert, from 'Easter' ll.4-6:

> ... thou likewise
> With him mayst rise;
> That, as his death calcined thee to dust,
> His life may make thee gold, and much more, just.

Palmer seems to think that 'calcyn'd' is a positive word to do with the Resurrection.

38

(p. 234) ll.5-6 I Corinthians 15.55.

39

(p. 234) This dark warning about 'fair shews' and deception on a grand scale may be related to the Declaration of Indulgence earlier this year, which, given her views on current events, Palmer might have realised was a strategy to appease the Nonconformists so that they did not oppose the Dutch War, rather than the generous act of toleration as which it was represented. The imagery of the shipping trade is well-developed in this poem: stanza 3 clearly relates to ships she has seen embarking from harbour.

(p. 235) ll.19-24 Matthew 7.21-23.

(p. 235) l.30 *ciphors*: mere numerical symbols without meaning.

40

(p. 236) Title: *compaint*: complaint. Note the similarity of ideas in this poem to Herbert's 'The Familie'.

(p. 237) l.43 *thurst*: thrust.

41

(p. 237) l.11 *let*: hindrance.

42

(p. 238) The 'sabbath rest' which is the subject of this poem is treated in Hebrews 4.1-11. For Julia Palmer, this 'rest' promised to believers is to be expected after death, in heaven.

(p. 238) l.6 Revelation 21.23.

(p. 238) l.15 *clog*: 'a block attached to the leg or neck of a man or beast, to prevent escape or impede motion' (OED).

(p. 238) l.29 *church. militent*: the church after the ascension of Christ and before his Second Coming in a state of continual militancy against Satan.

(p. 238) l.30 *chore*: choir.

43

(p. 239) Title: *that day*: the Day of Judgement. Revelation 20.11-13.

(p. 239) l.5 Revelation 20.13.

(p. 239) l.20 *gad*: in the seventeenth century has the meaning 'to leave the true path'.

44

(p. 240) l.9 *campensurate*: compensate.

(p. 241) l.26 *woorwood*: wormwood.

45

(p. 241) l.2 *inshutting*: shutting is the close of a day or nightfall: *in* perhaps functions as an intensifier.

(p. 241) l.3 *shourd*: shroud.

(p. 242) l.18 Matthew 16.18.

47

(p. 243) l.1 *prience of this world*: prince of this world, i.e. Satan: John 12.31, 14.30, 16.11.

48

(p. 244) l.9 *If here hee have not where to lay his head*: like Christ: Matthew 8:20.

(p. 244) l.10 *he veiws his mansion prepared*: as Christ promised in John 14.2.

(p. 244) l.19 *within the vaill*: see note on 'First Century', 14, l.50.

(p. 244) l.20 *apale*: appall.

(p. 244) l.29 *cecreet*: secret.

(p. 244) l.34 *Each providence*: see note on 'Second Century', 6.

(p. 244) l.38 *sublunary*: mundane, material, gross.

(p. 245) ll.54, 81 *free grace*: see note on 'First Century', 30, l.56.

49

(p. 246) A poem based on 1 Peter 5.8: 'The devil like a roaring lion walketh about, seeking whom he may devour'.

(p. 246) l.4 *be*: probably 'he'.

(p. 246) l.14 The chaining of the devil is described in Revelation 20.1-2.

(p. 246) l.15 *on*: one.

(p. 246) l.18 *thurst*: thrust.

50

(p. 248) l.61 *improve*: Nonconformist jargon meaning 'make the most of'.
(p. 249) ll.66-8 II Peter 1.11 (as in 'First Century', 40, 'Second Century', 31 and 32).

51

(p. 249) Title: This poem is a vivid portrayal of the importance of the doctrine of the believer's mystical union with Christ, a nonconformist doctrine under attack in the 1670s. See Introduction.
(p. 249) l.6 *indenture*: see note on 'First Century', 22.
(p. 249) l.25 *the white stone*: Revelation 2.17.
(p. 250) l.33 Referring to I Peter 1.12, describing the mysterious benefits of union with Christ: 'which things the angels desire to look into'.
(p. 250) ll.35-6 Colossions 1 26-7, which defines the hidden 'mystery' of the gospel as the union of Christ with the believer.

52

(p. 251) l.27 *hold*: in the context, this must mean 'prison' (Palmer's favourite adjective for 'prison' or 'cell' is 'durty', as here). The OED does not record this meaning of the word until 1717.
(p. 251) l.36 *word*: world.

53

(p. 251) This poem is based on a conceit very similar to that of Herbert's poem, 'Whitsunday', ll.21-22:

> Thou shutt'st the door, and keep'st within;
> Scarce a good joy creeps through the chink.

(p. 251) l.9 *Zion hill*: heaven.
(p. 251) l.17 *top*: to cut off the top of a plant: Sense 3a, OED.

55

The second, third and fourth stanza of this poem end with a couplet which is a variant of Herbert's refrain in his poem 'Home':

> Oh show thy self to me,
> Or take me up to thee!

(p. 253) l.23 *allfulnese*: possibly 'all fullness'.

56

Mr. H. seems to have offended Palmer by saying (54) 'tis good to live, here many a day'. Her irritation is understandable in that she will have heard many Nonconformist preachers saying the opposite. He also seems to have questioned her love for God, suggesting it to be a kind of self-indulgence ('Laze', 87). This poem is an indignant—and Biblical—rebuttal.

(p. 254) l.11 *clog*: 'a block attached to the leg or neck of a man or beast, to prevent escape or impede motion'(OED).

(p. 255) l.30 *evedence*: Nonconformists were encouraged to collect their 'Evidences for Heaven' which consisted of spiritual experiences such as the one Mr. H. is disputing here, and which Palmer writes about continually—her desire to die and be with Christ.

(p. 256) l.73 *tole*: probably 'toll', summon with a bell.

(p. 256) l.76 *sweet Sharons Rose*: Song of Songs 2.1. Jesus Christ, as the Bridegroom as the Song of Songs, is equated with the Rose of Sharon.

(p. 257) l.86 *Zion hill*: heaven.

(p. 257) l.87 *Laze*: laziness: self-indulgence.

(p. 257) ll.93-4 Revelation 14.13.

(p. 257) ll.95-7 Romans 8.19-22.

(p. 257) ll.99-100: 'We are confident, I say, and willing rather to be absent from the body, and to be present with the Lord'. II Corinthians 5.8.

(p. 257) l.104 Revelation 22.20.

58

(p. 258) Title: the 'complaint' here seems to be that fellow Christians are jealous of her spirituality and are attributing it to earthly pride rather than heavenly grace. This reduces Palmer to bewilderment and spiritual paralysis. Palmer appears to be coming under the accusation that her love for God is not authentic (ll.5-6).

(p. 259) l.7 *cecurity*: see note on 'First Century', 26, l.14.

(p. 259) l.18 *talent*: coin. This seems to be a glance at the parable of the talents in Matthew 25, in which the talents given by God were taken away if not used wisely.

59

(p. 261) l.18 *throp*: throb.

60

(p. 262) l.20 *baiting place*: place at which travellers stop for refreshment. It can also mean the location of bear-baiting.

(p. 263) ll.27-30 The parable of the wise and foolish virgins: Matthew 25.

(p. 263) l.40 *sublunary*: mundane, material, gross.

61

Another poem in praise of predestination and election 'Oh separating love'(13), 'distinguishing grace' (l.14), 'electing love' (l.20).

(p. 264) l.19 *On*: one. Psalm 42.7.

(p. 264) l.21 Jesus calls his followers 'litle flock' in Luke 12.32.

(p. 264) l.30 *Zions cacred hill*: Zion's sacred hill, heaven.

63

(p. 266) l.10 *non-such*: a person without parallel.

(p. 266) l.13 *let,* 36 *lett*: hindrance.

(p. 267) ll.31-2 Song of Songs 1.4.

64

(p. 267) l.10 *come away*: the common refrain of songs addressed to a lover in the many song books published in the seventeenth century.

(p. 268) l.29 *Sion hill*: heaven.

65

(p. 269) l.13 *evence*: evince, 'to prove the rightness of, vindicate'(OED, sense 4).

(p. 269) l.22 *in the room*: instead.

(p. 270) l.33 *earning bowels*: yearning bowels, as in I Kings 3.26.

68

(p. 271) Title: this poem seems to be a response to some event or experience, indicated by the shorthand symbols in the title.

(p. 271) l.8 *cecreet*: secret.

69

This poem is a rare insight into Nonconformist spirituality: that God's grace to the believer is not always indicated by an experience of peace and joy. She reaches the interesting conclusion that she will aim for grace, which will indicate the reality of holiness, rather than the experience of peace: she will 'invest', as it were, her meagre experiences of peace and joy, hoping that one day she will be able to claim a large amount of both.

(p. 273) l.7 *fullest mese*: presumably a large portion, such as Benjamin's fivefold mess mentioned in 'First Century', 55, l.43.

(p. 273) l.28 *in bank*: an interesting indication of the growing impact of early capitalism. The Bank of England was not founded until 1694, but obviously ideas of investment banking were common earlier in the seventeenth century.

70

(p. 274) l.11 *unmost*: probably 'utmost'.

(p. 274) ll.21, 27 *evedence*: technical term describing the experiences that convince the believer she is saved as in 'evidences for heaven'. This poem reifies 'evidence', extending the metaphor of 'clearing' of evidence (meaning to make it plain): in ll.25-27 'evidence' becomes something that can also be 'blotted'. Perhaps she is using a metaphor such as handwriting on paper, which would be appropriate, as Nonconformists were encouraged to write down their 'evidences'.

71

(p. 275) Title: this 'particular meditation' seems to be written in answer to slightly bewildered and perhaps irritated questioning by fellow-believers, who seem to be perplexed by the endless expressions of unsatisfied desire from this woman: 'Why ask you me, what tis that I would have/What would content, what is the thing I'de crave' (ll.1-2). In answer, Julia Palmer seems to display a rare sense of humour and objectification of her own incessant longing: ll.17-20 ask for all the perfections of every single exemplary Christian (presumably not Catholic 'saint'), and conclude that even that will not do. The tone indicates that even she realises how inappropriate her desires must seem.

(p. 275) ll.13-15 There seems to be a contrast set up here between 'grace and holiness' and 'attainments'. Perhaps the former is her spiritual experience of God, and the latter holy deeds in the outside world.

(p. 276) l.29: *cheak* check.

(p. 276) l.30: *Where* were.

72

(p. 276) Title: Matthew 5.16.

(p. 277) ll.13-18 Palmer is conscious of a gendered taboo on speaking out, which here she seems to equate with writing poetry: only God's express intervention, to 'unty' her tongue, overcomes this.

73

(p. 277) Title: this poem purports to sketch 'The devills picture' but it becomes clear by stanza 7 that in fact she is describing herself. This is why, in the final stanza, she tries to flee the sight she has conjured up, but can't: 'And if I knew, which way to run/From itt, away, I would be gone'. The sin that she has in common with Satan is spiritual pride.

74

(p. 279) l.10 *carve*: serve up.

(p. 279) ll.17-19 Romans 9.20-21, in the context, as here, of predestination.

(p. 279) 38 *Zion hill*: heaven.

75

A poem which encapsulates the Christian gospel as Palmer understands it.

(p. 281) l.30 *remi'ding*: remedying.

76

(p. 281) l.5 *cotten*: i.e. cotton: to 'get on' with each other, to harmonise or agree.

(p. 282) l.22 *thawrt*: thwart.

(p. 282) l.25 'The world hates me because God above has (I hope) chosen me out of it'.

78

A poem that demonstrates vividly the Nonconformist imperative to be cheerful.

(p. 283) l.2 *carnall*: wordly, unspiritual.

(p. 284) l.22 *do*: probably 'to'.

79

(p. 285) l.21 *cructh*: crouch.

(p. 285) l.25 *Jugle,* i.e., juggle: an act of deception, a trick.

81

(p. 286) Title: this poem is bases on a consideration of 'merit'. The Christian does not have to earn his salvation by merit, but can depend on the superlative merits of Christ, promised us in the Bible. This is one of the most important insights of Reformation Christianity.

(p. 287) ll.8-10 *we now more, firmly stand/ In our converses mediate/ Then Adam in his sinlese state*: We are on stronger ground communicating with God through the mediation of Christ than Adam was, despite his unfallen condition.

(p. 287) l.21 She seems to see God's promise as a kind of 'guard'.

(p. 287) l.23 *improve*: Nonconformist jargon meaning 'make the most of': here, referring to a promise (l.24).

(p. 288) l.39 *them*: promises.

83

(p. 289) l.4 *let* hindrance.

(p. 290) l.40 orthography unclear: *unsuiing* (ensuing) or *unsining* (unsinning). Probably the latter.

84

(p. 291) l.1 See note on 'First Century', 24. Also 'Second Century', 93.

(p. 292) l.6 *losser from it sitt*: i.e. looser from it sit. 'To sit loose' to the world is to care less for its 'delights' (2).

85

(p. 292) l.11 *vill*: possibly 'vilify'.

(p. 292) l.20 *art, of contentation*: see note on 'First Century', 69.

86

(p. 293) l.17 *as knowing him, to my friend:* 'be' missing here.

(p. 293) l.25 *give in*: see note on 'First Century', 11, l.51.

87

(p. 293) l.1 *free grace*: see note on 'First Century', 30, l.56.

88

(p. 294) Title: Romans 8.28: 'And we know that all things work together for good to them that love God, to them that are the called according to his purpose'.

(p. 294) l.5 *cecreet*: secret.

(p. 294) l.6 *free grace*: see note on 'First Century', 30, l.56.

(p. 295) l.18 *lees*: dregs.

(p. 295) l.38 *providences, most adverse*: see note on 'Second Century', 6.

(p. 295) l.42 *terene*: earthly.

(p. 295) l.48 *sublunarys*: here used as a noun, presumably to mean all material, worldly things.

89

(p. 296) l.3 *a stand*: a state of checked or arrested movement.

(p. 297) l.48 If *Then* in the next line means as it usually does in the seventeenth century, 'than', this line should read 'content me more' rather than *content me lese*.

90

(p. 298) l.13 Palmer is comparing her most vivid experiences of the presence of Christ to the experience of the disciples on the Mount of Transfiguration, who saw Jesus in his glory, yet had to face difficult problems on their descent from the mountain (see Matthew 17).

(p. 298) l.23 *Zion hill*: heaven.

(p. 300) l.32 *duty*: the taking of the Sacrament.

92

(p. 300) Title: I John 3.2: 'Beloved, now we are the sons of God, and it doth not yet appear what we shall be, but we know that, when he shall appear, we shall be like him; for we shall see him as he is'.

(p. 300) l.11 *face to face*: I Corinthians 13.12.

(p. 301) l.20 *imediate*: unmediated.

93

(p. 301) ll.1-2 See also 'First Century', 24, 'Second Century', 84.

(p. 301) l.29 *the creture*: she means 'any other human being'.

94

(p. 260) ll.9-10 Revelation 6.16.

(p. 260) l.13 *cecreet*: secret.

95

(p. 260) l.2 *this white, or yelow drose:* silver and gold.

96

(p. 303) Some event has provoked these two vehement poems on 'this black day', 11 July 11 1673, but we have not been able to establish which. They stand as appeals to God for vengeance. She attacks 'that sad generation/Which doe delight, to feed upon/The flesh of thine, and drink ther bloud' (19-21): this must refer to the persecutions of the 1660s and 1670s. She invokes the fate of Babylon, the city that is also the great whore of Revelation chapter 17: anti-Catholic tradition equates Babylon with Rome, as George Herbert did in 'The Church Militant'. The focus of this poem, which seems to be the government of Charles II and his openly Roman Catholic brother the Duke of York, is made clearer by the uses of the phrase 'mistery, of inniquity' (41) which from the early seventeenth century had been used for the Catholic church.

97

(p. 306) l.27 *what eres:* whatever is.

(p. 306) l.31 *canopy:* the 'banner' of Song of Songs 2.4.

98

(p. 306) l.4 *druges:* drudges.

(p. 306) l.14 *sandy ropes:* c.f. George Herbert's 'rope of sands' ('The Collar', l.22).

99

(p. 307) ll.4-6 *thou somtims, my evedence/for glory, when I goe from hence/Dost clear:* Nonconformist vocabulary. Again, she is talking about her 'evidence for heaven', experiences which convince her she is saved. These are necessarily subjective, so it was important to have 'clear' evidence. Here God is clarifying such experiences for her.

(p. 307) l.7 *dutys:* religious duties such as the Sacrament.

(p. 309) Epilogue.

Julia Palmer's final words echo those of the Spirit and the Bride at the very end of the Bible: Revelation 22.17.